DIGITAL
LEADER

5 SIMPLE KEYS TO
SUCCESS AND INFLUENCE

erik qualman

New York   Chicago   San Francisco   Lisbon   London   Madrid   Mexico City
Milan   New Delhi   San Juan   Seoul   Singapore   Sydney   Toronto

1 2 3 4 5 6 7 8 9 10 DOC/DOC 0 1 6 5 4 3 2 10

ISBN   978-0-07-179242-4
MHID   0-07-179242-2

e-book ISBN 978-0-07-179244-8
e-book MHID   0-07-179244-9

Interior design by THINK Book Works

McGraw-Hill books are available at special quantity discounts to use as premiums and sales promotions, or for use in corporate training programs. To contact a representative please e-mail us at bulksales@mcgraw-hill.com.

This book is printed on acid-free paper.

CONTENTS

SECTION FIVE: PEOPLE

ACKNOWLEDGMENTS

I would love to thank the all the people who have helped me along the way. As this would make the book longer than *War & Peace*, if your name isn't listed, please know I appreciate all you have done for me and I hope to someday soon return the favor.

My Family Leaders   This book was particularly rewarding for me as I was able to work closely with my Dad. It was an unforgettable lifetime experience. Aside from his great technical skills, he brought incredible insights and an unbridled passion to this project. Most importantly, it was fun. Thanks, Dad! Of course Mom was always ready at a moment's notice to provide invaluable input with a smile. Whenever called upon, my brothers Matt and Jay would give me unfiltered feedback; even when I didn't want to hear it—which is when it's most valuable. Their wives and kids are also a constant source of support. My family in Miami was incredibly patient and encouraging, while also providing a nice break from the intense nature of the work. Thank you to my grandparents for your wisdom and warmth. To my closest friends—you know who you are and I hope you know how much you mean to me.

To Ana Maria, my partner for life, thank you for making countless sacrifices to make this book possible and for always, always being there. To my beautiful 14-month-old Sofia, thanks for listening when you had Daddy's MacBook dangling over the full bath tub.

You all mean the world to me.

My Publishing Leaders   Thanks to my incredible team at McGraw-Hill. We were quick with this book, but never in a hurry. An ideal combination and I couldn't be more pleased with the outcome. To Zach Gajewski, my development editor, I still think you have a clone, as I couldn't believe the amount of great suggestions and reworks that kept coming my way. Thanks for caring so much about this particular book. Marketing star Julia Baxter—thanks for your openness to trying new ideas and following through on them. Of course, without my acquisitions editor Stephanie Frerich reaching out to me for lunch this never would have happened. Your Midwest values were a constant rock we could lean on.

My Inspirational Leaders　These are some of the busiest people I know, yet they have always been generous with their time and advice—thank you: Tony Hsieh, Guy Kawasaki, Scott Monty, Tom Izzo, Chris Brogan, Dave Kerpen, Angelo Pizzo, Angel Martinez, C.C. Chapman, Ron Jones, Mike Lewis, Ann Handley, Jeremiah Owyang, David Berkowitch, Alex Hult, Hakan Sjoo, Brian Solis, Chris Loughlin, Sean Cook, Mari Smith, Michael Stelzner, David Meerman Scott, John Hill, Mark Hollis, Lon Safko, Philip Hult, Cristina Teuscher, Josh Linkner, Dan Zarella, Paul Gillan, Mike Volpe, Dean Gilligan, Ralph Bartel, Lutz Bethge, Bill Hallock, Brian Reich, Michael Lewis, Stephen Kaufer, Dean Gilligan, Gary Kusin, Seth Godin, Corey Perlman, Eli Cox, Steve Kaufer, Jane Wooldridge, and Dan Heath.

Must Reads　Tony Hsieh, *Delivering Happiness* • Dan and Chip Heath, *Made to Stick* and *Switch* • Tony Dungy and Nathan Whitaker, *Uncommon* and *Quiet Strength* • Stephen Covey, *7 Habits of Highly Effective People* • Bill George, *True North* • Dale Carnegie, *How to Win Friends and Influence People* • Dale Carnegie, *How to Stop Worrying and Start Living* • Jim Collins, *Good to Great* • Marcus Buckingham, *Now, Discover Your Strengths* • Brian Halligan and Dharmesh Shah, *Inbound Marketing* • David Meerman Scott, *The New Rules of Marketing and PR* • Dave Kerpen, *Likeable Social Media* • Howard Schultz, *Onward* • Guy Kawasaki, *Enchantment* • David Kirkpatrick, *The Facebook Effect* • Charlene Li and Josh Bernoff, *Groundswell*

CHAPTER ONE

Life, Leadership, Legacy

"A man is the sum of his actions, of what he has done, of what he can do, nothing else."

—GANDHI

At one time, if you reached a certain level of celebrity or significance, you may have been immortalized on a postage stamp. Neil Armstrong, for example, was the first man to walk on the moon and a stamp was created, chronicling the event. Few people, however, attained this level of notoriety. The digital age has changed this concept: now *every single one of us* has a *digital* stamp. This new stamp is not simply reserved for the Gandhis and Elvises of this world and has greater reach than ones derived of paper and glue.

Digital footprints and shadows constitute our permanent imprint on the world: a detailed summary of our life for our contemporaries and for people of the future to view and consider. Digital footprints are the information we post about ourselves online, while digital shadows are what others upload about us. Collectively, these two items have changed the world forever, and as current or aspiring leaders it is necessary to adapt to this new reality. While others will help or hinder along the way, *you* will ultimately determine how effective a leader you become and your overall stamp on life.

With the advent of radical and accessible technology, each one of us, for the first time in history, is creating an influential mark forever—we are all mini-digital celebrities and heroes to someone. The fact that what we do today will be recorded for eternity is new to most of us and it can be downright overwhelming. Where exactly does our privacy end and our legacy begin?

As leaders, how does this new world affect the way we lead? How do we not only successfully lead our own lives, but those of others, whether they be our children, employees, church members, teammates, or beyond? What habits do we need to embrace to be effective digital leaders, knowing that our actions can be influential today, tomorrow, and 100 years from now? If you truly want a life that inspires, you need to change your leadership habits to adapt to the new digitally open world. This adjustment needs to start today.

The five habits of digital leadership form the acronym STAMP, referring to your personal stamp on your life and others. Each of these principles are discussed in depth throughout the book:

SIMPLE: success is the result of simplification and focus
TRUE: be true to your passion
ACT: nothing happens without action—take the first step
MAP: goals and visions are needed to get where you want to be
PEOPLE: success doesn't happen alone

A legacy of leadership isn't something far off in the distance, it is created by what you do now. Starting today, we will embrace our digital world and choose to lead a passion-filled and purposeful life, putting you on a path to success. By engaging in the five habits of digital leadership, we will empower others to achieve their best. In return, we will benefit from our followers' success—one needs to "give in order to get."

Whether you are a soccer mom or a CEO, to effectively lead you must understand how to properly navigate in a fully transparent society. Today, anything you say or do online or off will find its way into the digital realm. You can no longer have both a private and public life—they have become one and the same. The footprints we leave in the sand will be washed away with the coming tide, but our digital footprints last forever. For most of us, this shift is a radical one.

For example, Howard Schultz, while chairman of Starbucks, was disturbed when an internal digital memo leaked out to the press, social networks, and various blogs. Schultz approached his head of global communications, Wanda Herndon. "Did you hear about the memo?" asked Schultz. Wanda said yes, she knew about it. Schultz shook his head in disbelief and spoke about how hurt he was with the breach of trust. "Howard," Wanda said in the matter-of-fact way that Schultz had come to expect and appreciate from her, "Nothing is confidential. This is the new reality."

> "We don't get a chance to do that many things, and everyone should be really excellent. Because this is our life . . . life is brief, and then you die, you know?"
> —STEVE JOBS

Schultz admitted as such, "The leaked memo helped me comprehend the *enormous sea of change* occurring in how information was flowing as well as what was being communicated. *Technology was redefining the nature of relationships* and how people spend their time. The fundamental societal shift was affecting the psyche of our own people and our customers. But not until the memo leaked did it affect me, and none too soon."[1]

Internet security company AVG surveyed mothers in North America (USA and Canada), the EU5 (UK, France, Germany, Italy, and Spain), Australia/New Zealand, and Japan. The survey found 81 percent of children under the age of two have a digital profile, with images of them posted online. In the US, an astounding 92 percent of children under the age of two have an online presence.

According to JR Smith, AVG's CEO, "It's shocking to think that, while a 30-year-old has an online footprint stretching back 10-15 years at most, the vast majority of children today will have an online presence by the time they are two years old. A presence that will continue to build throughout their whole lives." He cautions parents to think about the type of information they upload about their children to the Web, since that content *"will follow him or her for the rest of their life."*

"Our research shows that the trend is increasing for a child's digital birth to coincide with and in many cases pre-date their real birth date. A quarter of babies have sonogram photos posted online before they have even physically entered into the world." Smith recommends parents think about two things:

"First, you are creating a digital history for a human being that will follow him or her for the rest of their life. What kind of footprint do you actually want to start for your child, and what will they think about the information you've uploaded in future? Secondly, it reinforces the need for parents to be aware of the privacy settings they have set on their social networks and other profiles. Otherwise, sharing a baby's picture and specific information may not only be shared with friends and family, but with the whole online world."[2]

Whether you are Howard Schultz or a concerned parent, this new reality can be daunting. The pages that follow will attempt to simplify what modern leadership means, both online and off.

Many technophobes that hear the term "digital" immediately believe it doesn't pertain to them. Make no mistake, even if you have never physically touched a computer, your life is being digitally chronicled by others right now. For example, a granddaughter posting a mobile video to her favorite social network of grandma singing karaoke is an example of a digital shadow.

A digital legacy has the capacity to highlight all the wondrous and shocking things that represent a life, not only in the future, but currently as well. Despite the term "digital," this idea is not simply about technology. If our offline behavior is being chronicled online then it affects our offline behavior as well. Whether we are digital savants or neophytes, all of us have the capability to accomplish our best life. A happy and purpose-filled life ultimately means that generations to come will view our legacy with awe and admiration rather than with empathy or apathy. In the present, it also means we have the capability to lead those within our physical proximity and those halfway around the world. Simply put, *word-of-mouth* has transformed into *world-of-mouth*. As a result of advances in technology, a leader's influence is now boundless.

Now more than ever, what is of upmost importance is not what we take from this world, it is what we leave behind. We need to collectively ask ourselves as individuals and leaders: Are we leaving the world better off than we found it?

> *"As we look ahead, leaders will be those who empower others."*
>
> **—BILL GATES**

Experienced writers advise that if you want the next big idea, you should first write a book. About midway through writing the international best-selling *Socialnomics*, I found this idea. Around the same time, I started getting questions from my MBA students, Fortune 500 businesses, small business, churches, non-profits, friends, and family. As I toured the world and gave keynotes on the same stage as prime ministers, celebrities, CEOs, and heads of charities, these leaders' and the audiences' questions and needs started to feel the same. The concerns centered on personal privacy, the overwhelming amount of messages they were inundated with, the want to produce more and respond less, and how to maintain relevance and standout. These people wanted to know how these issues played into their ability to maintain, or enter, a leadership role in this changing world. The pattern that was emerging to me was how do I achieve my best life, leadership, and legacy in the digital age? So I set out to determine the answer.

This book is not intended to be a "one-and-done" read. The hope is that you take notes and highlight the portions most relevant to you, then revisit them frequently. You will find "Digital Deeds Sidebars" peppered throughout the book as well. These practical and digital suggestions are designed to provide helpful tips and applications in understanding the available online and digital tools. New tools come out often, though, so please check my site, equalman.com, for the latest information and updates.

While others will help or hinder along the way, *you* will ultimately determine how effective a leader you become and your ultimate stamp on life. The following poem may say it best:

My Life Stamp

As a youth with little a plan,
My dad oft asked,
"What footprints are you going to leave in the sand?"

It meant little then,
But with time,
This became a motivating line.

If up to me,
What will be,
My ultimate legacy?

A legacy for me,
It would seem,
A far off, lofty dream.

After all, who am I?
I'm just average,
Somewhat shy.

Then I realized something you see,
It is up to me,
My ultimate legacy.

Social media, search,
Mobile, and more,
Leave digital footprints on the floor.

Digital shadows,
If you will,
Following all that I fulfill.

My grandchildren and great grandchildren,
What will they see and think of me?
What is my digital legacy?

Will they see that I pursued my dream,
Or that I settled,
For something in-between?

That I lived a life doing things I loved,
Or one filled with,
Should of, could of?

Digital footprints remain for all time,
So I can'l commit,
The ultimate crime.

What is that crime, you say?
It is, of course,
Not seizing the day.

Yes, before I die,
I'd rather fail,
Than not even try,

I will reach for the sky,
Laugh,
And cry.

I'll cry from joy not sorrow,
Because I lived for today
And planned for tomorrow.

My legacy,
You see,
Is truly up to me.

That's my view,
But, now I ask,
What will **you** do?

—Erik Qualman

> "The need to leave a legacy is our spiritual need to have a sense of meaning, purpose, personal congruence, and contribution."
>
> —STEPHEN COVEY, Author of *7 Habits of Highly Effective People*

This book will be there for you when you need inspiration to live a fulfilling life and will act as a guiding light to help you lead others—please use the material as such. In many ways, I have written this book as much for me as I have for you. While I do my best to adhere to the principles laid out here, I'm still a long way from following them consistently.

For those of you at the pinnacle of your career or personal life, this book will serve as a reminder that even the most accomplished people need to revisit the principles that were the foundation of their success. If not, their stay at the top will be short. This statement holds particularly true today and in the digital decades ahead.

Let's start the continuous journey of improving your life, leadership, and legacy.

SIMPLE

1. Life is complex, those that simplify it win

2. Complaining is toxic for a digital leader

3. We all make mistakes; it's how we digitally handle them that separates us

---

SIMPLE: success is the result of simplification & focus

TRUE: be true to your passion

ACT: nothing happens without action—take the first step

MAP: goals and visions are needed to get where you want to be

PEOPLE: success doesn't happen alone

CHAPTER TWO

Remove and Improve

"The trick isn't adding stuff, it's taking away."
—**MARK ZUCKERBERG,** Facebook Founder.[1]

Sean Parker, the cofounder of Napster and early advisor to Facebook, had this to say about Facebook founder Mark Zuckerberg: "Really great leadership, especially in a start-up, is about knowing when to say no—evoking a vision very clearly, getting people excited about it, but knowing when to draw the line, especially with products. You can't do everything. That's a lesson Mark didn't know yet. That's a lesson Mark learned."[2]

Like Mark Zuckerberg, we all need to learn and constantly revisit this "less is more" mantra. The saying "small is the new big" has been around for some time, yet many of us find it difficult to put into practice. Whether you run a billion dollar company or are just trying to run your life, in a digitally paced world success is dependent on simplification—a task which is far from simple.

Multitasking Inhibits Performance (More than Smoking Marijuana)

There is a great t-shirt that reads, "Multitasking, the best way to screw up both jobs." Many people would argue, however, that with all the tweets, texts, status updates, phone calls, and social gaming, we *must* multitask. Increasing workloads, dreams, and ambitions further force us to attempt to cram more and more into the limited time we have. You may ask, "But don't we need to multitask?" The answer is no, we don't. We believe this process makes us more efficient, but ironically, improper multitasking actually leads to less efficiency.

Decreasing Productivity

A study at The British Institute of Psychiatry showed that checking your email while performing another creative task decreases your IQ in the moment by 10 points. This decrease is the equivalent of the effects from not sleeping for 36 hours— and exhibits more than twice the impact of smoking marijuana.[3]

In a study of 1,000 of its employees, Basex, an information-technology research firm, found striking data showcasing inefficiency. It was determined that 2.1 hours per day is lost to interruptions. This figure indicates over 26 percent of the average workday is wasted due to multitasking and unwanted interruptions.[4] Jordan Grafman, chief of the cognitive neuroscience section at the National Institute of Neurological Disorders and Stroke, explains, "There's substantial literature on how the brain handles multitasking. And basically, it doesn't . . .what's really going on is a rapid toggling among tasks rather than simultaneous processing."[5]

Another study, conducted by professors at the University of California, observed the workflow and time-on-task of employees at two high-tech corporations. They discovered that the employees only spent an average of 11 minutes before being interrupted or having to move on to something else. It then took them 25 minutes to work their way back to their original task.[6]

Microsoft Research Labs ran a different type of study, but the results were similar. It found that following an interruption, such as an email or phone call, the participant then moved on to something different 40 percent of the time. It is incredible that only 60 percent of people stayed focused on their original task after an interruption.[7]

A study by Stanford psychologists Anthony Wagner and Eval Ophir found college students who often juggle many flows of information, such as checking status updates, reading email while Web texting, and chatting on the phone, performed significantly worse than those college students that limited their multitasking activity. As for what caused the differences—whether people with a predisposition to multitask happen to be mentally disorganized, or if multitasking feeds the condition—"that's the million dollar question, and we don't have a million dollar answer," said Clifford Nass, a Stanford University cognitive scientist.[8]

Researcher David Meyer, Ph.D., helped conduct a multitasking study at the University of Michigan. "People in a work setting," says Meyer, "who are banging away on word processors at the same time they have to answer phones and talk to their co-workers or bosses—they're doing switches all the time. Not being able to concentrate for, say, tens of minutes at a time, may mean it is costing a company as much as *20 to 40* percent" in terms of potential efficiency lost, or the "time cost" of switching. Meyer indicates, "It's kind of like one of the *Dirty Harry* movies with Clint Eastwood. At the end of the film Clint says, 'A man's gotta know his limitations.'"[9]

> "If you have more than three priorities, then you don't have any."
>
> —JIM COLLINS, Author of *Good to Great*

Our Digital Connectivity

When it comes to our own personal limits, it's always good to have some baseline statistics on what some of the averages are in relation to our digital connectivity and time constraints (below based on U.S. data):

- ▶ 20 = The average number of digital devices in a household
- ▶ 95 percent of families are online
- ▶ 43 percent of adults think they spend too much time online
- ▶ Adults interrupt meals more than kids via being online or on mobile phones
- ▶ 64 percent of adults think kids spend too much time online

- 18 percent of adults have considered a tech-free day
- 86 percent of people feel more informed and knowledgeable because of the Internet[10]

Staying abreast of statistics and research like the above is helpful for our own self-awareness as we forge ourselves into leaders. For example, if you are a parent, it's good to know (from above) that adults allow technology to interrupt meals more often than kids and teenagers. It would be difficult, as a parent, to lead your household if you are badgering your teenager about texting too much throughout the day, yet at the dinner table you are the one interrupting the meal by taking phone calls.

Tim Ferris author the *New York Times* Bestseller, *The Four Hour Work Week*, is also adamantly opposed to multitasking, specifically in regards to digital connectivity. When asked by Princeton students how he handles multitasking Ferris replied, "I try to eliminate multitasking. When I try to do more than one thing at a time, I wind up not getting anything done. Most emergencies are not emergencies. Focus on output more than input, because reading email all day is evil."

DIGITAL DEEDS

Let Technology Make Life Easier, Not Harder

Use technology to simplify your life, not complicate it. A few tips:

1. Batch process your various inboxes from 10-10:30 a.m. and 3-3:30 p.m.
2. If you don't know the sender, don't immediately accept the call, text, or chat.
3. Don't read the device/applications/software manual; these are cumbersome and poorly written. Do read online tips, forums, and/or watch short product videos. Simple tips learned here can save you many hours in the future.
4. Buy groceries online. The incremental delivery cost (roughly $7-$10) is minimal compared to the cost of your time, gas, stress, and physical transport (unloading the car, walking up stairs, ice

cream melting, etc.). Take advantage of the option that allows you to reorder your same list each week.

5. Treat digital conversations like a tennis match: quickly put the "ball" back in the other person's court by returning a concise message (two sentences or less) and, when appropriate, hit the winning shot that politely ends the conversation. Just as a cluttered desk makes you less efficient, a cluttered electronic inbox does the same thing.

6. Most digital inboxes have priority tools that sort by sender helping to visually sort the important from the unimportant—make sure to utilize this function to your advantage.

7. A keystroke in time saves nine: learn the shortcut keys for the programs you use most.

8. Give key people a different avenue to reach you than everyone else (e.g., "text me"). This relieves stress since truly urgent messages will not be lost in the clutter.

9. Emphatically use digital tools such as on-demand television and podcasts to view electronic content *on your schedule* and your terms. This avoids wasting time on things such as advertisements or segments of a program that don't interest you.

10. The bathroom, car, gym, or subway are all great places to listen to recorded material like podcasts. For the bathroom consider purchasing a small portable speaker that your phone or music device can plug into

11. Adjust your Web browser so your five most frequented sites automatically load when you open your computer or phone.

12. Purchase a good wireless/Bluetooth ear piece for your phone so you can perform minor, non-mental tasks while on the phone (e.g., wash dishes, fold laundry).

13. Don't constantly monitor items. For example, unless you are a day-trader, the act of incessantly checking the fluctuation of stock prices is a waste of time and energy.

14. When buying a new computer, select one that will close in "sleep" mode, rather than shutting down completely (e.g., "hibernate" mode). This avoids you having to wait for your computer each time it boots up or shuts down.

15. Download a free text recognition application/software for your phone. You speak and it types. This hasn't been perfected

yet, but it is very handy for taking down quick notes. It makes sending texts to friends and family effortless. It's not only a big timesaver, but it eliminates the typing difficulties associated with touch screens.

16. If you travel a lot, buy a portable scanner that can scan the receipts and business cards you receive and, most importantly, uploads them to Excel and your contacts list automatically, so there is no more manual data entry when you return.

Taxing Your Health

While multitasking can decrease productivity, it can also tax your health. Constantly switching between tasks is strenuous on the brain—similar to when you run multiple programs on your computer it slows down significantly. Managing two mental tasks at once reduces the brainpower available for either task, according to a study published in the journal *NeuroImage*. "It doesn't mean you can't do several things at the same time," says Dr. Just, co-director of Carnegie Mellon University's Center for Cognitive Brain Imaging. "But we're kidding ourselves if we think we can do so without cost."[11] Feeling overwhelmed, burned out, or full of anxiety due to multitasking can eventually lead to depression.

"Human lives have become too complicated—people have too many simultaneous goals and are always multitasking," Dr. Andrew Rosen, founder and director of South Florida's Center for the Treatment of Anxiety Disorders, told *Key Biscayne Magazine*. "Some text message and watch the news while having dinner. This is the worst for the brain, yet some people actually believe that multitasking improves their brain's ability like exercising a muscle. When, what it really does is overload the neurons, deplete the brain chemicals we need, and overload the central nervous system."[12] In a study published by *Reader's Digest*, volunteers played a computer game while having dinner. Cookies were offered as dessert. These people ate twice as many cookies following the meal than those who didn't multitask while eating.[13] With multitasking, our quality of work suffers and our sense of fulfillment and achievement decreases—a virtual double whammy.

These negative consequences from multitasking and interruptions can be easily avoided. They are a result of one not properly setting priorities. A key step in becoming a digital leader is the realization that you can't and shouldn't try to complete every single task that is "screaming" at you to be completed. Once you accept the fact that your aren't going to get everything done, then you can better address what should get done.

Exceptions to the Rule

There are, of course, exceptions to the no multitasking rule. Most prominent of these exceptions is when we are trapped somewhere unexpectedly resulting in idle time. Efficiency expert Michael Fortino offers the following troubling data for the average life lived in the United States. In your lifetime it is likely you will spend:

> "Once you accept the fact that you aren't going to get everything done, then you can better address what should get done."
> —@EQUALMAN

- ▶ Seven years in the bathroom
- ▶ Six years eating
- ▶ Five years waiting in line
- ▶ Three years in meetings
- ▶ Two years playing telephone tag
- ▶ Eight months opening junk mail
- ▶ Six months sitting at red lights

In an average day you will get interrupted 73 times, take an hour of work home, read less than five minutes, talk to your spouse for four minutes, exercise less than three minutes, and play with your kid for two minutes.[14] Knowing these daunting statistics and pitfalls better enables us to avoid them and become more productive. Being delayed at the airport is a great example: responding to emails and texts while you wait in the customer service line is a good use of your idle time.

Technology is a lifesaver when it comes to long waits at the supermarket or doctor's office as well. In such cases, checking on your friends via social media, replying to email, or sending a quick text is a better use of your time than fuming about the wait. But if you need the mental break and aren't upset by the wait, a mini-break from technology might be therapeutic.

Consider performing these positive multitasking combinations:

- ▶ Folding laundry while watching TV or talking on the phone
- ▶ Listening to a podcast at the gym
- ▶ Cleaning the bathtub while taking a shower
- ▶ Rocking your baby to sleep while listening to French language instruction
- ▶ Reading in the bathroom

Avoid these negative multitasking combinations, which will decrease your efficiency while increasing your stress levels:

- ▶ Listening to a podcast while writing a memo to the Board of Directors
- ▶ Watching a YouTube clip while having a conversation on the phone
- ▶ Answering a phone call or text while meeting with someone else
- ▶ Texting while driving

Texting While Driving Is More Dangerous than Drinking While Driving

Information about texting while driving exposes the dark side of multitasking. If you have been imploring your teenager, husband, or wife to avoid texting or tweeting when they are behind the wheel and they haven't changed their habits, please show them the following arresting results from a test conducted by *Car & Driver* Magazine in which two drivers' reaction times were observed.[15]

TABLE 1.1: Reaction Times and Extra Distance Traveled at 35 MPH

Averages at 35 MPH	Reaction Time (seconds)		Extra Distance Traveled (ft)	
	DRIVER 1	DRIVER 2	DRIVER 1	DRIVER 2
Baseline	0.45	0.57	—	—
Reading	0.57	1.44	6	45
Texting	0.52	1.36	4	41
Impaired	0.46	0.64	1	7

TABLE 1.2: Reaction Times and Extra Distance Traveled at 70 MPH

Averages at 70 MPH	Reaction Time (seconds)		Extra Distance Traveled (ft)	
	DRIVER 1	DRIVER 2	DRIVER 1	DRIVER 2
Baseline	0.39	0.56	—	—
Reading	0.50	0.91	11	36
Texting	0.48	1.24	9	70
Impaired	0.50	0.60	11	4

Specifically, *Car & Driver* found that, compared to a baseline of attentive driving, impaired drivers traveling at 70 MPH (103 feet/second) took 8 feet longer to react to danger and begin braking their vehicle. By contrast, test results showed that texting drivers took 40 feet longer to react and begin braking.

Thus, the texting drivers reacted 5 times slower than the impaired drivers did. *Car & Driver's* results showed the same five-fold difference for drivers traveling 35 MPH. From these data points we can conclude that texting while driving is one of the most dangerous activities a person can undertake.

Alternatives to Multitasking

Interruptions often cause you to multitask. For example, how many times have you been typing a message when someone drops by for a chat? Many of us casually continue typing while holding the conversation with the interrupter. This situation isn't good for you, the receiver of the message, or the person standing in front of you. Try this next time immediately at the start of the interruption: "Jane, I'm glad you stopped by. I'd love to catch-up this afternoon. I'll swing over later." In some instances, you may be letting Jane off the hook. She may have felt compelled to stop and say something to you since she was walking by your desk and didn't want to be rude.

If you are constantly being interrupted by fellow employees, instant messages, or phone calls, reserve a small conference room for a little bit of time, grab your laptop, and crank away. If you are at your home go to a local coffee house or a park with your laptop or tablet. Another trick is to wear you phone's headset or earbuds even when you aren't on a call as people will be less likely to interrupt you.

One group we should look to for guidance on how to avoid the pitfalls of multitasking is writers. Writers have known for years that they need absolute focus and concentration to churn out their best work. Often they seek solitude in a remote location or summer cottage void of distraction so they can complete the task. We don't have to all become David Thoreau, who spent two years in the woods writing *Walden* (1854), but moving our lifestyles a little in that direction is certainly a positive first step toward increased efficiency.

Just like writers, teams from the National Football League and Major League Baseball teams go to remote locations for their training camps. The NFL teams go to small towns outside their respective cities for a few weeks, while baseball has spring training in small, warm weather towns. This concept is also seen when companies hold offsite meetings or retreats. The place chosen isn't downtown Manhattan, rather it's somewhere remote with less external stimuli.

In general, simplification of processes and concentrating on the basics will help you as a leader in the digital age. Consider the following story about Alan Mullaly, the CEO of Ford, who made a number of offline and online changes when he began working for the company to create an environment more conducive to productivity, creativity, and efficiency.

Alan Mulally and Ford

When Alan Mulally was early in his tenure as the CEO of Ford, I was fortunate to share the speaking stage with him in Arizona. During the discussion I was transfixed by his story. He indicated that when he first came to Ford from Boeing in 2006 he was struck by several issues within the company culture.

One item that stood out to him was when he pulled into the executive parking lot—there wasn't a Ford car in sight. Rather, there were Land Rovers, Jaguars, and Aston Martins—brands which Ford had acquired over the years—being washed, waxed, and buffed. Right there Mulally knew things had to change. They weren't going to have a chance of turning around the Ford brand if the executives were buffing so many different high-end luxury brands, cars that the average person couldn't afford.

Moreover, the amount of brands under Ford was causing confusion in the marketplace. As Mulally states, "Nobody buys a 'house of brands.'" Hence, from that day forward the teams concentrated on shining and buffing the Ford brand. Part of Mulally's plan was to bring the digital cockpit concept from planes at Boeing into the cars at Ford, but he knew he had to simplify and get some of the basics down first. Part of this simplification included eliminating the pervasive multi-tasking approach at the organization. He knew if they were too busy trying to grow Land Rover, Volvo, and Jaguar along-side the Ford brand it would be a challenge to simply tread water, let alone insert new concepts like the forward thinking digital cockpit in a timely manner. This idea is part of what becoming a digital leader is all about. It's just as important what you decide *not* to do as it is what you do.

In this instance Mulally put a stake in the sand that the executives and everyone else at the company was going to focus on growing the Ford brand across the globe. The concept is known as "One Ford." Mulally profoundly understood that we live in a global economy—a concept that all digital leaders grasp. For example, in the past it may have been more prudent to have different names for the same or similar product in different parts of the world. With technology shrinking the world, however, a commercial that goes viral will be seen globally. Therefore, the more you can grow one brand—Apple, Microsoft, or Google—the greater your return. Operationally, Mulally also wanted to build a global platform so that all parts were compatible across the globe. They were going to concentrate on smaller, more fuel-efficient vehicles.

To remind everyone at the company of the "One Ford" strategy, he had plastic plates printed up and distributed to all employees. One side read "One Ford" while the other side read "One Team. One Plan. One Goal." Mulally carries spares in case employees can't produce theirs if asked. Note that even though we live in a digital world it's still effective to utilize such physical items as reminders. We'll discuss this concept more in the chapters that follow.

Another item stood out to Mulally during his first days at Ford. He looked out the giant window at the top of the company's headquarters and he could see the Ford River Rouge plant, whose operations began in 1917. He turned to one of the top executives and said he wanted to go down and tour the plant that afternoon. The executive reacted to Mulally like he had made a joke. "With all due respect sir, that's not a place for us. We don't go there."

"What do you mean?" asked Mulally

"Well it just would be uncomfortable."

"How so?" asked Mulally

"Well, I mean many of the workers have tattoos."

As Mulally told this part of the story, he stated in his Midwest twang, "that executive is no longer employed at Ford." The executive made the wrong choice in deciding that he was not going to visit some of the rougher plants as it would take him out of his comfort zone. Success or failure when it comes to digital leadership is often decided by what you select to not do. In this instance the executive chose poorly. A good guide when you are simplifying items off your plate is that if it takes you out of your comfort zone, or others' comfort zones, then that is often a good sign you are pioneering. You are starting to think like a digital leader.

Having the mission of the company simplified down to One Ford, Mullaly's next focus was changing the culture and thinking at the organization. Mulally accomplished this focus by defining a simple but powerful mission—build higher quality, more fuel efficient, safer cars that employees could rally around. "The more each of us knows what we're really contributing to, the more motivated and excited and inspired we are," he says.[16]

Mulally also wanted to change the way of thinking at Ford from traditional to innovative in regards to digital connectivity and utilization of new technologies. One way to convey this plan, both internally and externally, was by speaking at technology shows like the Consumer Electronics Show (CES) in Vegas rather than simply giving keynotes at various auto shows. He also decided Ford needed to simplify the dealer showroom floor by making dealers look and function more like an Apple store. Although not an avid user of Twitter himself, he'd take question and answer sessions from customers with his head of social media, Scott Monty. Through these simplified steps, technology, and messaging he's been able to change the culture of Ford back to how innovative founder Henry Ford had started the business. Ford stock during this time went from $1.87 (January 2009) to $15.95 (January 2011).

Speaking at digital events was a step in the right direction, but Mulally also put his money where his mouth was. Although it was a difficult time to invest in innovation with the stock on the verge of being delisted, Mulally forged ahead with MyTouch—the digital cockpit—which utilized SYNC technology from Microsoft. Mulally realized that even in difficult financial times it's imperative to stay innovative.

It is important to note that, while Alan Mulally exhibits digital leadership, he isn't a digital native (i.e., grew up with technology and lives, breaths, and sleeps technology) like some other digital leaders (e.g., HDNet Chairman Mark Cuban, Zappos CEO Tony Hsieh). Just as Mulally morphed into a digital leader, you can as well.

Curse of Knowledge

Dan and Chip Heath brought the curse of knowledge to popularity in their book *Made to Stick*. In an interview with digital expert Guy Kawasaki they explain the theory:

> Lots of research in economics and psychology shows that when we know something, it becomes hard for us to imagine not knowing it. As a result, we become lousy communicators. Think of a lawyer who can't give you a straight, comprehensible answer to a legal question. His vast knowledge and experience renders him unable to fathom how little you know. So when he talks to you, he talks in abstractions that you can't follow. And we're all like the lawyer in our own domain of expertise.[17]

Knowledge is a great thing, but we don't want to drown in it. We not only need to simply our lives, but we also need to simplify anything we project onto the world. When there are 48 hours of video being uploaded to YouTube and Twitter is limited to 140 characters of text you need to be as succinct as possible with your thoughts and messages. If you are lucky, your listening audience will remember one thing that you say or type, so make sure you provide messages in easy to digest formats. We can look at a few modern-day U.S. Presidents to see how challenging sticking with a simplified message can be.

Both Bill Clinton and Barack Obama exhibited great intelligence and charisma during their ascent to president. But, they often struggled trying to answer questions concisely and had difficulty clarifying points in their campaign platforms. They could see all the country's issues but also wanted to address and solve them all at once.

Bill Clinton

This problem of complexity was particularly apparent with President Clinton, as Dan and Chip Heath point out:

> As Clinton's key political adviser, James Carville had to cope with this complexity (Clinton trying to address everything)

leading up to the 1992 election . . .Carville wrote three phrases on a whiteboard for all the campaign workers to see. One of the phrases on the impromptu list was "It's the economy, stupid." This message would become the core of Clinton's successful campaign . . . "It was simple and it was self-effacing," Carville explained. "I was trying to say, "Let's don't be too clever here, don't come down here thinking we're too smart. Let's just remember the basics." . . . Clinton's advisers had to tell him, "There has to be message triage. If you say three things, you don't say anything."[18]

With all the digital mining and collecting of data available to us today we can easily decide we need to share everything with everybody. However, as a digital leader, part of your job is to curate what is the most important of all items at your disposal. Just like in Clinton's case, if you say three things you have said nothing. It is very difficult to break through all the information that is available digitally. To give yourself the best chance and to avoid confusing your followers you need to simplify what you stand for and your message around it.

Barack Obama

President Barack Obama faced similar challenges in his uphill battle to defeat Hillary Clinton in 2008. He was a first term senator and a long shot to gain the Democratic Party's presidential nomination. He and his advisors knew he needed a simple message. The Obama election campaign astutely understood that the country was mired in historic financial disarray and that the American people wanted change. His campaign effectively and accurately painted Hillary Clinton, and later John McCain, as part of the establishment that created the mess. Hence, the Obama camp's rallying cry was "Change You Can Believe In."

In particular, the younger generations wanted change and Obama recognized these individuals were a potential source of support. The fact that Obama actually used a smart phone separated him from Hillary Clinton and John McCain at the time. This difference was very symbolic to the young voter, showcasing a contemporary quality in the candidate.

Many experts indicated that, while the support of younger voters was an asset, they didn't have money, nor did they usually turn out on voting day. They agreed that it would be next to impossible for Obama to raise the money needed to compete with the Clinton political machine and its funding, especially if he was relying heavily on Generation Y. If Obama had listened to this negativity, he wouldn't have been elected President. However, he embraced the young potential voters, utilizing tools of the new digital generation. He reached out to twenty-something Chris Hughes to help him with the social media portion of his campaign.

Hughes was relatively unknown, but he was one of the founders of a new and upcoming social networking platform called Facebook. With the help of Hughes and others to properly leverage the new medium of social media, Obama's campaign garnered 5 million followers on social media sites and 5.4 million clicked on an "I voted for Obama" Facebook button. Most importantly, this resulted in donors contributing $500 million to the fundraising effort. A startling 92 percent of the donations were in increments of less than $100.[19] Even though Hughes knew all the inner workings of Facebook as well as a myriad of other hot social sites at the time, they kept the campaign simple by focusing primarily on basic offerings on Facebook and YouTube. The Obama team also created a clean and simple process to take online donations via social media in small increments. These small increments added up to more campaign funding than any of his competitors.

Obama pulled off an improbable victory over Hillary Clinton in the Democratic primary. He continued his simple strategy of "change" and appealing to the younger generation as he ran against Republican John McCain in the general election. Helped by the digital dissemination of information via Facebook, a record number of 18-29 year-olds (23 million) showed up at the polls, the majority backing Obama.[20]

It is important to note that even though we live in a hyper-connected world we can still learn from the past. Obama practiced this by studying John F. Kennedy's campaign. Kennedy leveraged the new medium of television to defeat better-known Republican Richard Nixon 49.7 percent to 49.6 percent in the popular vote. Instead of television, Obama leveraged social media to defeat Senator Hillary Clinton in the Democratic primary and then Senator John McCain in the general election. In the manner of JFK and Obama, consider creatively employing new technologies to help reach your goals. (Pay particular attention to the *Digital Deeds* suggestions in this book to help your pursuit.)

Ronald Reagan

Ronald Reagan's intellectual capacity may not have been as great as Clinton's or Obama's, but his ability to motivate and inspire citizens via simplicity certainly was. Being able to speak directly and express himself in clear, simple terms is a key reason why Reagan is one of the most beloved and respected U.S. presidents in history.

During his 1984 presidential campaign, Reagan, with the help of San Francisco advertising man Hal Riney, developed the now famous "It's Morning Again in America" campaign. Not only did it help produce a landslide victory over Walter Mondale, it also won numerous advertising awards. The ads highlighted a few simple, but strong, facts about what Reagan had accomplished in his first term. Below is the text:

> It's morning again in America. Today more men and women will go to work than ever before in our country's history. With interest rates at about half the record highs of 1980, nearly 2,000 families today will buy new homes, more than at any time in the past four years. This afternoon 6,500 young men and women will be married, and with inflation at less than half of what it was just four years ago, they can look forward with confidence to the future. It's morning again in America, and under the leadership of President Reagan, our country is prouder and stronger and better. Why would we ever want to return to where we were less than four short years ago?

Rather than focusing on his opponent (Walter Mondale), Reagan focused on what he believed was right for America.

Following his election, and true to his campaign promises, Reagan concentrated his attention on what was right for America and the world. He went on to achieve one of his greatest accomplishments; helping end the Cold War. The Cold War involved not only the Soviet Union and the United States, but also many other countries. While the danger was real, the "war" was amorphous and difficult for citizens to comprehend.

To clarify the Cold War, Reagan directed people's attention to something that was tangible and well known, the Berlin Wall. The Berlin Wall was constructed in 1961, was over 100 miles long and 12 feet high, and separated Soviet-controlled East Berlin from West Berlin.[21] The tall concrete and steel-reinforced wall was constructed to thwart the large numbers of East Germans fleeing to West Berlin. While people around the world couldn't feel, touch, or smell the cold war, the ominous Berlin Wall was tangible. Reagan understood this was a symbol of oppression that could rally worldwide support.

On June 14, 1987, Reagan stood in West Berlin facing the Berlin Wall at the Brandenburg Gate and applied tremendous pressure on the Soviet Union's General Secretary Mikhail Gorbachev by speaking these historic words, "if you seek peace, if you seek prosperity for the Soviet Union and Eastern Europe, if you seek liberalization: Come here to this gate! Mr. Gorbachev, open this gate! Mr. Gorbachev, tear down this wall!"

Reagan's genius of using the Berlin Wall to symbolize the tyranny of the iron curtain and communist oppression was a catalyst that helped end one of the most dangerous periods in the 20th century. Reagan's uncanny ability to simplify and connect with his audience rightfully earned him the nickname: "The Great Communicator."

Many leaders that achieve great success give much of the credit to others. This was certainly true of Ronald Reagan as is evident in his farewell speech on January 11, 1989:

And in all of that time I won a nickname, "The Great Communicator." But I never thought it was my style or the words I used that made a difference: It was the content. I wasn't a great communicator, but I communicated great things, and they didn't spring full bloom from my brow, they came from the heart of a great nation—from our experience, our wisdom, and our belief in the principles that have guided us for two centuries. They called it the Reagan revolution. Well, I'll accept that, but for me it always seemed more like the great rediscovery, a rediscovery of our values and our common sense.[22]

The crisp, principled, and substantive content of his communications and his bold, yet self-effacing style endeared him to the American public. In fact, as shown below, a 2009 *U.S. News* poll placed Ronald Reagan's popularity ahead of other highly regarded U.S. presidents:

1. Ronald Reagan   (24%)
2. Abraham Lincoln   (22%)
3. John F. Kennedy   (22%)
4. Franklin Roosevelt   (18%)
5. George Washington   (09%)[23]

Ronald Reagan's Legacy: How Does It Apply to Us?

So how does Ronald Reagan's legacy apply to us and digital leadership? We can all become masters of simplification. Consider what your Berlin Wall is. What can you tear down to achieve simplicity? What is your singular point of focus? Think of a focus/vision that is tangible and go for it: *write a screen play, become a better grandparent, complete a marathon, raise funds to add a new wing to the children's hospital, learn a new language, be the CMO of Coca-Cola, become president of the women's league,* or *start a new soup kitchen in your mother's name—the possibilities are endless.* (We will talk more about visions in Chapters 12–14.)

The Simple Genius of Forrest Gump

Forrest Gump, the lead character played by actor Tom Hanks in the 1994 film of the same name, is born with limited mental and physical abilities. His crooked spine makes even walking arduous for young Forrest. He has only been blessed with a meager IQ of around 75. As a result, his mother (played by Sally Fields) has to sleep with the school principal to get him admitted into the public school.

Yet, despite these deficiencies, Gump leads a rich, passion- and purpose-filled life. As we learn more about the character of Forrest Gump, we realize that he is closer to *genius* than simpleton. Gump's greatest weakness is also his greatest strength. He is a very simple man. This characteristic is the essence of the genius of the Forrest Gump character. Gump shows us that anyone can reach his or her dreams; success is truly a choice.

While Forrest Gump didn't grow up in the digital age, we will revisit him several times in this book as he exemplifies each of the five principles (**S**imple, **T**rue, **A**ct, **M**ap, **P**eople). As mentioned in Chapter One, these 5 leadership habits which form the acronym STAMP refer to your ultimate stamp on life. As the reader, use Gump as a guide to easily remember these 5 important concepts. One of the reasons Gump is used as an example is the counterintuitive concept that you (the reader) are being asked to emulate traits of Forrest Gump, rather than say a Julius Caesar.

A famous line in *Forrest Gump* is, "My momma always said, life was like a box of chocolates. You never know what you're gonna get." This quote is similar to the Yiddish proverb "Men tracht und Gott lacht," which roughly translates to "Men plan and God laughs." These sayings observe that life is uncertain. Because of this uncertainty, much of our success depends on the understanding that while we cannot control life's events, we are in absolute control of how we react to them. For exam- ple, can we control what someone digitally posts about us? We can influence it, but no we can't control it. What we can con- trol is our reaction and response to the post.

Forrest Gump embodies the power of positive reaction inherent in of all of us, yet few of us figure out how to unlock it. Most people have difficulty adjusting when things don't go as planned. Nobody likes change, yet the only thing constant in the world in which we live is change. Consider that more people are now accessing the Internet via mobile devices than via computers. This mobility enables a greater flow of information, resulting in evermore change in the way we interact, learn, and work.

If we dislike change but it is all around us, we are on a direct path to frustration. Have you ever found yourself screaming and swearing at the telephone when a bank's voice recognition system doesn't understand you, or you are abruptly disconnected after being on hold for thirty minutes? We don't see Gump complaining about his plight, which is much more serious than wrestling with a dreadful customer service system. Instead of getting upset, Gump bounces from one unexpected circumstance to the next, most of which begin rather unfavorably for him.

Ironically, those people close to Gump often become frustrated with him. They feel he is oblivious to how cruel the world is around him—how could he be so ignorant? They certainly would be complaining if they were in his shoes! Can't he see, as they can, that he should be miserable, or give up on what seems a hopeless situation?

Which leads us to another very important line in the movie: *"Momma always said, stupid is as stupid does."* Well, if "stupid is as stupid does" then Forrest Gump is far from stupid. All of us should be lucky enough to lead such a fulfilling life.

Let's take a look at what Gump accomplishes throughout the film:

- ▶ All-American football player at the University of Alabama
- ▶ Decorated war hero—Medal of Honor recipient
- ▶ International ping pong champion—defeats the Chinese
- ▶ Follows through on a promise to a deceased friend (Bubba)
- ▶ Jogs across the U.S. for three and one half years becoming famous in the process and creating a legion of followers
- ▶ Successful business man and billionaire (Bubba Gump Shrimp)
- ▶ Successful investor (purchases Apple Stock)
- ▶ Loving son, husband, and father

He is highly successful despite being labeled a "moron" by society. Forrest Gump faces more challenges in one day than most of us will face in a lifetime.

So what can we learn from Forrest Gump? *It is important to simplify our mission in life*. Consider the following scene from the movie:

> **Drill Sergeant:** Gump! What's your sole purpose in this army?
> **Forrest Gump:** To do whatever you tell me, drill sergeant!
> **Drill Sergeant:** God damn it, Gump! You're a goddamn genius! This is the most outstanding answer I have ever heard. You must have a goddamn I.Q. of 160. You are goddamn gifted, Private Gump. Listen up, people . . .
> **Forrest Gump:** [narrates] Now for some reason I fit in the army like one of them round pegs. It's not really hard. You just make your bed real neat and remember to stand up straight and always answer every question with "Yes, drill sergeant."
> **Drill Sergeant:** . . . Is that clear?
> **Forrest Gump:** Yes, drill sergeant![24]

The secret to Gump's success in the army, as well as in life, is his ability to hyper focus on one task at a time. He has simplified his life each step of the way. One thing in Gump's favor is that he doesn't suffer from the "curse of knowledge." If he did he might convince himself that he can't jog from New York to San Francisco, or it is foolish to use all your money to purchase a shrimp boat when you don't know the first thing about catching shrimp.

> *"Information is gushing at your brain like a fire hose pointed at a tea cup."*
> **—SCOTT ADAMS,** Dilbert Cartoonist

Author Tim Ferris, mentioned earlier in this chapter, does the same thing when he focuses first thing in the morning on the one or two "outputs" he needs to get done that day. Ferris has a firm understanding of how complex the world can be. However, he also understands that the complexity of the world is often the result of our own doing. In order for Ferris to avoid falling into this trap, he has employed the simplification trick of focusing on one or two outputs he wants to accomplish each day. Outputs are objects that you tangibly produced or items that add value to your life and society. Responding to one hundred emails is not a tangible output—that is more "input." For example, writing a blog post is a tangible output. Learning how to do a full turn in Salsa or a headstand in Yoga is an output. By focusing on just one or two outputs per day, Ferris has simplified his life and in turn has become more productive, happier, and famous.

Like Gump and Ferris, we want to get our lives to a simplified state. We want to be focused on a well-defined mission that we can attack with vigor. The modern world demands that we behave more like a Mini-Cooper than a cement truck. We need to be small and nimble with the ability to quickly shift gears when an opening presents itself. We can't be towing an eighteen-wheeler behind us—it's not feasible. We need to remove excess baggage before improvement can begin.

CHAPTER THREE

Complain = Digital Pain

"If you don't like something, change it. If you can't change it, change your attitude. Don't complain."

—MAYA ANGELOU

Inspired by the nonprofit group A Complaint Free World (www.acomplaintfreeworld.org), Republican Sam Graves of Missouri submitted House Resolution 404 to the Committee on Oversight and Government. Graves proposed that the day before Thanksgiving should become a national "complaint free Wednesday."[1] Why was Graves so compelled to stop people from complaining?

Complaining is negative energy that is counterproductive to greatness. To achieve success we need to eliminate excess weight from our life's backpack and the first thing to remove is the heavy box labeled "complaints." Imagine all the items jammed into our backpack of life; we can almost feel the weight of the straps digging into our shoulders. Now imagine how much lighter the backpack becomes when we remove the negative complaint box.

The primary reason we complain is that we feel insecure or powerless. The practice then becomes habitual. Offline complaints will permeate your digital communication, opening a doorway to a seemingly infinite audience. To be a leader in the changing modern world, it is imperative to break this habit.

Reducing Your Complaints

Ironically, the first step in reducing our own complaints is to look outside ourselves. We need to find the influencers and enablers of complaining. We needn't look far—these people are all around us. According to a survey by the Gottman Institute,[2] across all conversations there is a ratio of 1 to 6 in terms of encouragement to criticism. So for every one "good job" there are six "why can't you be more like your brother?" "he doesn't listen," "when you do that it gets on my nerves," "you never," "they don't get it," or "you can't" type statements.

For the next week pay close attention to who in your life is constantly harping. As a baseline, the average person complains 15-30 times per day.[3] Listen carefully for those that may be above 20 complaints per twenty-four hour period. If you can limit your contact with the top complainer, this is a great step in the right direction to start reducing the amount you complain (a topic covered more in Chapters 15–17 where I discuss how we can surround ourselves with great people). You can follow this advice digitally as well.

> "I had no shoes and complained, until I met a man who had no feet."
>
> —INDIAN PROVERB

Look at posts via email, chat, social media, and more and you'll easily see the top complainers. Also, keep in mind that people who complain offline generally complain digitally, too.

If the center of negativity is within your immediate family, your task will be a little more difficult. In this instance, you will need to focus on yourself first and help influence their behavior through your changed, positive one (which can take time!). Start by eliminating the daily number of complaints you exhaust. Ideally you'd take it to zero, but this will take practice and time. The key is to start the reduction process.

Be Part of the Solution

A good rule of thumb is to be part of the solution rather than the problem. Specifically, if you find yourself or others complaining, stop, you are simply becoming part of the problem you are complaining about. Instead, offer some solutions or, better still, contribute effort toward a solution. Despite what we might think, most people don't want to hear our complaints. They are already burdened with their own problems, which they care about much more than ours! When you ask someone how he or she is doing, do you really want to hear about how much he or she hates his or her boss? No, you don't. This doesn't indicate that you aren't a caring person, it's simply human nature.

Don't enable chronic complainers by joining the chorus of negativity. If you take on someone else's burden today you aren't really helping that person for the future. It's similar to the old proverb, "Give a man a fish; you have fed him for today. Teach a man to fish; and you have fed him for a lifetime." The best way to improve other people's lives around you is to ensure that you are happy—your positivity will influence others. Maintain an outlook of optimism, geared toward action to change a negative situation. Provide potential solutions to an issue, as compared to simply supporting complaints. John Woodall's father, a pastor, was always fond of saying, "Don't wait to give roses of encouragement at someone's funeral, give them roses of encouragement when it is still called today."[4]

Optimists have additional health benefits as well, they:

- ▶ Live an average of 9.5 years longer
- ▶ Are 9 percent less likely to develop heart disease
- ▶ Have a blood pressure that is 5 percent lower on average[5]

When faced with a challenge try to remember the Spanish saying "es parte de paseo," which translated, means, "it's part of the passage." It's particularly imperative to have this mindset when leaving our digital footprint. We don't want a trail littered with complaints and negative comments. If your digital trail is strewn with pessimism it reflects poorly on you today and tomorrow. Most poignantly, complaining undermines our ability to lead in the here and now. If you are already in a leadership role, you must assume anything you do offline and online will eventually be digested by your current and future followers. If you habitually complain you will either a) have your followers leave you since people like to follow individuals that inspire hope, or b) have a legion of chronic complainers. Neither of these resulting scenarios will benefit you and you will cease being an effective digital leader.

If you are like most people, you are in the process of developing your leadership skills and base of followers. Anyone can offer a complaint or criticism—those that offer solutions are thinking differently and becoming leaders. As a result, their digital legacy will ultimately stand out above the rest. Let's look at a few examples of people who have learned the hard way that digital complaints can have negative consequences.

Twitter Bird to Jailbird

Paul Chambers, a U.K. based tax accountant, was planning to fly out of Robin Hood Airport. To his disappointment he discovered the airport was closed and his flight canceled. An avid Twitter user, Chambers immediately posted: "Robin Hood airport is closed. You've got a week and a bit to get your **** together otherwise I'm blowing the airport sky high!"

While Chambers later indicated he was satirically messing around, a Robin Hood Airport employee didn't find it such a laughing matter. He immediately alerted the authorities about Chambers' post. Chambers was apprehended by police at his office, was convicted and fined 3,000 British Pounds for a post deemed "menacing" in its content. Chambers also lost his job.

> *"You can overcome anything if you don't bellyache."*
>
> **—BERNARD BARUCH**

Many bloggers came to his defense, indicating it was an attack on free speech. "What has been on trial is the possibility of humor itself, the right of a freeborn Englishman to be facetious as and when he feels like it, about any subject whatsoever," says Heresy Corner blog under the heading, "With the conviction of Paul Chambers, it is now illegal to be English."[6]

While many support Chambers, it's a reminder that we need to be careful using satire and threats via digital avenues.

Such posts, even in jest, obviously can lead to major repercussions. While Chambers may have thought his sarcastic complaint was humorous, he should have considered the amount of people who would be viewing the remark. In this new digital world, it is imperative to keep the universality of online posts and conversations in mind. All leaders need to keep this concept in mind both in their personal and professional online presence—everything stated is there for all to read.

DIGITAL DEEDS

Lost in Digital Translation

Here are two lists to consider before you decide to post comments or material online.

Win:
► Common sense
► Passion
► Post like your mom is watching
► Some things are best-handled offline
► Punchy & positive
► Prudent & proper use at work

Fail:
► Sarcasm
► Complaints
► Off-color jokes
► Racist comments
► Illegal activity—even if it's a joke
► Arguing politics & religion is tricky (avoid making it personal)

Ketchum Vice President

Even "experts" in the field of digital communications can misstep in their online presence. Consider the case of James Andrews. Andrews was a vice president for public relations and communications firm Ketchum. One of their main clients was FedEx, who is headquartered in Memphis, Tennessee. Andrews, based in New York City, flew down to Memphis for a meeting with FedEx to help discuss, among other things, the proper use of digital communications. During his stay in Memphis, Andrews posted this statement via Twitter: "True confession but I'm in one of those towns where I scratch my head and say 'I would die if I had to live here!'"

A FedEx employee discovered the post, was rightfully offended, and quickly responded to Andrews. In this response they copied both FedEx and Ketchum management. Andrews soon discovered the passion that many FedEx employees have for Memphis.

Mr. Andrews,

If I interpret your post correctly, these are your comments about Memphis a few hours after arriving in the global head-quarters city of one of your key and lucrative clients, and the home of arguably one of the most important entrepreneurs in the history of business, FedEx founder Fred Smith.

Many of my peers and I feel this is inappropriate. We do not know the total millions of dollars FedEx Corporation pays Ketchum annually for the valuable and important work your company does for us around the globe. We are confident however; it is enough to expect a greater level of respect and awareness from someone in your position as a vice president at a major global player in your industry. A hazard of social networking is people will read what you write.

Not knowing exactly what prompted your comments, I will admit the area around our airport is a bit of an eyesore, not without crime, prostitution, commercial decay, and a few potholes. But there is a major political, community, religious, and business effort underway, that includes FedEx, to trans-form that area. We're hopeful that over time, our city will have a better "face" to present to visitors.

James, everyone participating in today's event, including those in the auditorium with you this morning, just received their first paycheck of 2009 containing a 5% pay cut . . . which we wholeheartedly support because it continued the tradition established by Mr. Smith of doing whatever it takes to protect jobs.

Considering that we just entered the second year of a U.S. recession, and we are experiencing significant business loss due to the global economic downturn, many of my peers and I question the expense of paying Ketchum to produce the video open for today's event; work that could have been achieved by internal, award-winning professionals with decades of experience in television production.

Additionally Mr. Andrews, with all due respect, to continue the context of your post; true confession: many of my peers and I don't see much relevance between your presentation this morning and the work we do in Employee Communications.[7]

Andrews's response:

As many of you know there has been a lot of online chatter around a recent situation that has unfortunately spiraled. As an active practitioner in the space, I felt the need to both address the situation and offer my perspective on the practice of social media. Two days ago I made a comment on Twitter that was the emotional response to a run in I had with an intolerant individual. The Tweet was aimed at the offense not the city of Memphis. Everyone knows that at 140 characters Twitter does not allow for context and therefore my comments were misunderstood. If I offended the residents of Memphis, TN I'm sorry. That was not my intention. I understand that people have tremendous pride in their hometown.[8]

The Andrews example further highlights a number of problems inherent in the ability to complain to a mass-audience by a tweet or status update. Similar to the lesson of Paul Chambers, it is imperative to consider the global reach of your online presence before posting a complaint that may come across as highly negative to a certain audience (in Andrews' case, FedEx and Memphis residents).

Another issue is the difficulty that may arise in articulating your point in a small amount of words. Potentially, Andrews could have better explained the situation that triggered the complaint, instead of writing a short quip that ended up offending many and potentially costing his company the FedEx account.

Lastly, having access to social media at the tip of our fingers means we are likely to make emotionally charged posts in the heat of the moment, instead of stepping back and considering our actions. If Andrews had a run-in with a particularly "intolerant individual" and his immediate response was to tweet a complaint, he would have been better off waiting until fully removed from the situation physically and mentally. At that point, he would have had enough time to consider not only his wording, but if there was any reason to even make such a complaint or comment that would be read by his entire social network and beyond.

The Power of Encouragement

To truly see the influence of complaining and criticism, it sometimes is helpful to look at their converse, the power of *encouragement*. Many executives overlook this concept, which is astounding for a number of reasons, including that encouragement is free.

Digital tools make the distribution of encouragement easier. Don't wait: Shower your friends, family, employees, and co-workers with digital bouquets today. Many find it difficult or uncomfortable to tell someone face-to-face how much they like them, mean to them, or what a great job they are doing. Heck, the receiver even often has a hard time receiving praise face-to-face. Conversely it is easy to give and receive comments like, "You Rock!," "Jane is always a positive force of good," "Great chat with Joe, I always learn something new," "Great Yoga class, thanks Jess," "Our marketing team's new campaign is brilliant!" "Jealous of all the great places Jack travels to," "Proud to work with such a great and passionate team," and "Love my foodie friend Zach, he has great restaurant recommendations!"

Creative Encouragement

Jeff Henderson, a former marketing executive at Chick-fil-A, constantly preaches encouragement during his sermons. One particular story is from his time at Chick-fil-A:

> One day I walk into the office of the president, Jimmy Collins. I see him with a Bic lighter out and he's burning paper, which by the way is never a good sign, seeing an executive burning paper. I observe him burning the paper on the edge of his desk and placing the cooled paper into an envelope. Intrigued, I asked him what he was doing. He looked up with a smile and said, "Well I'm burning sales reports and sending them to the sales operators and telling them that their sales are on fire and to keep up the good work and that I'm behind them."
>
> Months later we had our annual Chick-fil-A conference, which covers many things over a few days, one of which is recognizing top performers within the company. It was amazing how many of the sales operators that won an award during their speech mentioned these letters. Most went something like this, "About three quarters of the way through the year I look at our sales goals and said there is just no way we can make these numbers, they are just too big. We were about to give up. Then I receive a letter with ashes in it and Jimmy Collins saying your sales are on fire and I believe in you. Well at that point I was all in. If Jimmy Collins believes in me then I believed in me. The reason I'm standing here on stage today and have won a car is because of that letter with ashes in it."[9]

Though encouragement via new technologies is now abundant, just like Jimmy Collins you can consider creative ways to be supportive of your team offline as well. Some employees or other executives may even find such gestures more personal in the digital age as compared to a tweet or quick email.

Whether digitally or not, instead of always focusing on being critical, think of how you can further encourage others by highlighting their successes, rewarding their achievements, or simply recognizing a job well done.

1000 Awesome Things: The Power of Personal Encouragement

Neil Pasricha was living a good, quiet life when in 2008 he hit some speed bumps. First, his wife approached him in tears indicating she had fallen out of love with him and would like a divorce. Shortly after, one of Pasricha's best friends lost his battle with mental illness and committed suicide.

It would have been easy for Pasricha to create a negative blog to release his frustrations onto the world, but he did the exact opposite. To help relax his mind, he started the blog *1000 Awesome Things*. The concept is simple: "1000 Awesome Things is just a time-ticking countdown of 1000 awesome things. Launched June, 2008 and updated every weekday."[10] Pasricha admits that at first only his mom read the blog. As the weeks rolled on, however, the site's traffic skyrocketed. Over 50,000 blogs are started each day, yet Pasricha's was standing out.

Parts of the below are paraphrased from Pasricha's talk at the Technology, Entertainment and Design Conference (TED) in September 2010:

> So I see my blog traffic start to grow exponentially when one day I receive a call: "You have just won the best blog in the world award." To which I reply, "That sounds totally fake." Yet a few weeks later I'm walking on a red carpet with Jimmy Fallon and Martha Stewart to receive my Webby Award.

Pasricha then received numerous calls from Literary Agents to help turn the blog into a book. *The Book of Awesome* was put together and quickly ascended in popularity, becoming a #1 International bestseller for 65 weeks. The sequel, *Book of (even more) Awesome* has enjoyed similar success. Below are a few items pulled from the blog:

> #992 Being the first table to get called up for the dinner buffet at a wedding

#851   Your family car growing up

#841   When the categories on *Jeopardy!* are right in your wheelhouse

#796   The sound of rain from inside the tent

#697   When chopsticks come apart perfectly

#572   Learning a new keyboard shortcut

#464   When characters in movies visit a place you know

#388   When a stranger laughs at a joke between you and a friend

#329   Twisting the lid off the jar after nobody else could

#313   Showing old people how to do something on a computer

> *"You will never be as young as you are now . . .see the tiny joys that make life so sweet . . . You will live a life that is truly awesome."*
>
> **—NEIL PASRICHA,** Author of *The Book of Awesome*

Simply put: Digital posts like the ones above make people feel good while providing personal encouragement in an unexpected way. At the writing of this book Pasricha's blog had accumulated nearly 30 million visits.

Three As of Awesome according to Pasricha:

Attitude: The future is not going to go as planned. Between the extreme highs there will be extreme lows. During these extreme lows you have two choices: a) swirl in gloom and doom or b) grieve, face the world with refreshed eyes, and take baby steps to move on.

Awareness: Three-year-olds are great to observe because they are seeing the world for the first time. Having a sense of awareness is simply embracing your inner three year old.

Authenticity: It's hard to be awesome if you are trying to be something you aren't—be yourself.

Instead of twirling in gloom and doom, Pasricha engaged in a form of digital therapy via the *1000 Awesome Things* blog, encouraging himself and millions of others, and changing his life for the better.[11]

Kick Your Complaint Habit: Don't Complain for a Week

One way to start moving out of a complaint mindset is to see if you can avoid complaining for seven days. To do so, try placing photos of your loved ones as your phone's background image. Save one image on your phone where they are smiling ("no complaints") and one where they are frowning ("complaints"). Then, every time you complain, switch the photo from the "no complaints" to "complaints" image. Let your loved ones know what you are doing or take photos of them specifically for this purpose. The more people that are aware of what you are trying to accomplish, the more they can help you succeed. You can even make a friendly competition out of it by having them get involved. The goal is to go an entire day without changing the photo on your phone's background, then striving to work your way up to an entire week without complaining.

If that sounds too technical or you need a more physical reminder than your smartphone, wear a rubber band on your wrist. Grant yourself the first day, so everyone starts with one rubber band. If you go an entire day without complaining then add a rubber band to that wrist. If you get to three rubber bands (i.e., three complaint free days in a row) and you complain then you need to "reset" back to one rubber band. The hope is that some day you will have seven rubber bands on your wrist, meaning you made it an entire week without complaining!

People will ask you about the rubber bands (we suggest cheap & colorful) and they will also help police you (i.e., positive peer pressure). Don't think peer pressure works? Have you ever been in a certain circle of friends and someone says, "Wow you are always so elegantly dressed—it's impressive." The next time you go to meet with this particular group don't you go out of the way to dress up and continue this reputation? Digital peer pressure works the same way: it's just easier for people to reach you. (The people behind A Complaint Free World, mentioned at the beginning of the chapter, offer similar advice and solutions to avoid complaining, including free purple wristband reminders.)

Lead by Example

In your effort to positively embrace challenges over complaints, remember to lead by example. Don't be the annoying person at the airport when a flight is delayed for 6 hours due to a massive thunderstorm to walk up to your fellow travelers and say, "Isn't this delay great!" Instead, be the one that doesn't make sarcastic comments. Listen to others, but don't add your own log to the fire of complaints. This action, or inaction, will help keep the complaint fire at a manageable burn and will help relax those around you or traveling with you. Ever notice if an adult cries that a baby mimics this cry? The same can often be said about complaints and adults.

> *"A smooth sea never made a skillful mariner."*
> —ENGLISH PROVERB

Take on the responsibility of leading by example. You can wallow in despair for the next 6-hour wait at the airport, or you can, for example:

- ▶ finish that book you've been dying to read or write
- ▶ grab a beer and catch the game with your travelers
- ▶ meet someone new
- ▶ complete the action item you have been putting off

Complaining offline and online undermines your leadership capability and is, frankly, beneath you. Just the simple fact that you complain less than others will immediately separate you from 95 percent of the crowd. Remember the average person complains 15-30 times per day and make the effort to avoid being average.

CHAPTER FOUR

Integrity and Reputation: Avoiding Digital Blunders

"When I do good, I feel good. When I do bad, I feel bad. That's my religion."

—ABRAHAM LINCOLN

Super Bowl winning coach Tony Dungy does a great job of describing the difference between integrity and reputation in his book *Uncommon*:

> Integrity is what you do when no one is watching; it's doing the right thing all the time, even when it may work to your disadvantage. Integrity is keeping your word. Integrity is that internal compass and rudder that directs you to where you know you should go when everything around you is pulling you in a different direction. Some people think reputation is the same thing as integrity, but they are different. Your reputation is the public perception of your integrity. Because it's other people's opinions of you, it may or may not be accurate.

Others determine your reputation, but only you determine your integrity.[1]

With our hyper-connected world the amount of difference between your integrity and reputation becomes smaller and smaller. In the digital decades ahead, your integrity and reputation will be one and the same. Why is this the case? Let's take a quick look at Dungy's words *"Integrity is what you do when no one is watching."* A key premise of this book is that someone is in fact watching you all the time. These are the realities of our fully transparent world. People start to think twice about committing adultery when they see the ramifications with public figures like Bill Clinton, Tiger Woods, Andrew Weiner, or Eliot Spitzer. Phones with high definition video cameras that port to social media sites instantly are becoming more prevalent, not less.

As the lines between integrity and reputation blur this is a great thing for the world, meaning that your reputation becomes more accurate. Think of reputation as your digital shadows (what others are saying and posting about you). The best way to influence these shadows is through your integrity, which is reflected in your digital footprint. The more you can simplify what you stand for in life, the easier it is not only on you, but on others that are contributing to your online reputation by developing your digital shadow. For example, someone posting photos of his or her kids at the Church bake sale that later accidentally checked in via a geo-location tool during a KKK rally is sending mixed signals that will be discovered and revealed.

> *"Integrity does not come in degrees—low, medium, or high. You either have integrity or you do not."*
> —TONY DUNGY

The easiest way to avoid digital blunders is to believe in your mission in life and stand by that mission. This concept of integrity and reputation isn't new; it's just even more important today as a result of more information being publicly posted. Most people's and companies' reputations will be more accurate than in any time in history. Being fully transparent and having integrity is the starting point to managing your online reputation, digital legacy, and leadership role.

Privacy 101

You know those thousands of scrolling words that are labeled "User Agreement" or "Privacy Policy?" The majority of us simply skip to the end and check the "I agree" box. Even if you did take the time to read these items, they are often difficult to comprehend. At one point Facebook's privacy policy had more words than the American Constitution, which may explain why only 25 percent of users have adjusted their privacy settings on Facebook.[2]

Rather than becoming an expert on privacy policies, the best approach is to assume that everything you do digitally will be found out by the person you least want to find out. Taking that one step further, everything that you do *offline* will be digitally discoverable as well.

For example, the looters and rioters in Vancouver following Game 7 of the 2011 Stanley Cup Finals learned this lesson. Photos and video posted online helped police conduct "Facebook justice" and arrest hundreds of violators. Many of these citizens not only received criminal punishment, but also subsequently lost their jobs. Unlike in the offline world where there may only be a handful of eyewitnesses, online there are millions of digital deputies. Further, consider how it is now possible to digitally scan an old photograph and post it for the world to see. During the 2008 political campaign, Barack Obama's kindergarten essays (from Hawaii) were even dredged up and posted digitally.

Make sure you are aware of what you are posting and to whom you are posting. We can't go back to make a new beginning, a world before the digital explosion, but we can start today to make a new ending. While you may not understand the policies of some social network websites, try to understand your personal settings on each tool. Many tools allow for you to selectively decide where to send messages and other posts. A positive example of selectivity would be for global companies posting in a foreign language like Italian or Chinese to select the relevant markets they want to target (e.g., Italy, China). A negative example would be if you, as an individual, post a picture mocking the Mona Lisa in the Louvre—you may want to avoid sending it to your art-loving friends. Nonetheless, we need to assume your art-loving friends will eventually discover the photo.

Considering this universality and transparency of your comments, conversations, and photos, you need to fully think about the material you are transmitting prior to posting. By taking some steps, you won't be blasting people with irrelevant or, in some cases, offensive content. Mistakes, however, do occur, in which actions online and off end up reaching a huge audience digitally. As leaders, our reputations can easily be tainted by a seemingly small error in judgment, and our leadership capabilities potentially called into question.

Would You Wear It as a T-Shirt?

Facebook founder Mark Zuckerberg's instant messages when he was starting to develop the concept of Facebook while attending Harvard have been damaging to his reputation. Controversy between him and three other Harvard students who claimed Zuckerberg essentially stole the concept of Facebook led to litigation in which Zuckerberg's personal computer was searched. Instant messages were found, and leaked, from Zuckerberg's time at Harvard that were less than flattering to his image. Among them, he made negative comments to a friend that came across as conniving and backstabbing toward these other early developers of a Facebook-like social network:[3]

> **FRIEND:** so have you decided what you are going to do about the websites?
> **ZUCK:** yea i'm going to **** them

In another exchange leaked to *Silicon Alley Insider*, Zuckerberg explained to a friend that his control of Facebook gave him access to any information he wanted on any Harvard student:

ZUCK: yea so if you ever need info about anyone at harvard
ZUCK: just ask
ZUCK: i have over 4000 emails, pictures, addresses, sns
FRIEND: what!? how'd you manage that one?
ZUCK: people just submitted it
ZUCK: i don't know why
ZUCK: they "trust me"
ZUCK: dumb *****[4]

Zuckerberg's digital footprint, however, didn't stop with the IM messaging. Also on his record are some drunken blog postings about his ex-girlfriend and some other more costly slipups. Digital posts were used against him as evidence in two separate lawsuits (around stealing the idea for Facebook). These lawsuits were estimated at over $50 million in payouts.

Plus, there are items like this snippet from the movie *The Social Network*—statement from then on-screen girlfriend—although fictitious the idea was derived from some of the aforementioned posts:

You're going to go through life thinking that girls don't like you because you're a tech geek. And I want you to know, from the bottom of my heart, that that won't be true. It'll be because you're an ******.

To Zuckerberg's credit, he owned up to these embarrassing comments and derogatory language. However, considering the black and white evidence of the IM conversations, what choice did he have? Zuckerberg's immature posts were a mistake, but he had the integrity to own his warts before someone else did—he went on to apologize for making these negative comments. If Bill Clinton would have owned up to the Monica Lewinsky issue right away he readily admits he would have been in a better place then and today. Americans were less upset about the act and more upset that he lied to them:

"I did not have sexual relations with that woman." Often it's not the crime, but the cover-up that gets leaders into trouble (e.g., Richard Nixon, Ohio State Coach Jim Tressel, Congressman Andrew Weiner). Like Zuckerberg, Clinton has been able to recover from this incident and has productively given back to the world with his Clinton Global Initiative.

We are all human, so we will make mistakes, especially digitally where we constantly have to learn new software and tools. We can take comfort in knowing that Zuckerberg was able to adjust his behavior in positive ways.

"Measure your words twice, post once."
—@EQUALMAN

Zuckerberg donated over $100 million dollars to help fix the Newark, New Jersey, public schools. He joined the billionaire pledge headed by Bill Gates and Warren Buffet to donate at least half of his wealth to charity. The ubiquity of Facebook resulted in Zuckerberg being named *Time Magazine's* "Person of the Year" for 2010. We, similar to Zuckerberg, will make digital and non-digital mistakes, the key is to learn from them and have our successes outweigh the blunders.

The fact that the founder of Facebook didn't fully understand the eternal nature of digital posts should wake us all up. If even he has struggled with digital leadership, then every one of us could potentially step on a digital landmine. To help avoid these landmines, a good exercise before you complete your IM chat thought or hit the send button is to ask yourself the question: would I be proud to wear my typed words on a t-shirt in public for the next hundred years? This extra step will slow your rate of messaging and help mitigate the potential for emotion overriding common sense.

When we do make a mistake, and we all will, to become a digital leader we need to get in front of it (potential negative backlash) and own the mistake (admit fault) before someone else does it for us.

As these digital missteps show, it's prudent to follow the old carpenters' saying "measure twice, cut once." With digital communication, measure your words twice, post once.

DIGITAL DEEDS

Live as if Your Mother Is Watching

As mentioned earlier, according to *The Facebook Effect* by David Kirkpatrick only 25 percent of us change our privacy settings on Facebook.[5] Make sure you are aware of your privacy settings for all the websites and digital applications you use and adjust them to your comfort level.

Though this practice is a good one, still keep in mind there is *no hiding from anything* in the new digital world. Your best course of action is to assume whatever you post will eventually be seen by millions. Even beyond that, you need to assume that anything you do *offline* will be posted by someone digitally, causing that action to become part of your permanent digital shadow. Your best plan is to live as if your mother is watching you.

Why even adjust your privacy settings at all then? Setting adjustments are mainly used to prevent the wrong information flowing into the hands of the ill intentioned. Websites in the past like www.pleaserobme.com and others in the future can aggregate data about us and publicly broadcast items like: "Bob is in Tokyo right now, but his house is in London at 2 Downing Street" (the site is meant to raise awareness about issues with over-sharing such information online). We must face the fact that the privacy our grandparents enjoyed no longer exists.

Red Cross: From Hoisting Pints to Donating Pints

It's not a matter of *if* we are going to make a mistake in our online and digital presence. Instead, it's a question of *when* we are going to make this mistake and *how* we handle it. The Red Cross found itself in a situation in which an employee accidentally posted a tweet to the Red Cross Twitter account that she thought was going to her personal Twitter account. Here's what transpired.

The employee tweeted through the Red Cross Twitter account: "Ryan found two more 4 bottle packs of Dogfish Head's Midas Touch beer . . . when we drink we do it right #gettingslizzerd" (The term "gettingslizzerd" refers to getting drunk.)

Ryan found two more 4 bottle
packs of Dogfish Head's Midas
Touch beer.... when we drink we
do it right #gettngslizzerd

HootSuite · 2/15/11 11:24 PM

The Red Cross quickly became aware of the situation and removed the post. In a smart move, they replaced the tweet with another, injecting a bit of humor: "We've deleted the rogue tweet but rest assured the Red Cross is sober and we've confiscated the keys."

We've deleted the rogue tweet but rest
assured the Red Cross is sober and
we've confiscated the keys.

about 11 hours ago via Über/Twitter
Retweeted by 86 people

 RedCross
American Red Cross

The incident received an enormous amount of media attention and "#gettingslizzerd" was a trending topic on Twitter for the week. Red Cross decided to take advantage of the media coverage by running a fundraising campaign. In response, Dogfish Head Beer (the beer mentioned in the original tweet) asked its fans to donate blood and money to the Red Cross by posting across their various media properties messages like this one:

Please join Dogfish Head Craft Brewery in raising money for the American Red Cross. If you're interested in donating a pint, please click here to learn more about Red Cross blood drives. Note: Alcohol can often make you more dehydrated. Dogfish Head recommends not drinking immediately before or after donating.

The Red Cross further thanked its fans for understanding that it is a humanitarian organization *made up of humans* and has inevitably made mistakes over the past 130 years. They also reassured their fans and donators that, even though the organization may continue to make mistakes in the future, it has their best interests at heart.

This type of digital response would not have been possible a few years prior at Red Cross. However, in 2006 they hired Wendy Harmon to provide guidance on social media efforts. "I was hired in part because the leaders knew that people were saying really bad things about the Red Cross's response to Hurricane Katrina," Harman recalls, "and they wanted someone to make it stop."[6] Over time Harmon was able to instill best practices, social media trainings, and materials specific to the Red Cross. This type of cultural shift and training didn't happen overnight and was often fought with resistance, but, as evidenced from the above example, it eventually paid off.

Five Things We Learn from the Red Cross

The Red Cross managed to turn a digital blunder into something positive. Though this result may not always be achievable in such a situation, there are a number of lessons we can take away from their actions:

1. Instilling proper guidelines, policy, and training across the organization can dramatically help when a crisis eventually arises
2. Build and invest in your network continuously, so when a crisis arrives your network can, and will want to, support you
3. Own your digital mistakes quickly and openly
4. Turn a negative into a positive (e.g., the Red Cross increased donations!)
5. Humor and humility go a long way

The Red Cross team exhibited leadership in their ability to utilize their social outreach after a potential crisis. Where many leaders or employees might have been paralyzed by such a mistake, the Red Cross was able to respond quickly, openly, and with humor. As a result they turned a negative into a positive. The ability to harness and call to arms their *online* network, along with that of Dogfish Head Beer's, resulted in more people donating to and helping the Red Cross' efforts.

> *"To ignore the unexpected (even if it were possible) would be to live without opportunity, spontaneity, and the rich moments of which "life" is made."*
>
> **—STEPHEN COVEY,**
> Author of 7 Habits of Highly Effective People

Top 14 Digital "Oops" Moments

Unlike the Red Cross example, The below digital blunders are from various types of people and companies that created permanent blemishes on their record. I would like to present them to you in hopes that we can all learn from their mistakes and better tailor our online and digital presence. Further, remember that anything done in this technologically advanced world affects your digital legacy, so even actions that were previously considered private (text messages, instant messages, offline communications, and actions) can have a public online life.

1. *Congressman Weiner lives up to his name:* New York Congressman Andrew Weiner resigned from his post after it was discovered he'd been texting and tweeting nude and lewd photographs of himself to several women. The married Weiner adamantly denied any wrongdoing, indicating his account had been hacked. Weiner eventually admitted guilt when several incriminating "self-portrait" photos were revealed.

2. *Fitbit leaks sex stats to Google:* Fitbit is a small chip used to help record your exercise activity—information that is then put into an online profile. One of the exercise activities included is sex. A problem arose when it was found

that the privacy default setting on the online profiles was set to public. Therefore, when certain people's names were typed into Google's search box a history of their sexual activity showed up through Fitbit. Making it worse was the fact that terms like "moderate effort" were often associated with the activity.

3. **Tiger Woods:** A myriad of text messages, and related physical rendezvous, with multiple women cost Woods his marriage, millions in endorsements, and affected his performance on the golf course—causing him to lose his number one Professional Golf Association (PGA) ranking for the first time in five years.

4. **Chrysler flames Detroit drivers:** Similar to the Red Cross example, Chrysler's social media agency accidentally sent this tweet on behalf of the auto company: *I find it ironic that Detroit is known as the #motorcity and yet no one here knows how to f$%#@ng drive.* The agency employee that made the error—thinking he was sending via his personal account—was fired that day. Chrysler also fired the agency.

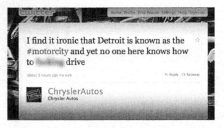

5. **Secret Service bored:** A member of the secret service mistakenly thought he was posting to his own Twitter account, but instead his disapproval of Fox News went out on behalf of the entire secret service: *Had to monitor Fox for a story. Can't. Deal. With. The. Blathering.*

6. **School teacher fired:** A Massachusetts high school teacher was fired for posting on Facebook: *I'm so not looking forward to another year at Cohasset Schools.* She added that the community was *arrogant* and *snobby.* "I made a stupid mistake, it may have cost me my career," she said.

7. **Google sets trap for Microsoft:** Google had a suspicion that Microsoft's search engine Bing was stealing and mirroring

the search results from Google. Google made up a few fake words and seeded them into the Google search results. Sure enough, Bing's search engine was soon showing these fictitious results.

8. **Craigslist Congressman:** Married Republican Christopher Lee sent a topless picture of himself to a woman he met on a "Women Seeking Men" forum on craigslist.org. *I'm a very fit fun classy guy. Live in Cap Hill area. 6ft 190lbs blond/blue. 39. Lobbyist. I promise not to disappoint.* Those disappointed were his wife and young son. Lee even lied about his age (he was 46 not 39). Lee resigned from his post.

9. **Kenneth Cole:** During the Egyptian Revolution which was being aided by Twitter and Facebook, Kenneth Cole decided to tweet: *Millions are in uproar in #Cario. Rumor is they heard our new spring collection is now available online.* Making light of a serious situation caused the company's pockets to be lighter as many protestors boycotted the clothing line (see screen shot below).

10. **NFL cheerleader:** An 18-year-old NFL cheerleader was kicked off the squad (New England Patriots) after photos on Facebook showed her posing with a passed-out man covered in offensive marker drawings.[7]

11. **Take the year off:** A U.S. employee of Anglo-Irish Bank asked his boss for Friday off to attend a family matter. Then

someone posted a photo on Facebook of him at a party the same evening holding a wand and wearing a tutu. Everyone at work discovered the lie.

12. **Embarrassing your son:** Andy Murray, a world-ranked British tennis star was embarrassed by his mother's tweet at Wimbledon. It used to be that your mom could only embarrass you by cheering too loud. But, when Judy Murray tweeted about Murray's opponent, Feliciano Lopez of Spain, *Ooooooooooh Deliciano . . . . looking good out there. As always,* it took embarrassment to a whole new level.

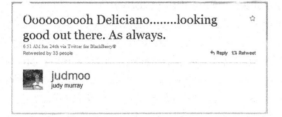

13. **Fired before starting:** A young woman was happy to receive a job offer from Cisco. Not sure whether to take the job she posted on Twitter, *Cisco just offered me a job! Now I have to weigh the utility of a fatty paycheck against the daily commute to San Jose and hating the work.* The company revoked the offer tweeting: *Who is the hiring manager? I'm sure they would love to know you will hate the work. We here at Cisco are versed in the Web.*

14. **Gottfried's own natural disaster:** Comedian Gilbert Gottfried started tweeting jokes about Japan right after tens of thousands were killed by the 2011 Tsunami. It cost him his job as the voice of the Aflack duck.

These examples show how both your personal and professional lives are effected by your digital presence, and how the line between the two has become blurred in this new age of technology. Your actions online have real-life ramifications, and if you value your leadership role, you will keep this in mind in all digital correspondence and offline actions for that matter as well.

Background Checks on Steroids

Many companies outsource to specialists for Internet background checks during the recruiting process. The information is gathered from large social networks, comments on blogs, posts on smaller social sites, user groups, e-commerce sites, bulletin boards, and even Craigslist.

"We are not detectives," said Max Drucker, chief executive of Social Intelligence, one such specialist. "All we assemble is what is publicly available on the Internet today."[8]

Mr. Drucker said that one prospective employee was found using Craigslist to look for OxyContin. Other background reports have turned up examples of people making anti-Semitic comments and racist remarks. One job applicant belonged to a Facebook group, *This Is America. I Shouldn't Have to Press 1 for English.*

Photos and videos seem to get the most people in trouble. "Sexually explicit photos and videos are beyond comprehension," Mr. Drucker said. "We also see flagrant displays of weapons. And we see a lot of illegal activity. Lots and lots of pictures of drug use."[9]

Joe Bontke, outreach manager for the Equal Employment Opportunity Commission's office in Houston, indicates that 75 percent of recruiters are required by their companies to do online research of candidates. And 70 percent of recruiters in the United States report that they have rejected candidates because of information online.[10]

Governments will even investigate your activity online. For example, if you apply for unemployment benefits in Sweden, the government will go to great lengths researching your digital footprint to see if there is any fraud.

Eye in the Sky

What if there was not a heaven or a hell (or equivalent in various religions), but simply one place? Imagine an infinite cinema in the clouds. For fun it could be called *Hellven* with a flashing neon drive-thru sign.

People would watch peoples' lives in 3-D (friends, foes, peers, acquaintances, strangers, etc.). How we lived our lives would determine whether we were in heaven or hell. If you were one that consistently talked behind others' backs, then that person could be sitting right next to you in the theatre as you say a snide remark or make fun of someone. Or imagine if you cheated on your wife or boyfriend? Or inappropriately shortchanged an employee's career so that you could get ahead. Something we "got away with" in our life would not be the case in Hellven. A daunting thought for all of us. Since nobody is perfect, a slip here or there is expected and tolerated. However, a nefarious lifestyle would be exposed and frowned upon.

With the digital explosion we see something approaching the fictitious Hellven. The digital revolution has connected our integrity and reputation in a way never seen before. Our online and offline lives have become inseparable. If you post something digitally, expect others to find it, even those people who you wouldn't want to. If you do something inappropriate offline, also expect people to discover your actions. Others will digitally post about your antics, creating digital shadows. (This is why at colleges we now see "shot rooms." Shot rooms are rooms in which no lights are turned on and no cameras are permitted in order for students to consume shots of alcohol without worrying about photos or videos of them being plastered all over cyberspace.)

The best way to handle this new digital age in regards to your reputation is to maintain your integrity and treat everyone you engage both online and offline as if he is the last person you might ever to speak to. People will, in return, influence your leadership capabilities and legacy.

In this digital world, still look for simple, little things that may cause a big smile offline. For example, unless you are late for a connecting flight, is there any reason to immediately jump up from your airplane seat upon landing? Is getting in front of one extra person going to make all the difference in your day? Look for opportunities to make someone else's day. Help an elderly lady remove her luggage from the overhead bin or yield to someone in a rush to make a connecting flight.

These things are little, but they can put big smiles on other peoples' faces—and yours as well! The greatest gift in life is to give of oneself, so look for opportunities to help others. When people are creating your digital shadow, your good deeds will often be reflected. Since it is no longer possible to have an offline identity and a digital identity, stress positive change in your *overall* life—true change within all of us doesn't begin in our fingertips, it starts in our hearts.

> *"The greatest gift in life is to give of oneself."*
> —@EQUALMAN

We have a tendency to hurt the ones we love the most. If we knew what we were about to say or type were going to be the last words exchanged with our mother or sister or a dear friend, we'd consider them more carefully. As Dale Carnegie suggests in *How to Win Friends and Influence People*: "Praise the slightest improvement and praise every improvement. Be hearty in your approbation and lavish in your praise." This statement is particularly true when it comes to digital posts, since electronic words can be easily misinterpreted. Take Carnegie's advice to err on the side of being sparse in your criticism and lavish in your praise.

CHAPTER FIVE

Simple = Success

"In character, in manner, in style, in all things, the supreme excellence is simplicity."
—HENRY LONGFELLOW

It's difficult to simplify today. But, the fact that simplicity is hard to achieve is a great thing. It gives you, the reader of this book, the chance to stand out. If simplicity were easy, then everyone and every company would be doing it. However, don't fall into the trap of believing that you, your business, charity, or other initiatives are too complicated to achieve success via digital, social, or mobile means. This belief is not only tired, it is false. We know two things for certain:

1. Technology is in a constant state of change
2. Those who embrace these changes will succeed

It is surprising to still hear comments today such as "we are unique and our business just doesn't translate digitally." I also heard this remark in the late 1990s while I was working at AT&T. Specifically, it was suggested that we accept orders for telephone service online. The corporate response was, "We can't take orders for phone service online, people will be able to put dirty names in the phone book." It's difficult to believe this was once the thought process (and also ironic that the use of paper phone books has fallen dramatically).

Have you ever heard an investor or venture capitalist say, "Wow that product concept and idea is complicated; so complex it will be difficult to translate digitally. I'll gladly invest in this because greater complexity is better"? No, you don't hear this, because savvy investors have learned that simplicity wins. Consider the technology conferences Demo and Finovate. The conference organizers have banned presenters from using PowerPoint and Keynote Slides. The thought is if your business model isn't simple enough to explain without slides, then your potential investors will not be interested.

"It's not about bullet points or the company, but what have you built?" says Finovate CEO Eric Mattson. "If you show your product to us, and we go, 'Wow, we can grasp that in seven minutes, and we want that,' then the customers will want it too."[1] The same holds true for our personal brands and relationships. Have you ever heard someone say, "I really like hanging out with her because she makes everything so complicated"?

Some corporations seem to wear a badge of honor for offering a complex service or product, but simplicity, not complexity, wins in this millennium. Consider Apple, Inc. Apple's success has been built on simplifying technology for the user. There were plenty of MP3 players on the market before the iPod came along, yet the iPod and iTunes software simplified things for the mass market. Profits soared on strong sales because customers were willing to pay more for the convenience and user-friendly devices and software.

Simplicity Online and Off

Innovation is imperative as both companies and consumers seek increased simplicity through technology. Great leaders and companies know what they are deeply passionate about and what they can do better than anyone else in the world. With the new digital world, we see how technology can be used to follow these passions and succeed, creating a better experience for consumers and higher profits for producers.

Zappos Simplifies Shopping

Before launching the No. 1 shoe website Zappos, every consultant Tony Hsieh hired predicted it wasn't possible to sell shoes online. Their research showed that people wanted to try on their shoes, see them, and touch them. What if the shoes ordered online didn't fit? What if the shoes looked different in real life than they did online? Customers also were tired of spending time ordering items online only to find out at the end of the process that the shipping costs were outrageous. The return process also was costly and cumbersome. Ordering shoes, and clothes, online was daunting for customers.

Fortunately, Hsieh and the Zappos founders ignored the consultants' advice and considered how to create a better shoe purchasing experience for the buyer. They simplified the entire process by making free shipments to the customer and even free return shipments. Customers could use the same box the shoes came in for returns, making a sometimes daunting task easier on the customer, and more sustainable for the environment.

Zappos also invested in digital tools that helped free employees from doing mechanical tasks, allowing them to spend more time "surprising" and "delighting" customers (e.g., handwritten thank you notes, remembering birthdays, staying on the phone with a customer who just wants to talk). They made the hard decision not to be in the shoe business, but to be in the *customer service business*. Everything else seemed to fall into place once this decision was made. In fact, one revolutionary element that Hsieh brought to Zappos was to treat customer service costs more like marketing ones, as he saw this as an investment in word-of-mouth. If a customer service agent could resolve a customer's issue for under $100 she was empowered to do so. This arrangement helped simplify things for both Zappos and the customers.

Zappos went on to sell millions of shoes and now sells various product lines. As a result, other companies attempt to emulate the Zappos business model and culture, and Amazon purchased Zappos for 1.2 billion dollars.

The NET-A-PORTER Experience

Similar to Zappos, people initially doubted it was possible to sell luxury goods online. Yet, fashion journalist Natalie Massenet, shortly after the historic technology bubble burst of 2000, decided to start a new company that June called Net-a-Porter. Her goal was simple: to make designer brands more accessible for everyone through a simple online buying process. She thought if someone can order a romance novel online why can't that person order a £1,300 Chloé bag online as well? Most people thought she was crazy. Boo.com, for example, an online fashion retailer, had spent $135 million in 18 months before going bankrupt in March 2000.[2] After a frustratingly complex experience trying to buy a pair of designer jeans online, however, Massenet was undeterred and went about launching her company to simplify the process.

"I thought, for a luxury brand, what better way to give the best service to clients than actually delivering to the door? I never thought it wouldn't work. I never once thought it wouldn't be huge." Huge indeed: after 10 years Net-a-Porter was such a raving success that Massenet was able to sell her portion for £50 million. To those doubters that thought she couldn't simplify luxury she says, "I'm sure their wives are having Net-a-Porter bags delivered to their homes every day."

Apple Takes a Bite Out of Complexity

Shown below in Figure 5.1 is Apple's homepage circa 2004. Notice at the top of the page there are 17 different tabs appealing to all of Apple's audiences (including educators,

professionals, developers, and businesspeople). This setup is inclusive as everyone is addressed, but the problem is that 17 tabs is equivalent to 17 different priorities. If Apple believed that all of these 17 products were equally worthy of placement on the home page then it was a sign that internally it needed to simplify its focus. Trying to focus on 17 different elements in such a highly competitive market, one in which Microsoft was dominating, was not a long term recipe for success

In 2010, Apple switched to eight tabs. This streamlining of the home page reflected Apple's strategy of simplifying its entire business—from easy to read instruction manuals to clean and open stores. Apple's slogan at the time was "Think Different" and it practiced this credo by deciding not to put every possible tab on its home page.

In 2011, Apple further reduced these tabs to seven. The more Apple simplified and focused its business, the better its business performed. The chart below shows the strong appreciation in Apple stock (APPL) during the World 2008-2011 recession, one of history's worst.

Are there tabs on your company site that can be reduced? What about on your personal blog? Are you trying to appeal to everyone and, as a result, appealing to no one? Or more importantly in life are you trying to be too many things? Are you trying to please everyone and as a result pleasing no one, including yourself?

In the manner of Apple, if we reduce the number of tabs in our life, success should follow. For example, say you decide you want to have more one-on-one meetings with your co-workers or friends, answer every email you receive within 24 hours, and spend an hour per day reading up on industry news, but you don't have the bandwidth to perform all these actions properly. You have a high probability of doing all three items poorly and making life more complex than it should be.

Rather, a better approach would be to simplify by prioritizing. In this instance you may decide to start with the personal one-on-one meetings, but make it a point to ask who you're talking with what they feel is making industry news (asking questions and listening also endears you to your audience).

This tactic will allow you to cut your reading of industry news to 25 minutes. You should tackle answering your email at two 30-minute intervals during the day and get through as much of it as you can. While you probably will not be able to answer everyone in 24 hours, you will be less stressed and more focused on responding to the most important emails first.

> *"If this were easy we'd have twenty more guys on this basketball team. But, it's not easy. You have made it here, on this team, because you simplified your life and committed yourself to this team and to being the best that you can be."*
>
> —**TOM IZZO,** Michigan State Basketball Coach

In-N-Out Simplifies Fast Food

Keep in mind that in this new era, simplifying as a mindset *without* the aid of new technologies can also still create serious results. Family owned In-N-Out Burger (1948) have used the model of simplification to watch their revenues soar. In-N-Out Burger is unique from other fast food establishments as it only uses fresh meat as opposed to reheating frozen hamburger. The company policy mandates each store be within one-day's driving distance of a regional distribution center (based in the Western United States). They simplify the supply chain and consumer ordering process by offering a simple menu consisting only of: hamburger, cheeseburger, "Double-Double" (double meat/double cheese), french fries, fountain drinks, and milkshakes.

Special K: Cereal Made Simple

Kellogg's and its advertising agency, Leo Burnett, made the difficult decision to reposition the Special K brand as a "diet cereal." Their goal was to target the brand specifically to women. Ignoring 50 percent of the market (males) is a gutsy thing to do. But once they simplified from broad to niche, everything became easier for both the brand and its consumers.

The Red "K" on the box was restyled in the shape of a woman's leg to present a more feminine image. Other elements of Special K's marketing mix were adjusted accordingly. This change even included the charities with which Kellogg's chose to associate the brand; e.g., the Susan Komen Foundation for the fight against breast cancer (pink ribbon).

Kellogg's introduced its *Special K Challenge Diet Plan* as well. This plan suggests replacing a regular daily meal with two bowls of Special K, and in only two weeks you drop a jean size. On the box of cereal is a yellow tape measure with the text "Drop a jean size in two weeks." This creates a tangible vision in the consumer's mind. Who wouldn't want to be wearing slimmer jeans in two weeks?

Five years after introducing the *Special K Challenge Diet Plan*, Special K grew from the brink of product cancelation to the company's No. 1 brand: [3] quite a feat in a company whose marketing spending eclipses $1 billion annually.[4] In 2009, branding specialists Landor Associates listed Special K as one of 10 breakaway brands from 2005-2008.[5] While the initial decision to change the brand direction was not easy, Kellogg's discovered a multitude of success when it simplified and repositioned Special K as a diet cereal.

While we are not boxes of cereal, we do control our personal brand and unique life story. Like Special K, we need to make the difficult decision to become smaller in order to become bigger.

Simplifying Our Personal Lives

While I have shown several benefits to companies simplifying, it's just as important for us as individuals to simplify our lives. This trait is essential if we are to become digital leaders. Many people think that to become a leader you need to do more, when in fact it's just the opposite. We need to *remove* more from our plate in order to concentrate on the things that are most important—the items that will ultimately make us successful and happy.

This action is not easy to do as we are constantly inundated with texts, tweets, phone calls, emails, and chats. If you think you are alone with these burdens, however, you are wrong! Almost everyone has too much to handle in this complex, digital age. The average person receives 41.5 texts per day[6] and sends/receives 141 email messages per day.[7]

However, complexity is often caused by us! This situation is great, though, because it means complexity can be easily removed by us as well. If you simplify, you will be able to stand out from the crowd, influence others, and reduce stress. At some point, all effective people, from school teachers to CEOs, figure out the following leadership habits discussed in the remainder of this chapter.

Don't forget that digital leadership starts with taking leadership of your own life first. Once you are comfortable, then and only then will it be easy to influence others and attract followers.

Just Text No!

Embrace the powerful habit of saying or typing "no thanks." Often our ultimate success is determined by what we decide NOT to do, as much as by what we decide to do. Get in the practice of initially saying no. If an opportunity does not inspire an immediate "I have to do this!" reaction, it will not be missed.

Those questions that elicit an "immediate yes," however, will be different for everyone. These types of opportunities will be the ones that you won't turn down and will find a way to make happen. Such questions could resemble, "Want a free ticket to the Super Bowl?" "Want to meet the Senator?" "Want to be a guest on Oprah?" "Backstage passes to U2?" "Drive my Ferrari for the weekend?" If it's not an "immediate yes" moment then start making it a habit to say "no." For most other circumstances, you can always circle back if you determine you really do have the time and want to do something to which you initially declined.

The habit of saying "no" is also a powerful way to avoid over scheduling. This is a difficult response to master, but stick with it and you will discover that you rarely miss the items you turn down. How often have you found yourself at a cocktail party or picnic and you would rather be somewhere else? Nobody wins in this scenario.

> "Often our ultimate success is determined by what we decide not to do, as much as by what we decide to do."
>
> —@EQUALMAN

The worse thing to do is to say "let me check on some things and I'll get back to you." Now both parties are in limbo. Make a decision. Consider these examples of how to appropriately say "no" in person and digitally:

Example Question One: Do you want to do the cancer walk with me this weekend?

Response: I'd love to, but at this time I'm going to have to say no. This month I promised myself I was going to dedicate all my charitable time to the soup kitchen. This is to be fair to that organization and myself. What you are doing is great, if there is a way I can contribute monetarily please let me know.

Digital Response: At this time I'm committed to another charity and have to say "no." Happy to contribute monetarily though!

Example Question Two: Do you want to grab dinner and some beers Friday?

Response: That sounds great, but I must decline. In preparation for my marathon, I'm running eight miles that day and cutting off the booze. When I complete the marathon, I hope the offer still stands.

The same holds true when you say "yes": get in the habit of being decisive.

> **Example Question Three:** Would you like two tickets to the Steelers game this weekend?
>
> **Your Response:** Yes, I'd love them! Count me in, but can you please give me until 5 p.m. to double check if a baby sitter is available?

Some people might argue that saying "no" too often lets others down. Sacrificing time for others is of course a good thing, but the best way to help others is to go long (time) and deep rather than wide and shallow. This maxim is especially true of the most important people in your life, your "A-List."

DIGITAL DEEDS

Last In, First Out [LIFO]

Life is not fair, so you shouldn't have to respond to messages in a fair manner. Here are a few tips to help:

1. Place messages from your personal "A-List" (e.g., your boss, reporter from BBC, your mother) above all others. Free tools like Gmail's priority inbox or Twitter lists can greatly assist this effort.
2. Treat your inbox using the LIFO accounting principle—Last In, First Out. For example, supply the "wow" factor to a person you'll respond to within minutes—a message sitting there for ten hours has lost that factor. It also feels good to answer a message that recently came in. Most of us make the mistake of answering messages via the converse accounting principle FIFO method (First In, First Out). Using FIFO, you will never "wow" anyone. Also, on tools like Twitter, minute delays are equivalent to day delays via other communication methods: people expect speedy replies. Hence, you might as well "wow" somebody with a quick response versus "wowing" nobody. If you received a tweet five hours ago and one five seconds ago, respond to the one five seconds ago first.

3. Just because you cannot answer everyone doesn't mean you should answer no one. Constantly remind yourself of what North Point Ministries senior pastor Andy Stanley recommends: "that you must do for one, what you wish you could do for all."
4. Most messages can be answered in one to two sentences—start making this a habit.

By Saying Yes to Everyone, You Say No to Everyone

We don't want to let people down by not being able to fulfill their requests. The more successful you become, the more requests you will have for your time. The below parable helps stress the importance of not saying "yes" to everyone.

Imagine you have a backpack and you are standing in South Africa. You hear about a family struggling in Botswana. The only means to get to this family is by foot. This family needs your help before the end of the month. You have a vision of getting there by November 30 and delivering the essentials for them: water, food, and a first-aid kit. You start on your journey with these three things to deliver.

After a few miles, you run into a very nice old man. "Where are you walking?" he asks.

"I'm off to the village in the mountains to help a family in need," you reply.

"That is wonderful. My daughter lives in the same village, do you think you would be so kind to bring her this package?"

The old man extends a wizened hand with a small package. There is room in your backpack for it and it doesn't weigh more than a few pounds.

"Sure, I'd be happy to take it to her."

You continue on your journey and after a few miles you are surprised how much of a burden the extra weight makes on your shoulders. As a result, you stop to take a rest earlier than expected in a small town. In that small town, you run into a young woman that owns a toy store. Upon hearing about your journey, she says, "How wonderful. Since you are seeing a family in bad spirits, wouldn't it be nice, besides the essentials for survival, if you brought them a new shiny toy?"

You agree with her that a toy would be a welcome distraction to the children's plight, and it would be nice to bring something other than water, food, and first aid.

"I'd be happy to give you this red truck for free," the woman tells you.

The truck is light so you make room for it by removing one of the bottles of water. You figure one less bottle of water can't cause that much harm. Plus, you don't have the heart to say no to someone that is only trying to help.

You continue on your journey when you pass by a small hospital. A middle-aged nurse politely asks where you are headed. You tell her about your vision and she is excited.

"Oh my, that is quite kind of you. I truly insist that you take this bottle of penicillin with you. It comes in quite handy in a village, and it is much too expensive for anyone in that village to afford on his own."

The bottle is tiny, you are able to stuff the penicillin inside the toy truck, and you start to make your way through the mountains to the village. By this point, with the added package, toy, and penicillin, the backpack is quite heavy (even though you removed one bottle of water) and your climb begins to slow.

Due to your numerous stops and slower pace, you arrive in the village three days later than scheduled. Upon arriving, you see three mounds of fresh dirt piled next to each other. You are crestfallen to discover that two of the children were victims of starvation and the mother died of dehydration. With the kids' passing, the shiny toy truck is of little use now. Worse, the town's well has gone dry and the most essential item they need is water. The village chief doesn't accept the penicillin, as they don't believe in Western medicine, they would rather be healed by natural means.

This parable is applicable to modern times: we cheat ourselves and, in turn, cheat others every day by not saying no. Like the parable, it is easy to do because we do not see or understand the ramifications until many days or years in the future.

Trying to help everyone often results in helping no one. We get more and more requests digitally since it's much easier to ask people for a favor via the safety of a keyboard than looking them eye-to-eye. Hence, the ability to say no, strongly and politely, becomes more and more important in the future. By all means, you should help people; that is really why we are all on this planet. However, we suggest going "long and deep" rather than "fast and vast."

We all have gone through a day, week, or sometimes even a year and said, "Wow! Where did all the time go? I'm not where I want to be." Perhaps these phrases sound familiar:

"Oh, this email from Nancy will only take five minutes to answer."

"There is an instant message from Luke. I can just take a two-minute break to deal with this."

"I'm just going to pull over to the side of the road to answer this text message."

Sound familiar? Sure it does. We all do this to ourselves to some extent. However, we need to train ourselves to say "no thanks" to the metaphoric woman with the shiny toy truck (parable). While we would love to help her, we would only be slowing our progress and hurting others dependent on our success by taking on the additional and unforeseen burdens.

We can look to doctors for tips on how to maintain this ability to say no. Many doctors start practicing medicine because they want to help people. For them it is difficult to turn away a patient in need. In some instances, these are life and death situations. Yet, they cannot expect to treat and heal everyone.

There are laws for the amount of time doctors can work in a week, because a tired doctor can make fatal mistakes. In fact, a study published in the *Journal of the American Medical Association* showed that patients of sleep-deprived surgeons faced an 83 percent increased chance of complications.[8]

Doctors keep regular office hours and some nights are on call for emergencies. They certainly aren't "on call" every night. Yet, many of us put ourselves on call every night, which is not sustainable. Start acting like a doctor and keep regular hours with occasional emergency duties.

Do you often find yourself staying at the office an hour or two longer than anticipated trying to reply to all the messages you received that day? If this is a constant problem you are shortchanging your family. Listen to what North Point Ministries senior pastor Andy Stanley recommends:

> Sit down your significant other and kids and look them in the eye and say: "I just want to apologize upfront to all of you, because I'm going to be home a few hours late each night this week. The reason is that I'm going to prioritize emails, phone messages, texts, and tweets that I don't know what they are about or who they are going to be from, but when I receive them in the future I'm going to put them ahead of you. What I am saying is, answering these messages is more important than you."

Sound ridiculous? This is exactly the message you are sending them.

For your own personal goals try this exercise: Write your goals on pieces of paper and tape them to a mirror. Address your goals and yourself in the mirror and repeat the above paragraph, essentially telling yourself that your goals will be secondary to the whims of messages and unknown requests that will be coming your way in the future. Sound like a silly exercise? It isn't if you aren't prioritizing your goals in life and, instead, are prioritizing future emails, texts, tweets, and more ahead of your passion and purpose in life.

Master Your Inbox before It Masters You

Life in general and digital life especially is not fair. Get over it. The sooner we realize this as leaders, the simpler our lives become and the more effective we become in our leadership roles. Even if we employ some of the simplification and digital timesaving tips discussed in this book, there will still be too much to do. This is a fact. Nobody has ever defeated Father Time, but successful people learn to work with him. In working with him in this digital age, mastering your inbox is a major component of managing your time.

Over 25,000 surveys compiled by Cohesive Knowledge Solutions, Inc. (CKS) indicate that professionals now spend 2.5 hours a day on email and consider 30 percent of that time to be wasted. Extrapolated across America's 100 million knowledge workers and assuming an average wage of $30 per hour this equates to a whopping $540 billion wasted each year.[9]

> "The only thing worse than being talked about is not being talked about."
>
> —OSCAR WILDE

If you are like most people, you have too much coming into your inbox. Whether it is email, text messages, instant messages, Skype video, Facebook chat, Twitter, or the next new thing— a lot of material is coming at you. You should relish this as it means someone else thinks you are important. Yet, often we view it as a dark cloud hanging over us, a cloud that never goes away.

Piling Up Messages and Spam

Some people suffer from a digital pack rat mentality. If you haven't read something in 10 days delete it. It must not be that important. If you cannot bring yourself to delete rigorously, then make a folder called "to read" and put them there. Most likely you will never read these, but it quickly clears your inbox of unnecessary clutter.

If you receive spam, do not simply delete it. At a minimum hit the spam button. It takes the same effort as hitting the delete button. The difference is that these tools track and remember spammers so that you will be less likely to receive spam from that same source in the future. In addition, if enough people report the offending spammer by clicking the spam button, the offender will be placed on a blanket "blocked" or "black list."

Better still, locate and click on the "unsubscribe" link within the message. If this link takes you to a page with several e-newsletters, unsubscribe to all of them. Then if it really is unsolicited spam go back in and hit the spam button. Taking the time to go through the unsubscribe process saves you from constantly deleting these incoming emails, which over time is a significant time and clutter savings. If the page you land on asks you to enter your email address and it is not a brand or URL you recognize, don't enter your email address, as this could be a scam or a malicious phishing site.

The Real (Lack of) Importance of Most Messages

Funny story on how unimportant email is. When I went on vacation for a week, I put an out-of-office reply that stated:

> This mailbox has exceeded its capacity and is temporarily full. New capacity will be added on 8/15. If the email is important please resend on 8/15, otherwise the intended recipient will not receive it. We apologize for the inconvenience.

I returned to 1,134 emails. I would have immediately lost any vacation mojo if I had to dig out from this digital morass. Instead, since I'd left the above auto-reply, I spent a total of 7 seconds selecting all messages and deleting! Hitting that delete button on 1,134 emails was disconcerting and I waited for the world to implode around me. When my world did not immediately implode, I felt a sense of liberation!

The next few days I still waited for the end of the world, but then a week went by, then two weeks, and nothing ill came of it. And, yes, I did receive 9 mails the day I returned (that had been resent) and they were all very important. Can you imagine only nine out of 1,134 emails were important enough for people to resend? Email, instant messages, texts, social posts, and other digital messaging can be abused by people pushing their problems and responsibilities your way: don't let them! Have the guts to simplify and hit life's delete button.

DIGITAL DEEDS

Efficiency

▶ Microsoft stresses the use of the 4 Ds: Delete it, Do it, Delegate it, Defer it. The key is to touch each message only once. Delete ruthlessly. Avoid "deferring" as much as possible. When you must defer, set up a dedicated folder so they a) don't get lost in the shuffle, b) don't clutter your inbox. Feel free to label this defer inbox, "To Read."

▶ Before you send a message determine if it's absolutely necessary. The more messages you send *the more messages you will receive.*

▶ Turn off the message alert functionality on all your devices and applications.

▶ Switch to Gmail (or technology that is more advanced in the future). Its tools (priority inbox, search functionality, labels) will make your life easier than Hotmail, Xfinity, AOL, or Yahoo, and more than justify the short-term switching costs.

▶ Set up copy and paste functionality for frequently asked questions (e.g., directions to your house, standing meeting time and location, hyperlinks to your YouTube videos).

▶ When appropriate indicate "reply not required" at the bottom of the message—this helps you and the recipients.

▶ Use this wording when appropriate "please don't reply 'to all,' please respond directly by calling my mobile." People normally only call if it is truly urgent or important. You do not have to answer every incoming call: the phone is there for your convenience not the caller's. If you are short on time indicate this right away. This helps the caller get straight to the point.

▶ Point people to your preferred means of communication. "This is my desk phone and I only check this a few times a week. If urgent please shoot me a text message to 555-787-555." Or, "I'm traveling right now, please don't leave a voicemail. The best way to reach me is to send me a short text—sorry for the hassle."

▶ Strive to end the message string. "Thanks, see you next week" or "Thanks, let me know if you ever get to Tokyo."

▶ If you cannot conclude the string, treat your digital correspondence like a tennis match—just get the ball back! In tennis, if you wait to get your feet aligned and racquet in position for the perfect shot before swinging, the ball may pass you by. Sometimes we don't reply to a post because we think we need the perfect response. Usually this is not the case. And by waiting we let the ball pass by—and nobody wins. The sender is upset with no response, and our inbox is cluttered with unanswered messages.

▶ Delete anything older than a week, or place in a folder labeled "Archive."

▶ Unsubscribe to newsletters you are not reading—you will not restart.

▶ Keep replies to 1-2 sentences.

Use more robust technology like Amazon's Mechanical Turk. Mechanical Turk gives your business access to a scalable, on-demand workforce. It can be used to break your work into smaller tasks that can be done simultaneously by multiple workers. For example, if you have considerable manual data entry—taking business cards and inputting them into a database, or having your website optimized for Google by having meta tags for all of your images—you can employ the Mechanical Turk at a minimal cost. The good news is that you can go to bed at night and the work gets done while you sleep. If you prefer to only deal with one person, explore hiring a virtual assistant from India or Thailand to help with your daily tasks. Best-selling author Tim Ferris swears by them.

If neither of these options sounds appropriate for your circumstance (they usually aren't the right fit for me) then I suggest you hire an intern. Yes, you can have your own intern. You may think this is crazy at first, but it's really a win-win for both parties. Interns are looking for hands-on experience and are willing to work for free. Reach out to a professor at your local university and develop a relationship. He or she will channel the best and brightest from his or her classes to you. If what you are doing doesn't entice interns, you should question what you are doing.

DIGITAL DEEDS

20-20-20 to Keep 20/20

When we work on our digital devices, the eye blink rate decreases by 70 percent. The eye blink average is 18 times-per-minute (tpm), but it goes to 4 tpm when working off a digital device. A simple rule is to take a break every 20 minutes by looking at least 20 feet or 6 meters away for 20 seconds (20-20-20 rule). Tools like EyeProtectorPro can remind you to take a break.

Never Stop Simplifying

Many people get frustrated in this digital world because they wake up thinking "today I'm going to get to that point where I have nothing to do, everything on my 'to do list' will be done! My inbox will be empty." If you are successful, you will never reach this point of completion. Nevertheless, many of us seem to define success as getting to this point, which is somewhat of a paradox. If your goal in life is to just sit on the couch then perhaps, yes, you can get to the point of having nothing on the "to do" list.

Life's frenetic digital pace makes it difficult for us to be great at everything. Constantly list your three most important items to focus on for the month. It will be very difficult at first (to narrow to three), but it's imperative that you remain disciplined. As author Jim Collins reminds us, any more than three priorities and we have zero priorities.

Make sure to keep it simple!

SECTION ONE: SIMPLE

Key Takeaways
- ▶ Life is complex, those that simplify it win
- ▶ Digitally complaining is toxic for a leader
- ▶ You are going to make mistakes; it's how you handle them that matters

- ▶ Multitasking makes you less productive
- ▶ Go from broad to niche
- ▶ Make decisions
- ▶ Learn to say "no" and to triage like an emergency room doctor
- ▶ Select a day per week to digitally unplug (i.e., no smartphone, TV, tablet, computer)
- ▶ Try the "no complaint day" approach
- ▶ Focus around the things you can do 3x better than others
- ▶ Type out three things you'd like to focus on
- ▶ Your inboxes are there for your convenience; not the sender's convenience
- ▶ Start to batch process your inboxes (suggest 10 a.m. and 3 p.m. for most people)
- ▶ Try answering all digital items in two sentences or less
- ▶ Life's not fair; respond to the most important messages first
- ▶ Your digital presence should be less "Chinese menu" and more "lemonade stand"
- ▶ Embrace challenges

TRUE

1. Decide who you want to be before you decide what you want to be

2. Being well-rounded is outdated in a globally competitive world—niche is the norm

3. Personal is powerful for digital leaders

SIMPLE: success is the result of simplification & focus

TRUE: be true to your passion

ACT: nothing happens without action—take the first step

MAP: goals and visions are needed to get where you want to be

PEOPLE: success doesn't happen alone

CHAPTER SIX

Who Before What

"The only way to do great work is to love what you do."
—STEVE JOBS

We realize far too late what life is truly about. Fortunately, if we're smart, we can learn a great deal about life, and our purpose, by heeding the advice of successful leaders. As Bill Clinton exhorts in a 2010 *Readers Digest* interview:

> Find something you care about where you can make a difference with whatever time or money you have. The older I get, the more I want to keep score: Are people better off when I quit than when I started?

As advice to recent college graduates on what vocational field they should enter, Clinton said:

> First of all, you have something that most human beings in history didn't have: the ability to make such a choice. The vast majority of people who have lived since we first stood up on the African savanna thousands of years ago had no choice whatsoever in how to make a living. So it's a great privilege to be able to choose what you do. So I would say, find something you care about; that's most important.[1]

Steve Jobs gave similar advice to graduating Stanford students:

. . . So I decided to drop out [of college] and trust that it would all work out OK. It was pretty scary at the time, but looking back it was one of the best decisions I ever made . . . You can't connect the dots looking forward; you can only connect them looking back. So you have to trust that the dots will somehow connect in your future. You have to trust in something—your gut, destiny, life, karma, whatever. This approach has never let me down, and it has made all the difference in my life . . . I was lucky I found what I loved to do early in life.

Right now, the new is you, but someday not too long from now, you will gradually become the old and be cleared away. . . . Your time is limited; so don't waste it living someone else's life. Don't be trapped by dogma—which is living with the results of other people's thinking. Don't let the noise of others' opinions drown out your own inner voice. And, most importantly, have the courage to follow your heart and intuition. Then somehow *know what you truly want to become. Everything else is secondary.*

When pressed for the most important advice to give to today's youth, two incredible leaders (Jobs and Clinton) of contrasting style both stressed the same point: be true to what you want to become.

Many of us don't heed this advice because we have bills to pay, a term paper to complete, or a boss to please. In the digital age we need to make certain we know who we are and what we stand for before we decide what we want to be. You may need to take two steps back before you can take a step forward, but it will be worth it in the end. We can take solace knowing that even Steve Jobs was scared when he dropped out of college.

Imagine if the person you sat next to on the plane, bus, or train asked you not "What you did?" but "Who you are?" It would feel a little uncomfortable. And it should, because this is personal. It gets to the core of what all of us stand for. What makes you laugh or cry? What puts a smile on your face? What makes you feel alive? We need to start with the who and then what we do becomes a direct extension and fulfillment of all that we stand for. Or, at a simplified level, if this were your last day on earth would you be happy with what you are doing and who you are as a person?

Discovering Your Passion

In the coming chapters we discuss taking action (just do it) and mapping (understanding your vision). Before we can do this, however, we must first understand what we are passionate about. Our passion is the fire in the engine that drives our ultimate purpose in life, and our digital legacy. As the head of North Point Ministries, Andy Stanley acutely states, "It's always a mistake to decide what you *want to do* before you decide what *you want to be*." This is an important point. If you don't know who you want to become, how can you lead others?

Pigskin, Needlepoint, and Ballet

Rosey Grier played in the National Football League from 1955-1967. He was a member of the Los Angeles Rams famed "Fearsome Foursome," which many consider one of the best defensive lines in history. Grier was a huge man. After retiring from football, he served as a bodyguard for his friend, U.S. senator and presidential candidate Robert F. Kennedy. The night Kennedy was assassinated Grier was assigned to protect Ethel Kennedy. And he was one of the men who subdued the assassin, Sirhan Sirhan.

Grier's history makes him unique, but one thing that also makes him authentic is his love for needlepoint and macramé. In fact, he was so passionate about the activity that he authored books on the subject, including *Rosie Grier's Needlepoint for Men*. Keep in mind that Grier was an African American football player and the book was released in 1973, not during today's more progressive society.

For any man in the 1970s, let alone an all-pro football player, needlepoint was considered a less than macho activity. Rosie Grier said his unusual hobby allowed him to relax while traveling and to be more comfortable around women. Rosie Grier is a poster child for authenticity according to Neil

Pasricha, author of *The Book of Awesome*, mentioned in Chapter Three. While the image of an alpha male hunched over needlepoint is comical, take inspiration from Grier—have the guts to stand up for what you enjoy in life.

> *"Heart Power beats Horse Power."*
>
> —H.J. HEINZ

Lynn Swann, another past football player, is a four time Super Bowl Champion of the Pittsburgh Steelers and was the first wide receiver to win the Super Bowl MVP. While he was in the NFL, Swann decided to take up the art of ballet to help improve his coordination and balance. Like Grier, Swann's interest in ballet received public criticism for being "un-macho" for such an athlete. To Swann's credit, however, he stuck with the practice.

Today Swann serves on the boards of H.J. Heinz Co., Hershey Entertainment, and Wyndham International. In 2006 he was the Republican candidate for governor of Pennsylvania but lost to incumbent Ed Rendell. If he'd won, he would have been Pennsylvania's first African American governor.

Though Grier's interest in needlepoint and Swann's in ballet may not have directly effected their successes in life, these somewhat seemingly offbeat hobbies exhibit the type of character that must be embodied in those who lead. These interests also may have required the necessary stress release points or developed complementary skills in both Swann and Grier so they could excel on the football field, in the board room, or in government. Following your passions in the face of ridicule or other barriers displays your worth as an individual. It conveys a publicly perceivable inner self-confidence that others will admire and want to follow. And, for those that are critics, well, you don't want them as followers anyway.

Oprah's Internal Guide

Oprah Winfrey often wrestled with what to include in her show and what not to include. However, she was always guided by what she felt would be best for the world rather than for her ratings.

"I taped a show with a guy who was a mass murderer. He killed eighty people. I did the whole interview, and I had the families of some of the people he killed. In the middle of it, flash, I thought, 'I shouldn't be doing this; this is not going to help anybody. It's a voyeuristic look at a serial killer, but what good is it going to do anybody?' And we didn't air it."[2]

Passionate about her show and the many causes that she has supported over the years through her three foundations, The Angel Network, The Oprah Winfrey Foundation, and The Oprah Winfrey Operating Foundation, Oprah has maintained her leadership role through following her heart. She has helped create substantial positive change throughout the world by helping others. Her actions endeared her to her viewing audience. While they enjoyed her as an entertainer, they felt as if she was looking out for their best interest and the world's. Even the best actor or actress in the world can't fake inner passion. Despite not being an early nor adamant user of technology, Oprah amassed millions of followers on her Twitter account within weeks of luanching it. People were enamored with how she, despite many challenges and difficulties, followed her passion to success. They, in turn, wanted to do the same.

DIGITAL DEEDS

Finding Your Passion

Finding your passion can be difficult, but this exercise will help.

Are you passionate about your work? The company you work for? Do you enjoy the people you work with? Do you feel inspired every day? Do you wake up and look forward to challenges or do you want to hide under the covers?

If you don't know the answers to these questions look to your digital footprint—your Facebook status updates, emails, photo uploads, what YouTube videos you forward. What you share most often with others, especially others whose opinions matter to you, gives you insight into what inspires and fulfills you. Take a day to go through the last two weeks of your digital activity and see which particular posts give you the most fulfillment. A theme should begin to emerge.

Another item that will help is this: each night, write down the two highlights of your day. What you write down every day will start to show a pattern and themes. These themes are what you are passionate about.

Google Yourself

What do you want the people who matter most to you to find about you when they search Google, or the Google replacement, in the future? Most people want to be remembered for the positive changes they created in the world and what they accomplished in their lifetimes. Without an understanding of what you want out of life, however, it is impossible to know where your passion lies to create change. So, what do you want your legacy to be? Reflect on this thought for a moment. Better still, stop reading, and type out what you would like people to see when they search your name. Before you start typing lengthy prose, however, it's important to comprehend the following parameters.

In 2011, the headlines in Google's search results stopped at 60 characters. The body copy, or details under the headline, totaled 150 characters. Twitter in 2011 only allotted 140 characters. In the decades to come we can expect these character limits to become even more restrictive as there will be more people, media, and technology vying for our attention. At the same time, people's attention spans will continue to shorten as they grow up as digital natives. To break through the increasing clutter our messages will need to be shorter and sweeter.

With these limitations in mind, type a single headline of 60 characters or less, followed by three personally descriptive words. For example, if Helen Keller were to do this exercise, it may look like this:

Helen Keller: Embodied the human spirit—inspiration to mankind
- Optimistic
- Determined
- Activist

As you work to develop how you want to live today and be remembered tomorrow, you will quickly realize that your desired headline will not be "Best Golfer in Tryon County" or "Richest Woman in the Family." Character traits such as honesty, passion, selflessness, inspirational, loving, optimistic, and generous will be what you want said about you. Take Dick Van Dyke, for example: when asked what he wanted on his Tombstone, he told *USA Today* simply "Glad I could help."[3]

> "No legacy is so rich as honesty."
>
> —WILLIAM SHAKESPEARE

DIGITAL DEEDS

Wikipedia—Where Are You?

If Wikipedia were made into a book it would be over 2.25 million pages long. Yet, many of us aren't listed on Wikipedia. Or, worse, we are listed and the write-up is unflattering. Wikipedia is important for individuals and businesses—a Pew Survey showed that 54 percent of adult American Internet users visit Wikipedia regularly and more than 400 million users visit each month. Wikipedia is also in 250 languages globally. In search engines, the top search result for you or your business will often be the Wikipedia entry, so it's imperative to put some effort toward it; being on Wikipedia gives credibility. So how does one get on Wikipedia or edit something written about you or your business?

If you were to start a Wikipedia account this morning and immediately post a write-up about yourself or your business it would most likely be taken down by the Wikipedia editors. It helps to have various contributions over a period of time before attempting to write about yourself or your business. If your Wikipedia account only posts about one person or one business it's too obvious to the Wikipedia editors that the content is coming from a biased source and it will be edited accordingly.

If there is something negative, but true, written about you or your company on Wikipedia don't immediately delete it. This censoring is another "flag" for editors and contributors and the retaliation can be ugly. Instead of removing the material, attempt to take the sting out of the negativity by telling the other side of the story.

Removing factually incorrect information, however, should be considered, but make certain to cite credible third-party sources in your response. Don't ever go as far as to write in a promotional nature on Wikipedia, as this will also quickly get scrubbed (Wikipedia lists what it considers promotional in nature).

Although Wikipedia is relatively simple to use, it's not as simple as using your iPhone so you may need to enlist someone to help you. Ask your friends and family if they know any Wikipedia contributors and go from there.

Healthy Smiles

As you strive toward a passion- and purpose-filled life, your attitude will naturally become more positive. Your physical health will often improve as well. Three separate studies have shown that healthy attitudes equate to healthy bodies.

Dr. Karina Davidson of Columbia University helped conduct a 10-year study of people in Nova Scotia, Canada. The results showed that those with a positive outlook on life were less likely to develop heart disease compared to those with a negative outlook. Davidson believes people with positive outlooks tend to sleep better, eat healthier, and are better able to cope with stress.

"The first principle is that you must not fool yourself, and you are the easiest person to fool."

—RICHARD P. FEYNMAN, Nobel Prize–winning physicist

A study published by *Psychological Science* examined the faces and smiles of baseball players from the 1950s. Those with wide grins lived an average of five years longer than those without big smiles.

Another study at the University of Kentucky followed 124 law students over a four-year period and discovered that those who had a positive opinion of the law school and were upbeat under pressure tended to have stronger immune systems. Researchers say this finding implies that entering stressful situations, like surgery, can have a better outcome if people go in with a positive attitude.[4]

DIGITAL DEEDS

Who Likes You Enough to Link?

If you have your own blog, company website, or Facebook page—after reading this book you should—a good way to find out who supports you is to determine who is hyperlinking from their page(s) to yours (i.e., they have a link that points to your site). To find out this information, simply go to a tool such as Yahoo Site Explorer (siteexplorer.search.yahoo.com) and enter your URL (Universal Resource Locater). Site Explorer will give you the number of people linking to your page and each site connected to yours. This tool is also great for businesses since you can enter your competitors' websites for comparative analysis. Why do they have links and supporters that you don't? In addition, the more inbound links you have, the greater chance you have to appear higher in Google and Bing, as the algorithms used by these search engines heavily reward sites with many inbound links.

Passion Propels Talent

Revisiting Ronald Reagan, CNN political analyst David Gergen made the following observation:

> Reagan had figured out who he was and liked it. He didn't just feel comfortable in his own skin; he felt serene. Reagan not only had a compass for his life, but a compass for his political beliefs, and he communicated both with a contagious optimism that stirred people across the land. Whether or not one agreed with his policies, it is pretty clear that he was the best leader in the White House since Franklin Roosevelt. Reagan didn't pretend to be the smartest man to serve, but he was smart enough.[5]

Gergen is the only man to serve in four different U.S. presidential cabinets (Nixon, Ford, Reagan, Clinton), and he readily allows that Clinton's IQ was superior to Reagan's. But here's Gergen's take on Clinton as excerpted from the book *True North* by Bill George:

> Instead of a struggle between light and dark [as with Nixon], my sense is that Clinton's central problem has been the lack of an inner compass. He has 360-degree vision but no true north. He isn't yet fully grounded within . . . . [He] isn't exactly sure who he is yet and tries to define himself by how well others like him. That leads him into all sorts of contradictions, and the view by others that he seems a constant mixture of strengths and weaknesses.[6]

We started this chapter showcasing Clinton's strengths, but when he blundered, as all humans will do, his mistake was often the attempt to define himself by external forces rather than internal ones. Over the years, Clinton has a better understanding of this notion and now stresses to younger generations to "find something you care about; that's most important." Notice he didn't say "find something that others care about; that's the most important."

You don't have to be the smartest person in the room to win; passion supercharges intelligence and talent. Thomas Edison realized this a century ago when he declared, "Genius is one percent inspiration and 99 percent perspiration."

We see this same idea in Michigan State Basketball coach Tom Izzo. Since 2000 Michigan State has had seven McDonald's All-American High School recruits join its program. Eight other programs garnered more All-American recruits during this same time period, including Duke (22), North Carolina (22), and Kansas (12).[7]

Yet, despite having less talent (based on the number of McDonald's All-Americans), Michigan State, over the same number of seasons, went to more Final Fours than any other program. Izzo believes a key reason for this success is that he recruits based on inner heart and desire, not just outward physical talent.

Izzo's methodology reminds me of an old saying relating to war: mercenaries will always beat draftees, but volunteers will beat both all the time. Hence a basketball player that is tall, has incredible speed and jumping ability, but is playing only to earn a scholarship or make money playing professionally, may not be quite as good as a player that is less talented but has a true passion for the sport. There is another old saying that directly relates to basketball coaching: talent and potential have gotten many a coach fired. Now, when you combine both talent and passion the results can be incredible, for example, Michael Jordan. However, keep in mind that Jerry Rice is considered the undisputed best wide receiver to ever play in the National Football League. Yet, there have been hundreds of wide receivers before and after Jerry Rice that were taller, faster, and could jump higher. Yet, because he was so passionate, he outworked all of them to become the best there ever was. The same idea applies to leadership in the digital age: leaders in the digital decades to come will be made, they are not born.

> *"You must believe in yourself, if you don't how do you expect others to believe in you?"*
>
> **—@EQUALMAN**

Forrest Gump: True

"I gotta find Bubba!" Forrest Gump cries out in the middle of an embattled Vietnam jungle during an air raid. Bubba is Gump's best friend and following the raid, he doesn't return with the rest of the platoon. Gump insists on returning for Bubba. But he is urged to stay put and not go back to save him since he is most likely already dead. Despite protests from others in his platoon, Gump remains true to his beliefs and goes in search of his friend in the blazing jungle littered with dead and dying solders.

In his search for Bubba, Gump encounters several other fallen and wounded soldiers that he drags to safety (for which he later receives the Medal of Honor). Gump is even shot before finally reaching Bubba who is barely alive. Gump carries his friend to safety, but Bubba dies in his arms. Gump returns from Vietnam and despite Bubba's death, he honors

Bubba's wish of starting a shrimping business together. They agreed everything would be split 50/50. And even though Bubba was gone, Gump was true to his word and gave 50 percent of the millions he earned in the shrimping business to Bubba's family.

People constantly reminded Gump that he was different, and not in a good way. Yet the thing that truly sets him apart is his ability to rise above the negativity of the naysayers. When people laughed at him, it hurt, but he kept on his path and stayed true to his beliefs.

> "It is not how much money we make that ultimately makes us happy between nine and five. It's whether our work fulfills us."
>
> —MALCOLM GALDWELL, *Outliers*

We need to stay true to our internal compass and not be dissuaded when others say words like "no," "can't," and "impossible."

We have metaphorically been given millions of digital oysters. The key to finding the one that contains the pearl for our lives is to open the one we are most passionate about.

CHAPTER SEVEN

Niche Is the New Norm

"If your only goal is to become rich,
you will never achieve it."
—JOHN D. ROCKEFELLER

In the past, well-rounded individuals were thought to be the most successful in life. However, in today's global economy, the playing field is far more competitive. Due to advances in communication the world is much more connected. Students from Germany entering the workforce now compete with students from Japan, China, India, the United States, and beyond. At the same time the global population has continued to increase. In 1960 there were 4 billion people. Today we are pressing over 7 billion.[1] That means if you want to become the best, you have an additional 3 billion people trying to knock you from the top spot. That's why you need to find your specific calling and hone your craft.

Jack Nicholas and Tiger Woods were successful in golf because they had the talent and singularly focused on one sport. Nicholas actually excelled in several sports growing up and was even recruited by some colleges out of high school to play basketball. However, while he attended Ohio State University he knew his best chance for success was to focus on golf. Woods grew up a few decades later and the times had vastly changed. Woods's father Earl knew that if his son wanted to become the best golfer in the world his best chance was to focus on the sport. From the age of two, Woods's singular focus was to become the best golfer of his era and hopefully all time.

Similarly, radio talk show host Colin Cowherd is adamant about focusing on content that delivers the highest broadcast ratings. His success in Las Vegas, Tampa, and Portland enabled him to land a national radio show with ESPN. He doesn't forget what got him to the top of his profession:

> I always find it humorous when listeners call or email us and they are upset that we don't talk more about hockey or soccer. Guess what, we don't talk about a lot of things on this show like women's field hockey or volleyball either. I'm rewarded based on my ratings; it's a simple numbers game. If soccer delivered the numbers, we would talk soccer all day. Or if the show were international, we'd talk soccer. But, I'm not going to discuss what the minority wants to hear; I'm going to discuss topics that the majority wants to hear, as simple as that. While we may grow tired of the New York Yankees or the Dallas Cowboys, the numbers don't lie; people want to talk about it. Just like in Los Angeles, they want to hear about the NFL, Lakers, and USC—that is pretty much it.[2]

Cowherd isn't beyond insulting people in small cities or rural towns saying things like, "If you are given the choice to live in Miami or Cleveland, you are taking Miami every day of the week. Cleveland is a dumpster fire."[3] He knows Cleveland isn't part of his listening audience, which mainly resides in New York City, Los Angeles, and Chicago. Like a politician that caters to his or her voting base, Cowherd focuses on what delivers the best ratings. To be successful, we need to focus on what we do best, no matter what business we are in. On a personal level, we need to focus on what delivers us overall happiness.

Marcus Buckingham in his bestseller, *Now, Discover Your Strengths*, puts the search for our true talents, our personal niche, this way:

Despite your achievements, you wonder whether you are as talented as everyone thinks you are. You suspect that luck and circumstance, not your strengths, might explain much of your success. The anxious little voice in your ear whispers, "When will you be found out?" And, against your better judgment, you listen.

In part this explains why, when asked to describe their strengths, people rarely refer to their natural talents. Instead, they talk about external things that they have gathered during their life, such as certificates and diplomas, experiences and awards. Here is the "proof" that they have improved themselves, that they have acquired something valuable to offer.[4]

Once we learn how to focus on our passions, we can leverage our unique talents to springboard from one profession to another, but only if it utilizes similar skill sets. For example, if your goal is to become the best advertising copywriter in the world, as you ascend to the top you may determine your skills translate nicely into becoming a world-renowned mystery novelist. Or you may determine you love writing romance novels more and are better at it than writing advertising copy. Being well-rounded, however, is different. Being well rounded would be setting a goal of being the best advertising copywriter, advertising account executive, and media buyer. You may become good at all three, but very few would ever become great at all three at the same time.

Focusing on Your Passion and Finding Your Talents

Joe Gibbs won three NFL Super Bowls as the coach of the Washington Redskins before going on to form Joe Gibbs Racing and wining three NASCAR Championships (one with Bobby Labonte and two with Tony Stewart). Both experiences required Gibbs to build a team, manage and lead that team, and get the players and crew to live up to their potential. The concept is similar to how top-level executives often succeed at various companies.

Consider James Patterson as another example. For years Patterson was a top Creative Director at the J. Walter Advertising agency before becoming a best-selling novelist. He honed his storytelling ability creating advertising before leveraging it as an author. He found his niche and used it to follow his passion of writing.

Before becoming the anchor of *Good Morning America*, Robin Roberts sharpened her broadcasting skills at ESPN. Sure, she liked sports, having played college basketball, but she loved discussing societal issues. She was able to develop her talents at ESPN, then use this experience as a springboard to move forward in her career. She became a co-anchor of ABC's morning show, *Good Morning America* in 2005. Roberts has won three Emmy awards for her work throughout her career.

These examples show that in today's world if we want something bad enough it is there for the taking. Sometimes it may require a stepping stone like in the Patterson and Roberts examples. However, today there is less hierarchy in the world due to technology. For example, it is much easier to now start your own company (consider Google, Toms Shoes, or Zappos). Technology has made the cost and risk of starting a new business or endeavor much smaller than previously. So, while a stepping stone may be required, it should be closer to the top than ever before.

Once at the top, things don't end, as from the Joe Gibbs example, unique skills can transfer to a different company, vocation or movement. Mark Cuban is an example of a person parlaying his entrepreneurial skills from founding Broadcast. com to creatively managing the Dallas Mavericks. His unconventional style took one of the NBA's most anemic franchises and delivered an NBA title in 2011.

Learning from Failure

Advice you commonly hear from successful people is: "Do what you love." As cited earlier, Steve Jobs put it like this: "Have the courage to follow your heart and intuition. They somehow already know what you truly want to become. Everything else is secondary."

This statement can be frustrating to hear. We often respond with a quip like, "Easy for you to say you have made it, I have bills to pay, kids to feed." In this frustration we forget one crucial fact—most of these people weren't overnight successes and failed at times on their journey to the top. At one point, they too had bills to pay, kids to feed, and the dangerous promise of leaving "solid ground" and going after their passion.

For example, when we see Tom Hanks winning another Oscar award, we don't think about the countless nights he toiled at his craft in seedy comedy clubs and bars. Lest we forget his stint on the sitcom *Bosom Buddies*, in which his character dressed up like a woman in order to live in a subsidized rental apartment. (As you might imagine, the show was canceled after two seasons.)

Author Dale Carnegie wasn't an overnight success either, which he discusses in *Dale Carnegie Training, Leadership Mastery: How to Challenge Yourself and Others to Greatness*:

> Carnegie trained to become a teacher at a state college in Missouri, yet as a young man he somehow found himself selling trucks in New York City. If that seems unlikely, it's no more unlikely than aspiring novelists who turn into corporate lawyers, or gourmet cooks who become accountants. One day it dawned on Mr. Carnegie that he was living a life totally unrelated to the one he had envisioned for himself. This was a very unsettling realization, but unlike many people, Dale Carnegie decided to do something about it.
>
> The first step he took was quitting his job as a truck salesman. That took some fortitude, but it was something he had wanted to do for a long time. The next step was a bit more complicated. Mr. Carnegie knew he did not want to sell trucks, and that his training had been in education. He saw that what he really wanted to do was write. As he considered his training and his aspirations, a plan began to form

in his mind. Perhaps he could find work as an instructor in adult education classes held at night. He could then have his days free to fashion novels and short stories. It was a good idea but it was not as simple as it seemed. Mr. Carnegie first applied to the most prestigious institutions of higher learning in the Manhattan area, including Columbia and New York University. Both schools, as he later described it, "somehow decided they could get along without me." Finally, a job teaching adult classes on salesmanship and public speaking skills opened up at the night school of the YMCA.[5]

Sometimes the worst job to have is not one you hate, but one you feel indifferent toward. A job you hate is much easier to quit than one that is simply OK. In Dale Carnegie's situation, one could argue that it was easier for him to leave the truck selling business since he woke up one day and knew with certainty it wasn't for him. However, most of us aren't this blessed, many of us muddle in mediocrity because it isn't "so bad," instead of searching out our niche in work and life.

A Quick Path to Failure

In life, sometimes the quickest path to failure is early or easy success. This statement may seem odd; after all don't you want early success? Well, the response depends on a few things.

First off, are you mature enough to handle success? Two years into their retirement, 78 percent of former NFL players are bankrupt or under financial stress because of joblessness or divorce. Within five years of retirement, an estimated 60 percent of former NBA players are broke.[6] Entertainers and celebrities have also had their problems with early fame and fortune. Consider Lindsay Lohan, Gary Coleman, Kurt Cobain, Anthony Weiner, Marilyn Monroe, Elvis Presley, Eliot Sptizer, Macaulay Culkin, Charlie Sheen—the list goes on.

The second potential problem with early success is that it might be in a field that doesn't inspire you. Yet, if we have success in a field, we feel we need to stay in that field, even if it's not our passion. The slang term for this situation is "golden handcuffs." It is imperative to find a niche that fulfills you.

Third, if success comes without hard work, we think that life is always going to work out that way for us. Many lottery winners, for example, can't handle their immediate newfound wealth. Lottery winners often immediately change their lifestyles, spend more than they are being paid and eventually go bankrupt. Ironically, many lottery winners' lives become worse, both financially and from a personal happiness perspective.

> *"Great spirits have always encountered violent opposition from mediocre minds."*
>
> **—ALBERT EINSTEIN**

Still, learning from these failures will help lead you on a path toward success. Even NBA star Michael Jordan was cut from his high school basketball team. Yet, Jordan stuck with basketball, because he loved it. In Jordan's Hall of Fame induction speech, he indicated he was motivated every day to prove people wrong, especially after that event. At the induction ceremony, he even went so far as to fly out the player from his high school team who was chosen over him.

Are you using your hurdles in life to motivate you like Michael Jordan? Or when life trips you up, do you choose an easier path? As legendary radio personality Paul Harvey once told me, "I hope one day to achieve enough success so that if someone asks me how I did it, I will tell them, 'I get up more times than I fall.'"

LIFE STAMPS

Wrestler Stands Tall

"He's always done everything; he hasn't let anything hold him back. He doesn't want to be different," says Anthony Robles's mother. Only her son *is* different, he's an NCAA wrestling champion. Few people have earned this title, and fewer still have done it on one leg—Anthony Robles was born without a right leg.

"I had a dream of playing football growing up, but I was too small for that so I decided on wrestling," says Robles. "I was a terrible wrestler, only about 90 pounds, but my mom told me God made me for a reason, and I believe that reason [God made me] is for wrestling."

Robles didn't see his condition as an obstacle. In fact, he has used it to his benefit. "It is a great advantage; my grip is extremely strong from walking on crutches all day using my hands and shoulders. My upper body strength is a huge advantage in my weight class."

He even ran his first mile on crutches in 10 minutes and then reduced his time to eight minutes. "I think he has a goal of doing it in six minutes on crutches and, knowing Anthony, he'll accomplish it," said an Arizona State teammate.

In 2011, Robles completed a perfect senior season by winning his final wrestling match 7-1. "I wrestle because I love wrestling, but it inspires me when I get kids, even adults, who write me on Facebook or send me letters in the mail saying that I've inspired them, and they look up to me, and they're motivated to do things that other people wouldn't have thought possible."

One Personality

One thought that struck a cord with many readers of *Socialnomics*, and one that many traditional leaders still struggle with today, is consistently expressing the same personality both online and offline. Many people still desire to have different personalities depending on what subset of friends they are with—both online and offline. They desire to behave differently in front of their softball team than in front of their church group. To become a true digital leader you don't have the freedom of having a multitude of personalities like in decades past. Your true personality is just a camera phone away from being discovered.

> *"Be who you are and say what you feel, because those who mind don't matter and those who matter don't mind."*
> —DR. SEUSS

This concept may be one of the most difficult ones to grasp, so I discuss it a number of times throughout the book. Even the creators of Facebook wrestled with the concept. David

Kirkpatrick's book *The Facebook Effect* provides insight on this idea:

> "You have one identity," he says emphatically three times in a single minute during a 2009 interview. He recalls that in Facebook's early days some argued the service ought to offer adult users both a work profile and a "fun social profile." Zuckerberg was always opposed to that. "The days of you having a different image for your work friends or co-workers and for the other people you know are probably coming to an end pretty quickly," he says . . . "Having two identities for yourself is an example of a lack of integrity," Zuckerberg says moralistically. But he also makes a case he sees as pragmatic—that "the level of transparency the world has now won't support having two identities for a person."[7]

We need to understand and accept this societal shift so we can adjust our behavior accordingly in our development path to becoming digital leaders. To become a leader of others we first must take control of our life. We need to start living our best life so that we are fulfilled and happy with the person we become. If we can do this, then we create magnetism from within that others are sure to follow. Become digital leaders of our life first and then digitally lead others, keeping in mind transparency is key.

For an even earlier example of the power of transparency, consider H.J. Heinz and the Heinz Corporation. H.J. Heinz understood the importance of truth and transparency in the 19th Century. He was the first to sell his Heinz Horseradish sauce in a clear bottle; the purpose was to show its purity. People, at the time, were skeptical of manufactured food and they had a right to be: many companies used substandard fillers or canned their food in unsanitary conditions.

Heinz was one of the first to allow tours of his plants to showcase their quality and cleanliness. For the first time ever, people were able to witness the actual production line. He would have 20,000 people tour the plant annually. Assume your once opaque bottle of privacy is now as clear as the Heinz bottles.

Conviction & Time

Staying true to your passion and finding your niche is often difficult. Achieving success at what you love to do can often take longer than you'd like. Taking shortcuts in life, however, is usually a shortcut to disaster.

I know this truth firsthand, because for 14 years I submitted query letters to publishers requesting their consideration of my manuscripts. The hundreds of rejection letters I received helped motivate me to become a better writer. Then, passion and persistence finally paid off with my international best seller, *Socialnomics*. I wouldn't have it any other way as the challenging path made me improve my craft and eventually led to success.

Young & Rubicam CEO Ann Fudge offers this advice:

> Struggle and tough experiences ultimately fashion you. Don't worry about the challenges. Embrace them. Go through them even if they hurt. Tell yourself, there is something to be learned from this experience. I may not fully understand it now, but I will later. It's all part of life, and life is a process of learning. Every challenging experience develops your core of inner strength, which gets you through those storms. Nothing worth doing in life is going to be easy.[8]

As leaders, this advice is imperative to keep in mind as we move forward in the new lens of the digital world. The challenges we face in implementing new technologies, competing globally, and finding success must be dealt with head on. The ability to follow our passion and find our niche will help us in this process by playing toward our strengths and individuality. Maintaining a sense of who we are contributes to our ability to stand out in this new world.

Wicked Good

Gregory Maguire, author of the successful book and musical *Wicked*, also needed time before he caught his big break. Success did not come quickly:

Before *Wicked* I'd been a writer for fifteen years, getting decent critical reviews and virtually no sales. Then, I accidentally hit upon the idea of using *The Wizard of Oz* characters as the context for my idea about the nature of evil—I like to say that I had the garment, and then I found the hanger to hang it on. But, if *Wicked* itself didn't have its own potency and cohesion, I think it would just be too ephemeral and unable to survive on Oz lore alone.[9]

Using Maguire's words, it often takes us a while to find our "hanger." When we do find it, we need to move full speed ahead. In the meantime, it's important for us to stick to our garment (craft/passion) so that we are ready when the right hanger comes along.

Or, put another way, luck is where opportunity meets preparation.

Golden Arches in Golden Years

One of the world's iconic businessmen didn't get his big break until he was 52 years old. Ray Kroc was a high school dropout who once played piano in bordellos and speakeasies. In 1917, when Kroc was a mere 15 years old, he lied about his age to the Red Cross in order to become an ambulance driver during World War I.

Throughout much of his career, Kroc was a salesman. In 1954, as a Chicago-based multi-mixer salesman, he was surprised to receive a large order for multi-mixers from a restaurant in San Bernardino, California. Kroc flew out to meet with the McDonald brothers. By 1955 Kroc had founded the McDonald's Corporation. Kroc opened his first McDonald's in Des Plaines, Illinois, with a simple menu consisting of a 15-cent hamburger, french fries, soft drinks, and milk shakes. These milk shakes were made in the multi-mixers sold by Kroc.[10]

Kroc was born in 1902 when the average life expectancy for men was 46.3 years.[11] Statistically, at age 52, Kroc was supposed to be resting in his grave. Yet here he was just beginning his legacy as one of the world's great business entrepreneurs. Today, research indicates the most recognized first word of babies in the world isn't "mama" or "daddy"—it's "McDonald's."[12]

We have a distinct advantage over Ray Kroc who lived in the pre-digital era. We don't necessarily have to wait as long for our big break—we have the digital means and access to succeed faster. Whether you are 21 or 71, you can start making your break after dinner tonight. Success may not come right away, but we have the ability to make it come faster than anytime in history. Also keep in mind that a person born in 2011 has a life expectancy of over 80 years. In fact, 1 out of 5 born in 2011 are expected to live to be over 100 years old. Many of us have the better part of a century to establish our digital legacy.[13]

While I performed multiple efforts to help promote my last book *Socialnomics*, by far the biggest contributor to awareness around this new word were a few videos that I produced on YouTube. In *one year's* time search results on Google for the term "Socialnomics" went from zero to over 1 million and this was primarily driven by people looking for and reposting these videos. I then made certain to focus on doing several revisions to these videos. In developing this specific concept and utilizing social media tools, I was able to create a great deal of attention for the book in a shorter time than may have been possible in the pre-digital world.

Feedback

Why do people want to engage with us? If you don't know why people associate with you, ask your best friends: *Why do you hang out with me, what do you like? Where can I improve as a person?* Don't be surprised when they are done answering your questions if they, in turn, ask you the same ones about themselves.

These are uncomfortable questions for most of us to ask, so feel free to use this book as a pretext. *I'm reading a book that has action items for me to do. One I thought was interesting involved asking a friend a few questions and I was hoping you could help me out.* It will be tough for your friend to laugh or say "no" when it is phrased as such. Don't wait. Ask your friends today—this type of feedback is invaluable.

I remember kayaking with my mom when I asked her the question "Where can I improve the most?" She, like most of us, was hesitant to answer, but I kept pressing her on the issue. Eventually she responded to my plea, "Well, Erik you have all of these wonderful ideas and plans, but I never see anything actually finished." Let me tell you, this was the tough truth I needed to hear to get motivated. Three months after our conversation my book *Socialnomics* was at the publisher ready to print, and since then I have always made a daily point to get things "out the door." Or, as Seth Godin discusses in his book *Poke the Box*, we all need to get in the habit of "shipping" stuff.

> "Tis great confidence in a friend to tell him your faults, greater to tell him his."
> —BENJAMIN FRANKLIN

My hope is that you have someone valuable enough in your life to tell you the tough truth. Ask your confidants about your strengths and where you can improve to help you find your niche. Verizon's Judy Haberkorn says, "They called me the feedback queen. The best thing you can get in this world is honest feedback from someone who cares about your success and well-being. Some of us are more self-aware than others, but few of us see the world as it sees us."[14]

This tactic should be applied to your business. Embrace the feedback that you receive through traditional and digital channels, whether it is a comment or request left on your Facebook wall, a tweet about one of your products or services, or a response to a post you made on your blog. Seriously consider what people are saying and how you can cater further to their needs or respond to negative feedback. Use these tools to your advantage by honing in on what you can do better than any other company to satisfy your current or potential customers.

As a leader, make sure that you are aware of what is going on in this digital realm and you understand what is being said about your product or service by your customers, employees, and colleagues. Take suggestions to heart and look for that small niche that will help your company get an edge on competition.

Inspirational Starbucks CEO Howard Schultz's niche idea for Starbucks came when he was traveling oversees:

> As I visited small espresso bars throughout Milan and Verona, I was taken by the power that savoring a simple cup of coffee can have to connect people and create community among them, and from that moment on I was determined to bring world-class coffee and the romance of Italian espresso bars to the United States.[15]

Schultz asked why shouldn't there be a place that focuses on supplying a romantic coffee experience. It was something he loved when he visited Europe and he figured others would love it as well.

Similar to Kroc, Schultz purchased Starbucks when it was very small and grew it into a global empire. When your Starbucks or McDonald's epiphany comes along, be ready to seize on the opportunity.

Successful Turnarounds

This book can serve as a catalyst to turn your life or business around and as an impetus for turning over the proverbial new leaf. As such it would be helpful to know what a successful turnaround CEO uses as a formula for success in this niche executive category. Ken Robbins (founder and CEO of digitally based Response Mine Interactive) recounted the following story to me:

> I was at a poker tournament and one of the other gentlemen seated near me was another lover of math. We immediately hit it off. When I asked him what he did, he simply replied "I'm a turnaround CEO."

> The response certainly piqued my interest. What exactly were the makings of a good turnaround CEO? It was obvious

this guy was not short on smarts or success (he even won the poker tournament). So, I asked him what his general formula for success was when turning these companies around in 18-24 months:

Q: Do you dramatically reduce headcount? Is it all about downsizing?

A: No, typically we don't have to downsize. Generally, I'll find one or two Lieutenants in the old regime that aren't willing to accept change. I'll typically remove these inflexible Lieutenants simply because they are causing major distractions for everyone else that has bought into the new plan.

Q: So it surely must be operational. You must come in and streamline the operational process from logistics to bill payment?

A: It's not that either.

Q: Is it technology then? Do you invest in new technology and eliminate inefficient systems?

A: No, it's not that either, that's not the quickest road to sustainable success. While they are tools that help, they aren't the quickest way to turn something around.

Q: OK, I give up, what is the secret then?

A: You are going to be surprised at just how simple this sounds. I ask for a list of our 40-50 best customers. If we don't have this list then that is a major warning sign and we fix that first. However, most companies do have such a list. I then personally go and visit each one of these customers and ask them two simple questions. What do you buy from us? Why do you buy from us?

I've been doing this for a long time and it's amazing that for each different company the 40-50 customers we talk with will have very consistent answers for that particular company.

I then return to the office and immediately adjust our focus on the products that are purchased by our top customers and why they buy from us. The reasons they buy from us are usually one of the following:

a. You have the product I need at a fair price
b. Customer service
c. Speed of delivery
d. Simple reordering process
e. Trust

From this story, we see that you must focus on the products your best customers want because that is what other new customers will want. Then you need to get everyone internally to focus on making those desired products and services the best they can be. Consider these products or services your company's talents, its niche that will help you succeed. Being true to your customers and your core competencies is the formula for a successful turnaround. Recall that this turnaround advice is in line with what is discussed in Section One of the book: successful people and businesses focus on simplification. While many businesses cannot afford a turnaround CEO, consider your company's strengths and abilities and how you can use them to your advantage in dealing with customers. What do customers want most and what can you provide that is unique and most helpful?

In another example, Howard Schultz, the founder of Starbucks, decided to return as the Starbucks CEO after a 10-year absence. He discusses at length in his book *Onward* the impetus behind his return after such a long break. In Starbucks's desire for growth they lost sight of the essence of their brand and disregarded what made the company so successful. As a result, they were no longer being true to the Starbucks values and, in turn, were no longer being true to the customer. They had lost their niche that had made them successful. Instead of simply focusing on great coffee and a great experience they were trying to sell music, DVDs, books, smoothies, hot made-to-order food, and other items. These items distracted them from their core mission and they were no longer being true to what had propelled them to success in the first place.

This lost vision eventually reduced Starbucks's profitability. When Schultz returned, his turnaround plan was not to find a silver bullet, but rather to set an aggressive agenda to return to Starbucks's original values. Within two years, and during a difficult economy, under Schultz's stewardship, Starbucks returned to profitable growth.

Be True to Yourself and Find Your Niche

No matter what goal you have in mind, be it personal or professional, success is not an overnight phenomenon. To succeed in the digital age, we have a number of tools that may help us in certain ways to speed up that achievement, but it still takes hard work and persistence. Overall, we need to concentrate on what we as individuals, and as companies, do best, and then consider how we can further improve. Without passion, however, it is unlikely we will ever find our specific niche that will lead to success. In leveraging our unique techniques, we have many more options, and opportunities, open to us than ever before. Utilize your strengths, meet challenges head on, and continue on your path toward success.

> "You must have the courage to be true to yourself."
> —JOHN WOODEN

Keep in mind it's always easier to start niche and then grow big (e.g., McDonald's) than it is to try and go for everything from the start. This idea applies to us both personally and professionally. It's much easier to have success on Facebook and then move onto Twitter, StumbleUpon, YouTube, Wikipedia, Google+, and others. Think about how it is easier to learn calculus once you've already learned algebra, geometry, and trigonometry first. Find a niche you are passionate about, hone it to the best of your ability, and you will be on your way to success in the digital days ahead.

CHAPTER EIGHT

Personal Is Powerful

"Passion, that intangible concept many businesspeople belittle, is essential."

—HOWARD SCHULTZ, Starbucks Founder[1]

As Kid Rock was composing his album *Born Free*, he asked legendary music producer Rick Rubin if his new songs were too Detroit-centric. Rubin encouraged him not to dilute his songs' hometown pride. "When an artist talks about something really personal," Rubin says, "the thing that connects with people and makes it relatable is the passion conveyed." Hearing Kid Rock croon about Michigan is like hearing Springsteen sing about New Jersey: people hear "Detroit" but picture their own hometowns.

Just as music listeners can discern and appreciate Kid Rock sharing his passion through music, your followers can appreciate your passions only if you share them. It's important for us to let go and not feel we have to tie our own hands on what we do and don't reveal to others about our personal lives. When I say personal, I don't mean it in the "fluffy" and lovey-dovey sense, but more in the way of giving potential friends and followers a glimpse into your soul via your passions. For example, say you love Ultimate Fighting Championship (UFC), yet you are the head caretaker at a tulip flower farm and you post videos about how to care for tulips. Your inclination might be to keep your passion for UFC a secret. Instead, you should embrace your passion and give relevant or funny analogies on how it does or doesn't relate to taking care of tulips. "To make sure your tulips thrive, when you start to see brown shading on the edges, make sure to snap the head off the flower like you're former UFC champion Chuck Liddell."

The old world thinking would be to not disclose something so personal that is unrelated to your business. Yet, in today's world with so much being shared, it is likely that employees, executives, or coworkers are going to find out your passions anyhow, so you might as well embrace them. What you will discover, just like in the Kid Rock example, is that to do so is not only powerful, but it's fun for you. People can feel that passion and want to know what other things excite you, even if there is no direct correlation to your job or leadership position.

In the same vein, you need to find out what your followers and potential followers are passionate about. If someone sends you a message liking something you've done, a simple thanks is nice. But what's even better is if you take a second or two to research this person's interests or background. For example, if you receive a tweet you can simply click on the person's profile and it may reveal he lives in Atlanta and is passionate about BBQ. Then your message back might be, "Thanks for the kind words, I hope you are enjoying some BBQ at the Horseradish Grill. I love that place."

Skeletons in the Closet

For many of us, the thought of having others know more about our passions and personal lives can be daunting, especially in the digital, online realm. If you become comfortable with this form of sharing, however, it can be powerful for anything you are trying to accomplish.

Some of us may be open to sharing but are concerned about potential skeletons in our closet. As a result of technological advancements, your "closet" now has a glass door. This glass door is going to be there whether we embrace the digital world or not. Almost everyone has some skeletons in the closets to varying degrees. We also all have enemies to one extent or another.

Combining those two elements (closets and enemies) there are probably some items online about us that we aren't happy about or there will be something revealed in the future. The first step to dealing with this issue is realizing that worrying about it will only produce unnecessary stress. Unless someone invents a time machine, we can't go back to fix something in the past. What we can do now is start to lead our best life. For the items in the past, or potential skeletons, instead of worrying you should figure out which items you are most concerned about coming to light and figure out a plan if they do in fact become posted digitally.

This exercise should help reduce stress, as once you know the "worst" thing that can happen, you can better deal with it. You will also be prepared to execute your plan when the time comes. A key focus of this plan should be owning up to the mistake without making excuses, helping everyone move forward. You should make efforts to proactively mitigate the damage. For example, if someone posts an unflattering picture on Facebook you should start by going and removing the "tag" of your name on the photo. This is very easy to do, you simply hit the "untag" button on Facebook for that particular photo. It's also an argument for having a Facebook account so you are aware of what is being posted about you via the alerts they send.

You should also call the person that posted the photo and see if she would be so kind to remove it (you'd be amazed at how often this works!). Moving forward, be aware when you are in the presence of this particular person, that she has a history of posting unflattering content about you. Above all, if you keep leading a great life, then when these items are dredged up, they will hopefully be drowned out by all the positive things you've contributed to society.

The Vaynerchuk Way: From $4 Million to $50 Million

Gary Vaynerchuk's parents immigrated to America from Russia and started a liquor store in Springfield, New Jersey. A young Gary developed a passion for wine, and his parents allowed him to carve out a small wine section in their store. Gary's wine business grew modestly. To stimulate sales he decided to start broadcasting an online show in 2006 called *Wine Library TV*. The premise of the show was Gary sharing his vast wine knowledge with the audience.

The content of Gary's first episode of *Wine Library TV* is what one would expect: Its tone is subdued and the set is fastidiously arranged. A shiny spittoon sits atop an elegant table encircled by three perfectly aligned wine classes. As the show's host, Gary sits smartly dressed in a black sweater with his hands folded on the table. He calmly introduces the show and begins discussing the virtues of wine in a soothing monotone.

If one compares episode #1 of *Wine Library TV* with episode #505, it would be difficult to discern that it was even the same show. The polished spittoon has been exchanged for one with a giant New York Jets decal, and toy action figures are randomly arranged on the table among a few bottles of wine. In the background is a New York Jets football jersey because Gary's dream is to one day own the National Football League's New York Jets. He talks incessantly about his love of the Jets with his wine-oriented viewing audience, which seems counterintuitive. Isn't professional football talk more appropriate for the canned beer crowd? And, yet, this counterculture approach to wine tasting is exactly what sets Vaynerchuk apart, and what his audience craves.

Rolled-up sleeves and a yellow sweatband on Gary's right arm have supplanted the more formal black sweater. In the background is a chalkboard with the hastily scrawled words, *"Who likes it?"* The broadcast opens with script dancing across the screen, Gary violently flicking a paper wad at the camera, and Gary shouting in a frenetic voice "Hello everybody and welcome to *Wine Library TV*, I am your host Gary

VAAAYY-NER-CHUK! Say it with me VAYNIACS, this is the 'Thunder Show,' aka the Internet's most passionate wine program!"

Gary concludes this opening with an emphatic fist pump. The bouquet of the episode's featured wine is described as being *akin to your girlfriend's hair after she returns from a weekend of cooking chocolate and marshmallow s'mores over an open campfire.*

Gary had found his sweet spot with the program's format and, as is often the case, it flowed naturally since it was Gary being Gary. If Gary had continued the stilted tonality of the first episode, he most likely would have never made it to episode #505, and he certainly wouldn't have sold $50 million dollars' worth of wine. By episode #505, Vaynerchuk had more than hit his stride; the audience wanted the real Gary, not a typical wine connoisseur. Vaynerchuk serves as a good example of being true not only to yourself, but also to your audience.

Gary didn't sell $50 million dollars' worth of wine because of heavy advertising spending or glitzy studio production. Gary's success resulted from his strong passion and his ability to connect with his audience. As a result of the success of *Wine Library TV*, Gary has gone on to write the best-selling books *Crush It* and *The Thank You Economy*.

DIGITAL DEEDS

Learn Shortcut Keys

Getting personal can take time, so it's important that we save time where we can digitally, affording us more time to be personal. Many programs and applications we use have shortcut keys. Learn the common shortcut keys today to save millions of minutes tomorrow.

For example, on Gmail if you desire to go to the next message turn on the shortcut key ability and simply hit "n" and it will take you to the next new message. If you are using an Apple MacBook Pro hitting F3 will open all the active windows in one place so you can easily toggle between programs. Or, if you are using Microsoft

Outlook, you can use the "ctrl" and "r" keys together to reply to a message, saving you the time of navigating via the mouse to click "reply." If you have a page open in Windows, you can press "ctrl" and "m" keys and it minimizes everything on the page (or the Windows logo button and "m").

Even if you learn just a few of these tricks, they will be major time savers over the long haul. Equally important, don't *use every tool* out there (e.g., Flickr, Yelp, Gmail, Yahoo, Twitter). Rather, use the tools with which you feel the most comfortable. This will help you know that specific tool better. Learning shortcut keys for three programs is much easier than learning them for 25 programs.

Steve Jobs: 9 Lessons in Leadership

The outpouring of sympathy and compassion that followed Steve Jobs's untimely passing was incredible to witness. Apple at the time had the largest market cap of any company and Jobs was at the top of this empire. When his death was announced, it was as if the whole world grieved for a close friend, even though he was a CEO most people had never met. Many, though, felt as if they knew him and understood his passion. Just like there will never be another Socrates, Wayne Gretzky, Winston Churchill, or Ghandi, there will never be another Steve Jobs. While we can never become Steve Jobs, we can all follow our hearts like he did.

We can also study what made Steve Jobs such a beloved leader and where these principles can be applied to help us in our leadership roles. You have already seen some of these habits mentioned and exuded by other leaders in this book and you will see others further developed in subsequent chapters. As you read the following nine lessons, remember that personal isn't about revealing that you have a tattoo on your left shoulder, it's about letting people know about the passions and principles in your life that you stand by. When they know this information about you, personal becomes powerful.

1. Simplify

Jobs demanded that the first iPod not have any buttons on it, including an on/off switch. This idea seemed implausible for the engineers working on the project, but Jobs wouldn't bend. The engineers were pushed to their limits and the famous scroll wheel resulted. Jobs indicates "that's been one of my mantras—focus and simplicity. Simple can be harder than complex: You have to work hard to get your thinking clean to make it simple. But it's worth it in the end because once you get there, you can move mountains."

2. The power of "NO"

Jobs is just as proud of the many products he killed over the years as the ones that were monumental successes. At one point he worked hard on a device similar to the Palm Pilot but appropriately killed it to focus on the cell phone market. What resulted was the iPod and iPhone.

3. Money is overvalued

Innovation has nothing to do with how many R&D dollars you have. When Apple came up with the Mac, IBM was spending at least 100 times more on R&D. It's not about money. It's about the people you have and how they're led. Jobs once said, "Being the richest man in the cemetery doesn't matter to me . . . Going to bed at night saying we've done something wonderful . . . that's what matters to me."[2]

4. It's not what you say, it's how you say it

Jobs's keynotes and product launches spellbound audiences. The missing "it" factor is palpable when he's not on stage. Not all products under Jobs were the most cutting edge on the market, but consumers perceived them to be. Part of this perception was Jobs's overzealous demand of secrecy around products. This secrecy helped feed consumers desires for the products once they were revealed. That is the critical point— perception becomes reality. Part of Jobs's success was based on the notion that "Your customers dream of a happier and better life. Don't move products. Instead, enrich lives."

5. Recognize good ideas

Jobs and Apple did not create the computer mouse, podcasting, or the touch screen, but they recognized their value and integrated these innovations into their products.

6. Shun the majority

Jobs's actions epitomized the mantra of *if the majority was always right then we'd all be rich*. Like Henry Ford before him, who indicated, "If I asked the public what they wanted they would say a faster horse," Jobs typically eschewed focus groups and gave the public what he thought they needed. This worked the majority of the time, but when it didn't work it was a chance for him to fail forward into the next project, taking the lessons he learned with him. As Jobs concedes, "Here's to the crazy one, the misfits, the rebels, the troublemakers, the round pegs in the square holes . . . because the ones who are crazy enough to think that they can change the world, are the ones who do."

7. Eat your own lunch

There is a saying in Silicon Valley that you need to "eat your own lunch before someone else does". Jobs had the fortitude to "eat his own lunch" with the introduction of the iPhone, knowing full well it would and did cannibalize the sales of the flagship iPod. Letting go of the familiar and embracing the unknown is a real test of digital leadership.

8. Strive for perfection

The night before the opening of the first Apple store, Jobs didn't like the aesthetics of the floor tiles so he had them all ripped up and replaced. Right before the iPod launch, Jobs had all the headphone jacks replaced so they were more "clicky."

9. Small teams

Jobs didn't want his iPhone team to be muddled with preconceived notions around the cell phone market and had the team placed in a separate building. While this rightfully rubbed some employees the wrong way, the results are irrefutable. The original Macintosh team had 100 members.

Whenever it reached 101 members they would have to reshuffle and remove someone from the team. Jobs's belief was that he could only remember 100 names.[3]

Edison Follows His Light

Another more distant example of following your passion and being open with your personality can be found in Thomas Edison. He famously said, "My mother was the making of me. She understood me; she let me follow my bent. She was so true, so sure of me; and I felt I had something to live for, someone I must not disappoint."[4]

Edison was credited with inventing the incandescent light bulb. In truth, he was responsible for perfecting it. On October 18, 1931, Edison passed away. The press waited outside his home for a signal and his wife, instead of turning off a light, turned one on. Now that is the type of legacy we should all strive to achieve. If we follow our passions and convey these passions to the world then we will all have such a legacy when the time comes.

> "I never worked a day in my life. It was all fun."
> —THOMAS EDISON

Trust Is a Must

When you exhibit your personality and openness with others, they are bound to trust in you more, both as an individual or a company. Better yet, make sure to be trustworthy. Reveal your secrets and mistakes before someone else does. Take this metaphoric weight off your shoulders. If you don't own up to mistakes, two things can happen:

1. Stress will result in your effort to hide them
2. They will eventually be revealed under circumstances beyond your control

It's a lose-lose situation. The truth will indeed set you free. At the end of the long-running Broadway show *Avenue Q*, the protagonist discovers happiness in life isn't about money or having sex with beautiful people. Rather, one feels best by making other people happy. How does a Broadway show comprised of Muppets relate to modern leadership? The answer is that digital transparency requires us to be happy with our own lives to effectively lead others. Otherwise, our body language on YouTube, voice inflections on podcasts, or the tone of our tweets will undermine our effectiveness as leaders.

Where Do You Excel?

In their book *Marketing Lessons from the Grateful Dead*, Brian Halligan and David Meerman Scott recommend that executives determine what their company can do three times (3x) better than their competition, and what they do three times (3x) worse. If this cannot be determined, the company's capabilities are not different enough. The same approach is applicable to individuals as you become a leader in the digital world and define your life stamp.

> "I am just a common man who is true to his beliefs."
> —JOHN WOODEN

A way to determine your area of personal strength is to assume that you had to appear on the quiz show *Jeopardy*. While on *Jeopardy* you would be allowed to select from any subject category in the world. Which category would you choose? Indian Ocean SCUBA? Antebellum Architecture? PHP Computer Programming? Nigerian Music? Your category selection would be determined by what you believe you are the best in and, most likely, what you find personally interesting or gratifying. Similarly, if you had to write a five-page essay in an hour without references or resources, what topic would you choose? Again, your choice reveals your key competency and interests.

Record everything you do for a day or two: Type your actions into the memo section of your smartphone or tablet, use speech recognition or audio record, or simply write it down on an index card you carry in your pocket. Next, review what you recorded. How frequently are you doing the things you love? Are there things you don't enjoy doing that can easily be eliminated? If so, eliminate them.

Now, write down what you can do 3x better than most other people. Place this alongside your favorite daily activity. If these two things are the same, count yourself lucky. However, if you are not currently 3x better than others at what you love to do, can you become 3x better? Don't be discouraged—Bill Walton, Barbara Walters, and Lou Holtz didn't become successful broadcasters overnight. All three have significant speech impediments or lisps that could have easily deterred them from this vocation. Instead, understanding that passion is the panacea for most roadblocks, they overcame the obstacles in their path and have enjoyed long and successful careers as broadcasters.

> "If you talk to a man in a language he understands, that goes to his head. If you talk to him in his language, that goes to his heart."
>
> **—NELSON MANDELA**

Is It Business or Personal?

The question of is something "business or personal" is outdated as the two are becoming one and the same. Recently a president of a company asked me if it would be a good idea for their sales team to have a link to the sales person's personal Facebook profile on their business cards. I asked him where he came up with the idea, and he responded that several of the people on his sales team had requested it. I guessed the reason they had done so was most likely because they thought it would help them increase sales. He agreed. To me it made logical sense, since personal is powerful.

We don't buy from logos, we buy from human beings because we trust or like them. A great way to increase trust is for that person to know more about you. I told the president that he should have some digital training for the sales team for some of the pitfalls and then go ahead and print the Facebook profile links on their business cards.

LIFE STAMPS

Stephen Hawking

Stephen William Hawking was born on January 8, 1942 (300 years after the death of Galileo) in Oxford, England.

He was educated as a theoretical physicist and cosmologist. His scientific books and public appearances have made him a worldwide academic celebrity. He is an honorary fellow of England's Royal Society of the Arts. In 2009, he received the Presidential Medal of Freedom, the highest civilian award bestowed by the United States government. Professor Hawking has 12 honorary degrees.

Hawking achieved all of this while suffering from a motor neuron disease that is related to amyotrophic lateral sclerosis (Lou Gehrig's Disease). The diagnosis came when Hawking was 21. At the time, doctors projected that he would only live three more years. Hawking gradually lost the use of his arms, legs, and voice, and today he is almost completely paralyzed. A wheelchair-mounted portable computer with special software and a synthesized voice box enables his genius to be communicated:

> I try to lead as normal a life as possible, and not think about my condition, or regret the things it prevents me from doing, which are not that many . . .although there was a cloud hanging over my future (with the disease), I found, to my surprise, that I was enjoying life in the present more than before. I began to make progress with my research, and I got engaged to a girl called Jane Wilde . . . It gave me something to live for. I have had motor neurone disease for practically all my adult life. Yet it has not prevented me from having a very attractive family, and being successful in my work . . . I have been lucky, that my condition has progressed more slowly than is often the case. But it shows that one need not lose hope.[5]

Stephen Hawking has three children and three grandchildren.

DIGITAL DEEDS

Videos Replace Manuals

Don't like to read instruction manuals? Then go on YouTube and watch video demonstrations explaining everything from how to activate the auto flash on your camera to building IKEA furniture. Unlike the manuals, these videos explain the most important things quickly and come across as more personal. The video assistance is particularly helpful for visual learners. This is more productive and enjoyable than leafing through an outdated 50-page manual in three foreign languages that's difficult to comprehend.

Building for Others

When you are true to your passion, it's much easier to overcome obstacles. A good example of this ability is seen in Mardy McGarry of Port Washington, Wisconsin. A special education teacher for 52 years, her heart always went out to her students with disabilities when sand, ladders, or other obstacles stopped their wheelchairs short on the playground. Her vision was to build a playground that allowed children with disabilities to play alongside other children.

The city donated the land for the project. An estimated $450,000 needed to be raised for materials. Families bought pickets for the fence at $30 apiece, bricks for the walkway went for $50 to $750 apiece, one woman even donated $25,000, and her company matched it. A few walkathons and silent auctions later McGarry had reached the goal of $450,000. Then she received the heartbreaking news that it would cost an additional $900,000 for the actual construction of the park.

Instead of being deterred, McGarry was able to rally the small town. Two women heard about the effort on the radio and took the day off to help. Kids sanded surfaces and stacked wood. A couple in their 80s helped organize the tools. Volunteers separated the work into groups according to experience and ability. Local restaurants and churches donated meals for the workers. Over 2,800 people volunteered, roughly a third of the town. "The site looked like an anthill. So many people can take ownership of this playground," said McGarry.

Because of Mardy McGarry's passion and vision, on a bluff overlooking Lake Michigan, there is a playground where children of all abilities play side-by-side. Possibility Playground is one of the most popular destinations in Ozaukee County. When you have a passion and a purpose, and are able to personally convey this externally to others, the possibilities are limitless.[6]

Money, Happiness, and Passion

Two studies published in the *Proceedings of the National Academy of Sciences* focused on self-satisfaction and overall happiness. The studies, which were both based on Gallup polls (2008 & 2009), found that an individual's sense of overall well-being didn't improve based on an increase in salary after a threshold of $75,000. Therefore, if you are fortunate to be in the position of earning more than $75,000 annually; statistics indicate your happiness will not increase by making more money. Hence, your efforts may be best focused elsewhere.

> "Only you can control your future."
> —DR. SEUSS

If you are making less than $75,000 annually, the study did show a correlation between increased salary and overall happiness. To that end, I would *still* suggest putting your passion ahead of the money, because, ironically, following your passion might well be your best way to earn above $75,000.[7]

Tim Ferris accurately assesses that "much is predicated on the assumption that you dislike what you are doing during the most physically capable years of your life. This is a nonstarter—nothing can justify that sacrifice." In short, most of us look forward to retirement, where Ferris acutely argues against waiting until we are old and physically incapable of doing certain things to "start living."[8] Live for today, not tomorrow. Retirement may never come and if we are doing what we love and following our passion, then we will never want to retire. Remember, your personal passions are powerful and will help you achieve a fulfilling life as a leader.

SECTION TWO: TRUE

Key Points

- ▶ Know who you want to become; everything else is secondary
- ▶ If you don't know what you are passionate about, start taking five minutes per day to journal something positive that happened to you that day, and detail why it made you happy. Feel free to share these positive thoughts digitally—the world needs your positive influence. By daily chronicling what makes you happy, your true passion will reveal itself.
- ▶ Success is a choice, but it usually doesn't happen overnight
- ▶ Take your daily action card and, beneath your two action items for the day, write down two things for which you are grateful
- ▶ Being well-rounded is an outdated ideal and can be an anchor; focus on what you can do 3x better than others
- ▶ In a globally connected world it's critical to know your audience
- ▶ Healthy attitudes = healthy bodies
- ▶ Letting others know your passions and personal side is powerful
- ▶ Research shows additional income above $75,000 per year will not increase happiness
- ▶ Sometimes in life the quickest path to failure is early and easy success
- ▶ If we love what we do we may never want to retire

ACT

1. Be decisive

2. Increase your rate of failure: fail forward, fail fast, fail better

3. Leverage inertia: people in motion tend to stay in motion

SIMPLE: success is the result of simplification & focus

TRUE: be true to your passion

ACT: nothing happens without action—take the first step

MAP: goals and visions are needed to get where you want to be

PEOPLE: success doesn't happen alone

CHAPTER NINE

Be Decisive

"An ounce of action is worth a ton of theory."
—RALPH WALDO EMERSON

Most of us understand that the world is moving at an ever increasing pace. Yet, many of us become overwhelmed by this pace and, as a result, are neither able to lead the life we want nor accomplish what we'd like in our limited time on earth. The basic concept that causes much of our unhappiness is indecision. *Being indecisive in a digitally paced world is akin to trying to win the gold medal in the 100 meters with an elephant strapped to your back.* Much of our indecision is caused by our fear of failure. The good news is our fears and indecisiveness are predominately self-made. Hence, we can self-correct these issues and be on our way to a happier, more fulfilled life. Once we accomplish this goal, then we can lead others both digitally and offline to do the same. The focus of this chapter is for us to better understand indecision and how to eradicate it.

The Cost of Being Indecisive

In a five-year study, researcher Piers Steel found that 95 percent of people procrastinate. "People who procrastinate tend to be less healthy, wealthy and happy than those that take action. This bad habit also affects friends, family, and coworkers," reports Steel. Americans that delay their tax filings cost themselves a cumulative $400 million dollars per year due to mistakes caused by being in a hurry. Being digitally ensconced makes putting things off even easier. "Having the Internet for a procrastinator is like trying to diet with a floating spoon of ice cream following you around," said Steel.[1]

Make a decision now—if it's wrong you can easily correct it later. We saw this possibility in the example of Gary Vaynerchuk and his success with *Wine Library TV*. He "failed forward" so that by episode #505 of the show he was well on his way to success. He certainly didn't sit in his parents' liquor store dreaming about the perfect *Wine Library TV* episode. Instead, he started the journey and began working toward perfection. As a result of failing forward his sales grew from $4 million to $50 million. Making decisions because you don't fear failure, in fact most times you learn from it, is what all digital leaders grasp.

Minor Decisions: The Shapes Experiment

A study in 2008 by *New York Times* columnist John Tierney and Dr. Dan Ariely, a cognitive psychologist and professor of behavioral economics at MIT, examined the issue of humans' flawed way of spending too much time on minor decisions. The Shapes Experiment was a game in which readers had to choose between two different shape selections (i.e., which shape is bigger or smaller). Players were rewarded for correct guesses. The game was played by thousands of participants. Sometimes players had to choose between two shapes similar in size—a difference in area of less than 2 percent. Other times they had to choose between shapes that differed in area by 25 percent. The game was timed, hence it behooved a player to complete as many trials as possible.

Yet, participants agonized over decisions that didn't make much difference—affecting their score in a negative way since they didn't get to as many trials. They spent 64 percent of their time deciding between similar shapes, and only 36 percent of their time choosing between dissimilar shapes, Dr. Ariely reports. Ariely went on to explain that most players could have garnered more points if they took into account the opportunity cost of time. In other words, people should have quickly submitted a response on the trials similar in size, increasing the amount of trials where the size difference was more obvious and helping to increase their scores.

Tierney pointed out that if a participant was going to devote time to making a choice, it was better to do so when there was a bigger payoff—when the shapes were dissimilar in size. However, most did the reverse: 94 percent spent more time on similar choices than on dissimilar choices even though it was likely they still might get it wrong.

Dr. Ariely indicated this lesson was a good one to learn for decision makers in the real world. In real life people are even more prone to wasting time on trivial decisions because the options and consequences aren't nearly as clear-cut as in this particular game. Dr. Ariely, in his book *Predictably Irrational*, cites a real-world example of this phenomenon:

> One of my friends spent three months selecting a digital camera from two nearly identical models. When he finally made his selection, I asked him how many photo opportunities had he missed, how much of his valuable time he had spent making the selection, and how much he would have paid to have digital pictures of his family and friends documenting the last three months. More than the price of the camera, he said. Has something like this ever happened to you? What my friend failed to do when focusing on the similarities and minor differences between two things was to take into account the consequences of not deciding.

Participants of the MIT Shapes Experiment were able to improve their scores when they were given feedback showing the costs associated with pondering over trivial decisions. Unfortunately in life we often don't have the luxury of experts pointing out how to improve our use of time via decision-making.[2]

The GMAT

The Shapes Experiment reminds me of an episode in my life. In preparation for taking the GMAT test, an exam necessary for application to top MBA programs, I took a Kaplan review course. The first day of class every student took a "mock" GMAT test. A majority of the students, including me, didn't finish the test in the allotted amount of time. It turns out this was a big "no-no."

At the time, the test scoring for the GMAT was based on how many right answers you were able to achieve; you weren't penalized for incorrect ones. The Kaplan instructors stressed the importance of answering *every* question and not allowing oneself to get stuck on any one specific question. They stressed "marking" any questions you were unsure of and if you had time after you completed the test then you could return and review them. This advice dramatically improved most of our scores on the real test. How many of us are lucky enough to learn this skill in our day-to-day lives?

> *"Things do not happen they are made to happen."*
> —JOHN F. KENNEDY

Although, an old adage, "he who hesitates is lost," is probably even more applicable in today's world. Consider a digital leader like Richard Branson, who, when a new tool like Twitter comes out, doesn't become paralyzed by all the bad things that could happen if he opens an account. Instead he makes the decision to dive right in and start tweeting great items like *From Great White Sharks to @virgingalactic Spaceport opening. More on that Monday, have a great weekend* and, eventually amassing over 1.4 million followers. You can't become a leader if you are indecisive. Your followers are looking for inspiration and direction and don't want to get lost—that's why they are following you in the first place. Make a decision: most are trivial and the cost of indecision is often far greater than making the wrong choice.

DIGITAL DEEDS

Activity Toolbox

Below are a few suggestions from various sources on getting things done.

> ▶ Ryan Wagoner of Lifehacker.com suggests setting a timer for 25 minutes and getting started on a new task or one you may

have been putting off. He indicates that you can do almost anything for 25 minutes. Others suggest even smaller intervals of 10 or 5 minutes. With ever newer technologies, it's amazing what you can accomplish in such a short time, but you need to get started.

▶ Timothy Pychyl, Ph.D., a psychologist at Carleton University in Ottawa, Canada, suggests breaking the task down into smaller, more manageable pieces. For example, instead of writing "buy a new car," start with "research cars online for 25 minutes." Or instead of "complete taxes" jot down "buy online TurboTax software." Pychyl also suggests not letting "planning substitute for real action." Make sure you are taking concrete steps, even if they are small ones, to your goals. Conquer mountains one pebble at a time.

▶ There are free online time management tools that alert you to get back on task if you start randomly surfing the Web.

▶ Sites like stickK.com are great because they make your goals public and you can even optionally set what you are willing to pay (usually a charitable donation) if you don't achieve them in the time frame set. You can even select referees and virtual cheerleaders. The inherent pressure enables people to achieve all sorts of goals.

▶ Some people find it helpful to post an unflattering picture of themselves on their Twitter, Facebook, or LinkedIn profiles and don't allow themselves to remove the picture until they have reached their goal.

▶ Select a friend and have him periodically text you or post on your Facebook wall asking if you have completed a planned task you have told him about (e.g., mailing your Christmas Cards). The more public you can make it the better.[3]

State Your Opinion: The Abilene Paradox

The Abilene Paradox and other Meditations on Management was written by management expert Jerry B. Harvey.[4] The well-known "Abilene Paradox" fable is taught in graduate classes around the world. Harvey's anecdotal story was even made into a film.

The basic plot and lesson of the story are as follows:

On a hot afternoon in Coleman, Texas, a man, his wife, and his wife's parents are comfortably playing dominoes on the front porch. The man's father-in-law suggests that they all take a trip to Abilene that evening for dinner. The wife says, "Sounds like a great idea." The man, despite having doubts about the 53 mile drive north in the brutal Texas heat, thinks his preference must be out-of-step with the group, but instead of raising any concern, he says, "Sounds good to me. I just hope your mother wants to go." The mother-in-law responds, "Of course I want to go. I haven't been to Abilene in a long time."

The drive from Coleman to Abilene is hot, dusty, and long. When they get into town, the family picks out a restaurant and sits down to enjoy their meal. The food, however, is as bad as the drive. After they finish eating, they get right back in their car and head home, arriving in Coleman four hours from when they had initially left, but now exhausted and unsatisfied.

The mother-in-law dishonestly says, "It was a great trip, wasn't it?" even though she would rather have stayed home but went along since the other three seemed so enthusiastic. The man says, "I was delighted playing dominoes on the porch and would have been happy to continue doing so. I only went along to satisfy the rest of you." The wife says, "I just went along to keep you happy. I would have had to be crazy to want to go out in the heat like that." The father-in-law then says that he only suggested going to Abilene because he thought the others might be bored.

The group sits back, perplexed that they collectively decided to take a trip which none of them wanted to actually go on. They each would have preferred to sit comfortably and happily enjoy the afternoon as they were, but none of them admitted it.

There are many interpretations of Harvey's anecdote, but the key takeaway for the purposes of this book is that you must make a decision and speak your mind, which isn't always easy to do. Consider the mother-in-law's position in the story above: she is the last in the decision tree. How many of us act as she did? It's polite to be agreeable and go along with the crowd. Think about the many times you may have said to yourself, "Well, I don't want to rock the boat or rain on everyone's parade," or "Everyone will think I'm a cantankerous jerk if I state what I really feel."

Keep in mind the parable is set in a simpler time. With more options today, it's even more imperative to state your opinion directly and honestly. Look at the multitude of potential decisions at our disposal in this day and age. A modern day Abilene Paradox might involve a multimedia lounge that opens out onto a covered porch. We probably wouldn't be playing dominoes. Instead of considering whether to stay at home or drive 53 miles away, the question might be should we drive to a restaurant nearby, head out of town, or simply order food in from Domino's? Should we watch the game broadcast live or watch the game we have digitally recorded on 3-D high definition, or should we play a virtual social video game with each other, video chat with those not able to be there? The possibilities are endless. One trick to stating your opinion easier is learning how to do so without coming off as a malcontent.

If the mother-in-law had to relive the situation, she would be better off stating: "The most important thing to me is that we are together, that is what makes me happy. I'm perfectly happy staying here. I believe that the drive to Abilene will be long and hot and that we're better off given the climate staying here. However, if I'm the only one that shares this opinion then I'm happy to go with everyone."

Notice she didn't say, "That's a dumb idea" or "I don't agree with you." She merely stated her opinion and did a good job of bracketing it by stating what is most important to her ("being together") while at the same time making others around her feel good ("being with you *makes me happy*"). This is her taking an active leadership role.

Next time you lead a meeting, it's imperative that you foster a level of openness so people are willing to state their true opinion. Alan Mulally, the CEO of Ford Motor, tells a great story that relates directly to this idea. For an update meeting with his top executives he wants to keep items easy to identify. All executives report on initiatives as either green (everything is fine and on time), yellow (things looks OK for now but need to keep in eye on it), and red (trouble spots or items may be getting behind schedule). For the first few meetings everyone came in and it was all green. Mulally was a bit befuddled by this, as one of the main reasons he was brought in as CEO was because Ford was struggling dramatically and needed to be turned around.

Then one meeting, someone with apprehension presented a few items in red. What did Mulally do? He started clapping. The next meeting, almost everything from every executive was in red. Mulally indicated from there they were able to really make progress as the employees felt comfortable stating not only what was going on (even if it was bad), but how they truly felt they could fix certain problems. Mulally as a leader fostered this openness which then allowed for more rapid decisions on how to fix the trouble spots.

You never hear someone say, "I really respect that guy, he agrees with everything I say and I therefore never know where I truly stand with him. What a great YES man." But you do often hear, "I *don't* always like what she has to say, but I *respect* her, because she always speaks her mind."

Make it a habit to make decisions and speak your mind. If you do this then it will be the exception, rather than the rule, that you end up somewhere you don't want to be.

My Personal Decision and Indecision

I'm reminded of an instance in my own career while I was the Head of Marketing at Travelzoo. As the Internet travel industry exploded, we were faced with a difficult decision. Our core product was our weekly Top 20 List. This was, and still continues to be, a list of the week's 20 best travel deals. If we wanted to continue to grow as a company we considered if we should change into more of an Expedia, Orbitz, or Hotwire type of model that actually took the bookings on site.

This idea had potential for much more revenue and gave us greater control than relying on travel companies and online travel agents having enough great deals and the willingness to pay Travelzoo to include these deals in the Top 20 List. Spearheaded by founder and CEO Ralph Bartel, the decision was made to continue our current core business model. No radical changes would be made, but we would expand into various foreign markets (Europe, Asia, and others) with this model. Since that time, Travelzoo has increased its subscribers from 8 million to 22 million and counting. It's not that the decision was right or not (it was), it was that a decision was made. Knowing this decision enabled the employees to better focus on the mission.

> "It's better to be boldly decisive and risk being wrong than to agonize at length and be right too late."
>
> —MARILYN MOATS KENNEDY

By making this tough decision, Ralph Bartel was being a digital leader. If he had made the final decision to replicate more of the Orbitz business model and later discovered that perhaps that wasn't a good idea, he would be a few months or years ahead to admit failure and change direction. The key to being a digital leader is making the decision.

As the CEO of Deckers Outdoor Corporation, Angel Martinez also needed to make a difficult decision. One of the company's brands, UGG Australia, was well positioned and dominated the female footwear category. Martinez saw an opportunity in the men's footwear market for the brand. However, it would be a difficult transition and it could potential hurt the UGG position in the female market. Instead of being cautious or indecisive, Martinez and his marketing team launched an aggressive campaign with Tom Brady. It was risky, but the risk paid off as the Deckers stock rose from $56.75 to $118.53 in 2011, the year the campaign launched.

For our digitally paced lives being decisive will help us all become leaders. Our time on this planet is much too short to not be decisive in what we want and what stamp we want to leave behind.

CHAPTER TEN

Fail Forward, Fail Fast, Fail Better

"I failed my way to success."
—THOMAS EDISON

Often the biggest misstep we can make in life is to simply stand still in hopes of avoiding failure. The cost of inaction, however, is often greater than the actual failure we fear. Postponing tasks or items can cause emotional, financial, and physical strain. If you wake up each morning expecting not to face challenges throughout your day, you are setting yourself up for disappointment. You must assume challenges are coming and, instead of avoiding them, welcome and embrace them. Life would be boring without the difficulties we face on a day-to-day basis, and, in the long run, these consistent challenges will make us stronger, smarter, and better leaders.

Challenges are simply a chance for us to improve and bring out our best and should be viewed as such. If we were studying for a spelling bee we wouldn't review easy words. We'd test ourselves with more difficult spellings. We need to take this approach in our day-to-day lives and be invigorated by modern challenges.

Too often we don't learn from our experiences and either quit from frustration or don't fail forward, neglecting to apply potential new knowledge to future initiatives. We must,

145

however, fail fast, fail forward, and fail better. We need to learn from our failures and keep heading in the right direction to succeed in this digital world.

Facing Challenges in the Digital Revolution

We need to break items into smaller chunks so that if we fail it doesn't take as much time or money and isn't a big deal (fail fast). This approach allows for more experimentation, which is crucial in our digitally paced environment. Founder and CEO Jeff Bezos helped build Amazon into the global empire it is today by applying this concept.

Bezos wanted to change the book-selling world, so he solicited many experts in the publishing industry prior to, and during, the launch of Amazon. He readily admits that Amazon sometimes made mistakes by turning down good advice. But he also indicates that some of these mistakes—like starting off with a massive inventory of books, rather than focusing on the best sellers—hurt in the short term, but turned out in the long term to be incredible powerful "mistakes." Bezos said, "Every well-intentioned, high-judgment person we asked told us not to do it. We got some good advice, we ignored it, and it was a mistake. But that mistake turned out to be one of the best things that happened to the company."[1]

Bezos indicates that, "We are willing to go down a bunch of dark passageways, and occasionally we find something that really works."[2] He even took breaking items into smaller tasks beyond product experimentation and into meetings. He also famously instituted the two pizza rule for meetings (meaning that a meeting should never have more people in it that could be comfortable fed by two pizzas).

There was concern when Amazon was about to launch a feature enabling customers to sort user ratings by the most helpful positive and most helpful negative ratings. The concern was that the most helpful negative ratings might drastically curtail sales across all of Amazon. However, since Amazon over time had perfected taking chances and testing in smaller chunks, it was comfortable rolling this out to a portion of its audience. The feature was so popular that it is now available to everyone and some estimates have it helping increase Amazon's annual revenue by $2.7 billion dollars.[3]

Active Digital Communication

The digital revolution has increased the pace of life's changes and challenges. On a micro scale, just think about how many digital messages you receive and have to respond to daily. How many of us dread seeing we have voicemail or 100 emails in our inbox? I used

> *"Life is either a daring adventure, or nothing."*
> —HELEN KELLER

to be in this camp, until I decided to change my attitude and train myself to take a different vantage point.

First, the fact that someone respects us enough to want our input or opinion is always important to keep in mind. We should be happy that we are worthwhile enough for someone to take the time to reach out to us. Start thinking less about what you can take from this world and more about what you can give back. Look at responding to these digital communications, be they texts, blogs, emails, or any other kind, as an opportunity to give back. We may not have all the answers or be able to give back to everyone, nor should we, but we can definitely help some people.

Active Non-Digital Communication

Of course, non-digital communication is still imperative to your success as a leader in this new world. The same type of traits and values should be applied to both, and with the ever decreasing barriers between your "online" and "offline" life, digital and non-digital communication have become much more similar. Face-to-face interaction, however, is still necessary.

When I give keynote speeches I'm always disappointed when I'm instructed not to take Questions and Answers (Q & A) from the audience. Why do I love Q & A so much? Aside from being able to interact with others, it challenges me.

There may be a question I never thought of or a question I don't know the answer to—yet someone in the audience has the answer. Such challenging questions serve to advance my knowledge and that of others in the crowd.

Wasted Energy

The task we dread performing is the one we typically should tackle first as it is often the most important. Additionally, having something hanging over our head is wasted energy. Think about college. When you had a big paper due on Monday and you completed the paper a few days in advance, how much more enjoyable were the football games and parties or hanging out with friends that weekend?

Professor Randy Pausch (author of *The Last Lecture*) shared similar advice with the students at the University of Virginia months before he passed away from pancreatic cancer: "Do the ugliest thing first. There is an old saying: if you have to eat a frog don't spend a lot of time looking at it. If you have to eat three frogs, don't start with the small one."

Life is so much more enjoyable not having a dark cloud looming in the distance—slay the dragon today, not tomorrow.

Failing Fast, Forward, and Better

Some of Thomas Edison's teacher's implied he was "too stupid to learn anything." Edison was also fired from his first two jobs. He put forth over 1,000 attempts at inventing the light bulb before getting it right. Instead of viewing this as 1,000 failures, however, Edison viewed it as failing forward. He quipped, "I didn't fail 1,000 times. The light bulb is an invention with 1,000 steps." The creation of the light bulb epitomizes the concept of failing better. What does failing fast, failing forward, and failing better look like?

- ► Fail Fast: break items into small chunks which allows for more experimentation, leading to more chances for success
- ► Fail Forward: learn from what didn't work, but continue toward what will work

▶ Fail Better: the best way to increase our amount of learning is to increase our amount of failure

Let's take the simple example of flying a kite to illustrate these types of failure.

Jane

A mom gives her daughter Jane a kite and tells her to literally "go fly a kite."

Day One (rainy & windy): Jane looks out the window and decides she will wait for another day.

Day Two (rainy): Jane looks out the window and decides she will wait for another day.

Day Three (sunny): Jane heads outside, places the kite on the ground, and nothing happens for five minutes so she returns inside.

Day Four (cold & windy): Jane heads outside, places the kite on the ground, and the kite gets blown around a little. She decides to pick it up and toss it into the air. The kite blows around for a few seconds before crashing to the ground. At this point Jane's little fingers are cold, so she goes inside.

> "Going through life with caution is like driving with the breaks on."
> —@EQUALMAN

Day Five (cloudy & windy): Jane heads outside, places the kite on the ground, and the kite gets blown around a little. She decides to pick it up and toss it into the air again and the kite floats softly back to the ground. She does this a few more times before becoming frustrated and going in to tell her mom that the kite simply will not fly and she's tried everything.

Hope

Another mom gives her daughter Hope a kite and tells her to literally "go fly a kite." She also tells her to try every day and to keep a log of her daily progress.

Day One (rainy & windy): Hope takes the kite outside and notes: *Not able to fly, but notice when the wind blows the kite lifts* *off the ground a little. Once the kite was really wet it no longer lifted at all even with the wind blowing.*

Day Two (rainy): Hope takes the kite outside and notes: *Not able to fly. Unlike Day One, the kite doesn't move at all today. Wind must be important. If the kite didn't fly when the kite became wet and heavy on day one, perhaps the wind lifts from underneath the kite.*

Day Three (sunny): Hope takes the kite outside and notes: *With the kite laying on the ground nothing happened. When I picked it up still nothing happened. Wind is definitely very important. Sun may not be so important.*

Day Four (cold & windy): Hope heads outside and places the kite on the ground and the kite gets blown around a little. She decides to pick it up and toss it into the air since she thinks the wind comes from underneath. The kite blows around much better than on the ground before crashing back down. At this point Hope's little fingers are cold so she heads inside and notes: *Definitely need space from underneath the kite to allow wind to help. Need to gradually let out string as it hurts my fingers once the wind catches. Notice kite goes up higher when facing the wind than with the wind.*

Day Five (cloudy & windy): Hope heads outside and reviews her notes:

1. Need wind
2. Avoid rain
3. Give space underneath kite for wind
4. Gradually let out string
5. Going against wind better than with

Hope faces the wind, lifts up the kite, and the wind starts to take it. In her excitement and to let out more string she starts to run. The kite is magically in the air and flying!

Applying the Analogy

This kite-flying analogy is a simple one that works great for parenting and trains your kids early how to fail fast, fail, forward, fail better. However take the above words and do the following:

Replace *daughter* with *employee*
Replace *mother* with *boss*
Replace *fly a kite* with *launch this initiative*

Surprised? You shouldn't be: this is how simple failing forward, failing fast, and failing better is. Yet so many of us don't practice this on a daily basis, so our proverbial kites never fly as high as they can. Either we only do as specifically instructed or we give up on something too easily saying it can't be done. Any head of a non-profit, CEO, or high school will tell you that there are hundreds of smart people willing and able to give great reasons and explanations on why something will not work. However, there are many less people ready and able to lead. People that aren't afraid to go against conventional wisdom are willing to admit when their idea was the wrong, but they are also willing to stick to a task, trying it from several angles, and staying with it until they get it right. *One way to soar high in life is to run against the wind.*

Magic Johnson Fails Forward in His Business Career

In 1990 near the peak of his professional playing career, Magic came up with the concept of *Magic 32*, a retail outlet that would sell sporting goods nationwide. Magic went to a few retail conventions to select products and negotiate price for his store. "I didn't ask a single customer what they'd be interested in," Johnson says. "I went there looking for products I'd be interested in buying. I had to learn that I was not my customer. Actually, I was taught that lesson by what happened after we opened."

One of the items carried were $1,500 leather jackets. The jackets never sold. Unfortunately that wasn't the only thing that didn't sell—the original store closed after only a year. "I'm sure I've made bigger business mistakes, but I can't think of one," said Magic.[4]

As the *Minnesota Spokesman Recorder* points out, early success wasn't easy for Johnson. While his fame opened doors he admits, "I'd go before the board asking for $150 million, and the board would say, 'Magic, you play that basketball game great. I want to take a picture with you, and my son wants an autograph. But we got to turn you down.'"

"I dealt with that for three years," said Johnson. Another investor asked: "If your business strategy and business plan is so sound, and you want to invest in urban America, why hasn't somebody else come here and asked us for money?'" Johnson admits, "I didn't know what to say to them."

To help sell an original deal to Starbucks's owner Howard Shultz. Johnson took him to a tough section of South Central Los Angeles to watch a movie. "I had about 500 Black women [in attendance]," recalled Johnson. "I tried to warn him that we [blacks] go to the movies a little differently than [whites]. The women all thought they knew Whitney Houston personally: *'Dump him . . . Why are you still with him, Whitney?'* they were shouting at the screen.

> "It's fine to celebrate success but it is more important to heed the lessons of failure."
> —BILL GATES

"Howard says to me, 'I've never had a movie-going experience quite like this,'" Johnson continued, "he came out and gave me the deal." Johnson was warned that Starbucks stores wouldn't work in the black community. "Yes, we [inner city residents] will pay $3 for a cup of coffee—we just don't eat scones," Johnson said amidst laughter. "We don't know what scones are in my community. You take those scones out and [put in] sweet potato pie, pound cake, and sock-it-to-me cake—things that resonate with my customer base. When I did that, my customer base grew." [5]

Magic was fortunate to learn from this initial failure and overcome the naysayers—using the lesson to his advantage to amass hundreds of millions in other business ventures—a great example of failing forward.

Innovators Embrace Failure

Google is famous for allowing its employees to devote 20 percent of their time at work to their own innovation projects. Employees can take time to think about new initiatives that will help the company stay ahead of competition and, just as importantly, they are given the freedom to fail. As a business leader, providing your employees with an opportunity to confront failure will lead to a company embracing innovation.

Mark Zuckerberg, the founder of Facebook has this to say about innovation:

> A lot of people think innovation is having a great idea. But a lot of it is just moving quickly and trying a lot of things. At Facebook we built our whole company and culture around this. We have traditions called 'hackathons' which are events where all of our engineers stay up all night and build new things, whatever they want, not what they are currently working on, but rather trying things out and innovating.[6]

"If you are going through hell, keep going."
—WINSTON CHURCHILL

This quote from Zuckerberg is important in that we never want to put ourselves or others in a predefined box. We need to allow people to play in a sandbox that may not even seem tangential to an important current task that needs completion. If we do this, however, it may result in an unforeseen product (3M Post-It notes came out of a failed product initiative) or the break will help the creative thought process when workers are back on their normal daily projects. If you assign everyone, or even yourself, to one long, major initiative, you put all of your eggs into a very inflexible basket. Always attempt to break tasks into smaller ones.

Vivian Schiller, the CEO of NPR, has similar thoughts on simply going for it:

> We make sure everybody in the entire organization throughout the world understands everything that's going on. What's going on in the digital space, the radio space, what our audience likes, what looks good, what's the user experience. Then we let them experiment like crazy, we're big into test and learn, it's okay to fail, just keep trying stuff. As long as it's true to our core values, as long as it's quality journalism, as long as it's about good user experience, just go for it.[7]

Michael Bloomberg, three-term mayor of New York and one of the richest people in the world, believes:

> The public insists, and arguably has the right to insist, to know where its money is going. [They] have very high expectations and results [from the government]. That is not the way innovation works. Innovation—is you don't know what you're going to build, what it's going to be called, how much it's going to cost. You cannot use public monies unless you can answer virtually every one of those questions, which is why government tends not to innovate. The public wants that accountability in advance, that justification in advance. But that's not going to work for certain things.[8]

We need to increase our rate of failure to dramatically increase our rate of learning. Failure can often lead to greater things—Steve Jobs, who was forced out of Apple by the time he was 30 years old, believed being fired from Apple was one of the best things ever to happen to him. He went on to start the successful Pixar Animation Studios (*Cars, The Incredibles, Toy Story*) and in his absence Apple floundered. When Jobs returned to the company, he was responsible for helping launch the iPod, iPhone, and iPad, and Apple soared to new heights.

> *"Innovation distinguishes between a leader and a follower."*
> —STEVE JOBS

As stated before, Michael Jordan was cut from his high school basketball team. Warren Buffet was rejected by Harvard University. Lance Armstrong wasn't among the best triathletes, so he switched to cycling and won the Tour de France a record seven times. Michael Dell dropped out of the University of Texas to start his computer conglomerate. Retail giant Amazon.com went seven straight years before turning its first profit, yet founder Jeff Bezos believed in its prospects and kept tweaking the company until he got it right, Wilma Rudolph overcame infantile paralysis (at one point deemed a cripple) to go on to become the fastest woman in the world and win three gold medals. All of these people were great innovators who experienced plenty of failures on their way to the top.

New Challenges

Once you reach the top, you are faced with an entire new set of challenges. Many people at the top of their professions indicate staying there is much harder than getting there. Part of this difficulty results from them forgetting what got them there in the first place (failing better). Julien Smith (co-author with Chris Brogan of *Trust Agents*) states that you need tension once you reach the top:

> When you get rich and famous, you go on defense and, next thing you know, you've lost your way," Smith notes, "You don't produce relevant work anymore because your purpose is to defend what you've built and avoid mistakes. Those that are able to keep tension in their lives despite their success are those that will endure and have a chance to become great. Those that coast on their success will not.[9]

Oprah Winfrey wanted "for people to see within each show that you are responsible for your life, that although there may be tragedy in your life, there's always a possibility to triumph. It doesn't matter who you are, where you come from. The ability to triumph begins with you. Always, always."[10]

In *True North* Bill George discusses David Pottruck, former CEO of Charles Schwab, who relishes the opportunity to learn from every experience:

> Failure forces you to reflect. What went wrong? How could I have done this better? It's an opportunity for you to take responsibility. The path of least resistance is to blame it on someone else. I failed many times but learned from each experience and usually managed to come back stronger. I kept plugging away and eventually was successful.[11]

Whether we feel we are at the top or bottom of the ladder, challenges always present us with opportunities to learn and become better. Challenges are a gift rather than a curse, as they are often viewed. More often than not, we can turn failures into success later in life by asking what can I do better next time? What have I learned? It may help you to write these items down or share them digitally with your friends, family, or coworkers. This action sends a signal that you are not only secure in your missteps, but that you'd like others to learn from them as well.

> "We cannot change the cards we are dealt, just how we play the hand."
>
> —RANDY PAUSCH, Author of *The Last Lecture*

Forrest Gump

In the early years of Forrest Gump's life his legs were in shackles. He was designated a cripple. Then one day bullies start chasing him and throwing rocks at his head. Gump's survival skills take over and he starts running to escape. In this flight or fight scenario he breaks free from the shackles both literally and figuratively.

Gump's fear resulted in positive action. Ironically how many of us have our own mental shackles that we are afraid to break from? Or, how about psychological crutches that exist because people say we need them? If Gump had listened to the experts, indicating he'd never walk properly, then he would go through life shackled. It turns out in his moment of need he doesn't fall on his face and fail without the shackles. Instead it's a breakthrough moment and he indicates it as such: "Now you wouldn't believe me if I told you, but I could run like the wind blows. From that day on, if I was ever going somewhere, I was running!"

He later goes on to be an All-American running back at the number one college football program at the time (Alabama) and later jogs across the country. It's time to break away from our self-imposed shackles. Beyond running, when Gump decided to pick up ping-pong, he didn't read about it or analyze it. No, he picked up a paddle and started playing; and ping-pong became his central focus for an extended time period. Just like Gump, if we want to shed these shackles we need to take that proverbial first step, we need to take action.

DIGITAL DEEDS

Time to Move On

Even if you are a technophobe, you need to move on to more advanced programs once they gain mass appeal. You don't need to be an early adopter or a fast follower of technology, but you do need to conquer your fears and move forward with the times. For example, most of us many years ago moved away from Yahoo search to Google search. Or we moved from a hotmail email account to Gmail. Many people fear change and a failure to understand new technologies. But just as is being stressed throughout this chapter, it's better to face new challenges and learn from your flubs along the way.

So, if you are a baby boomer it's time to move from your AOL browser and onto using Firefox or Google Chrome and discover the beautiful world of having multiple windows/tabs open at once. Also, it's time to trade in your mobile phone for a smartphone, tablet, or both. Despite your fears, the benefits of these new technologies will make life easier.

Competition Brings Out the Best

Great athletes want to face the best, because they know it brings out the best in them. There is not much gained from thoroughly thrashing an inferior opponent.

Larry Bird and Magic Johnson had one of the greatest rivalries in sport. Yet, today they are great friends. Here is Bird's take on the relationship:

"I remember back in my days, I'd rather play against Earvin Johnson than play with him," he said. "I know he's a great player and you always want to play with the best, but I just loved to compete against him. He's a guy I always compared myself to. I'd rather stay in Boston and let him stay in L.A. and just

> "If you ever think there aren't going to be problems, you're fooling yourself. There are always going to be problems."
> —JOHN WOODEN[12]

compete every year in the Finals. That's what made me a better player. It would've been too easy if we played together."[13]

Life without challenges is certainly a boring one; take the attitude to welcome them. Life will become more enjoyable and you'll learn a great deal about yourself. Many start-ups move to Silicon Valley despite the high expense rate and difficulty finding programmers that aren't already hired. One reason that leaders of these companies do so is that they know they will be challenged on a daily basis. Venture capitalists, reporters, and competition will quickly identify the "warts" of the company. Although this will be difficult to take, if the issues are resolved it will only make the company better, and faster. It will also make you a stronger leader, because your leadership skills will be challenged as well.

> *"Practice isn't the thing you do once you're good. It's the thing you do that makes you good."*
> —MALCOLM GLADWELL, *Outliers*

When I give keynotes and receive tough questions from the audience, I relish the opportunity as I know it will make my next speech better. While it may be difficult and stressful at the time, if all the questions were easy then I wouldn't be progressing as a speaker and that would be unbeneficial to me and my future audiences.

The More You Eat the More You Want

Japan's Takeru Kobayashi is one of the world's top professional eaters—he once ate 95 hamburgers in a competition. When the competition from humans wasn't strong enough, the 5' 8" 150 pound Kabayashi challenged a 1,000 pound Kodiak bear to an eating contest. The bear won the competition eating 50 hot dogs in 2 minutes and 36 seconds to Kobayashi's 31 hot dogs in the same time. [14]

When leading up to a competition a reporter asked, how do you train the days leading up? You'd think he'd starve himself, but in fact it is the opposite, he stuffs his face. He indicates that the more you eat, the more you want. Just like Kobayashi, once you get in the habit of making and completing things it will inspire you to take even more action.

DIGITAL DEEDS

CEOs on Twitter

A study by Aaron Stout and Andrea Lipizzi showed that by June, 2011 less than 5 percent of the Fortune 500 CEOs had a Twitter account. Of these only half of them were truly active. Some of the standouts were Brian Dunn (Best Buy), Michael Dell (Dell), John Donahue (eBay), Eric Schmidt (former Google CEO, now Executive Chairman), and Douglas Conant (Campbell's). Notice how progressive the companies are on this list; expect in the future for more and more CEOs to face their fears and digitally lead via tools like Twitter.[15]

Listen First, Sell Second

We should always listen to others, and for the digital opportunities all around us, before trying to sell a product or service. As the famous saying goes, there is a reason God gave us two ears and one mouth. In the digital world, however, we often try to sell first, rather than listen first.

Selling first digitally is analogous to going to a friend's housewarming party, seeing a group of four strangers having a pleasant conversation, walking up them and saying, "Hello, I'm Jane Doe and I'd like to interrupt your conversation and tell you why I'm great for the next 20 minutes." Considering how socially unacceptable such an action would be it is unlikely you would do this, but yet many of us completely forget such etiquette when we enter a digital world.

> "Do or do not. There is no try."
> —YODA

Failing Your Way to Success

The myriad of examples contained in this chapter showcase that standing still in the hopes of avoiding failure is not a solid strategy. Inaction is often more costly than the actual failure we fear. Emotional, financial, and physical strain can result from putting off decisions. We will face challenges each and every day, so the sooner we embrace them the better off we will be; knowing they will make us stronger, smarter, and better leaders. They will only improve us, however, if we properly learn from them. So while in the midst of failure and frustration we must determine what is to be learned and move forward quickly. For a more rewarding life and to become leaders of our life and others, we must fail fast, fail forward, and fail better.

"Success consists of going from failure to failure without loss of enthusiasm."

—WINSTON CHURCHILL

CHAPTER ELEVEN

Leverage Inertia

*"Twenty years from now you will be more
disappointed by the things that you didn't do than
by the ones you did do. So throw off the bowlines.
Sail away from the safe harbor. Catch the trade
winds in your sails. Explore. Dream. Discover."*
—MARK TWAIN

When you get up in the morning, jot on a 3 × 5 Index card the two most important things you need to get done that day. The index card is good because it carries weight and can fit in your pocket as a reminder. Draw a little box next to each item and check each one off as you complete it. Even better, when you have completed both items crumple up the card and toss it energetically into the trash (feel free to take a basketball-like jump shot). If you prefer to use your smartphone to the index card then set an alarm every hour as a reminder to complete the task. Yes, this will be annoying if you don't do it, but that's the point! But, you may say, some of these items will take hours. Some tasks do take hours, but in most cases we should simplify the mountain down to pebbles (see Mark Twain's quote earlier in this chapter or reference Chapter 2).

You will be amazed at how often, unfortunately, you can't even complete one of these two tasks. Many of us start the day by rolling over in bed, grabbing our smartphone or tablet, and immediately answering emails and texts or responding to tweets. This situation is a procrastinator's dream—don't fall into this trap. Multitasking is junk food for the brain. Get your two things done first before doing other tasks. It's best if you attack these items of importance early in the day to avoid getting caught up with something unexpected. Get in the habit of shipping things as opposed to responding to things. Video recording customers in your restaurant asking them why they frequent your establishment and then showing this to the rest of your staff is an example of "shipping" or producing something tangible. Even better if you take the best of these clips and upload them to YouTube. Answering 50 emails you received over the course of the last day is an example of responding to things and is not as valuable.

Even attempt to get these goals done before noon. In a modern world, since challenges are going to arrive during the day, you can't bank on having that hour later or some time in the afternoon—double down your effort early. Too many unexpected things can occur to derail your best intentions. Completing the two most important items has a positive impact on your overall attitude for the rest of the day. It is a great feeling when everything else you accomplish beyond those two main items is an added bonus!

Make sure you delete tasks as you accomplish them. You will always have more than two tasks on your plate, but don't put them on the same list! Make a list called "parking lot" for these other tasks. You can then pull from this "parking lot list" each day for your two items.

Utilize the basic principle of inertia (Newton's First Law of Motion) to accomplish your goals: objects in motion tend to stay in motion. Buying a new bucket of paint for a room in your house is easy—the difficult task is starting that first brush stroke. It's hard to leave the rest of the room unfinished once you've started painting.

Most people are fast to shoot an idea down before it is fully understood, especially when it comes to new digital initiatives. Some people in high positions aren't digital natives and are therefore often uncomfortable around new ideas related to technology. At the same time, many of these same people are hesitant to get in the way if action has already been taken and success proven. Rather than looking for permission, consider taking some initiative. Get in the habit of asking for forgiveness rather than for total approval. If it comes to a point where you've used the "forgiveness card" one too many times, then you probably want to reconsider if you are in the right company or organization for your progressive thinking and attitude.

Construction of Disneyland began on July 21, 1954, and it was famously built in a mere 366 days.[1] This is truly astounding. When asked how he was able to accomplish this in only 366 days, Walt Disney simply replied, "We used every one of them." Are you using all your days like Walt Disney, forging ahead?

Digital Log

When setting your daily goals, not only should you verbalize your plan, but post it digitally to gain support from others. Posting more long-term goals is helpful as well: "I am going to be hiking Mount Kilimanjaro with my husband and our sons next year! Feel free to offer me encouragement along the way as I'm going to need it!"

In a company, this same idea can be utilized. Posting weekly, monthly, or annual goals for different departments or the organization as a whole provides common ground for all employees and executives. With the advent of social media, these goals can be sent out across a number of different platforms—some organizations are now even developing their own in-house social media networks similar to Facebook or LinkedIn. Goals can be posted to company or division blogs. When a major task or goal is completed, members of the organization can post this information and coworkers or bosses can respond with congratulations or positive feedback. This setup creates a supportive environment

> "There are costs and risks to a program of action, but they are far less than the long-range risks and cost of comfortable inaction."
>
> —JOHN F. KENNEDY

even if the organization is spread across different locations, time zones, or countries.

As a leader, you should promote the use of social media tools throughout your organization. Lead by example and be active on social networks where you know fellow employees will take note. Work toward your own personal goals while also helping the organization reach its overall ones. At Zappos their number one goal is customer service, which is evident if you ever take their free tour at their Las Vegas headquarters. They have updated graphs and charts (both digitally and handwritten) showing what their customer service score is for the day, the week, and the quarter.

The beautiful thing about being consistent in posting items digitally, especially within social media, is that it gives us a running account of our lives, both personal and professional. When executed properly, we will not look back upon wasted time and ask what we have done, or not done. Instead, we will constantly be reminded of our achievements.

Most religions discuss remaining "present." This idea roughly means don't focus on your life being better tomorrow (e.g., "when I retire things will be easy" or "next week I'll get that report completed") and don't focus on the past, (e.g., "things were so much easier and better in college" or "my last job was much less stressful than this one"). At some level, our digital posts help us remain "present" as they allow us to take a look at the digital footprint we are creating in the moment. Is your footprint on the rocky hills of Kilimanjaro or is it firmly planted on the couch watching reruns of an insignificant reality show? Have you made the best use of your time, contributing to the overall success of an organization, or are you spending your time hidden away in your office?

Don't Go Overboard

Consistently digitally posting is great, but we need to keep in mind that there are times when it may not be appropriate. It is one thing if you post a note right before you begin your hike and then one later after you reach the summit. If you are too busy posting every second of the hike and miss the sunrise, however, then you are living in an augmented reality rather than enjoying the one around you. Don't let your reporting of what you are doing get in the way of living the moment itself. Similarly, don't abuse posting in regards to your professional or work environment—work toward output, not idle input.

Consider this scenario: what are you most likely to hear at a cocktail party?

"My grandmother volunteered for the Red Cross in WW II at the age of 12 and continued service the rest of her life, receiving the highest honor the organization offers."

- or -

"My grandmother did a great job watching *I Love Lucy* and *The Honeymooners*."

- or -

"My grandmother sent more emails than anyone I know."

You are more likely to hear the first one: family members enjoy boasting about significant accomplishments of their relatives. There is nothing special about watching television or replying to email. The big difference in the future is that our grandchildren will *show* (digitally) versus *tell* about the significant accomplishments of those living before them. Imagine such a situation:

"Let me show you a blog my Nanna started when she was only 25 that lasted for 30 years and helped raise $45 million dollars for the City of Chelsea. They even have a few pages about her at the city's Website—check it out."

What they aren't going to be able to show is:

"My Nanna spent most of her adult life looking up funny videos about birds and playing casual video games online with people she didn't know."

It's important to note the item that discusses the charitable contribution of Nanna (*"helped raise $45 million . . ."*). Posts should not reflect a tone of narcissism; meaning they shouldn't be relegated to accomplishments that are a benefit *only to you.* Always look for activities that help benefit your company or, more importantly, society as well. For example, if you just got promoted and want to tell the world about it, make sure that you mention and thank others that helped you along the way. Or, if you are going to hike Mount Kilimanjaro, is there a creative way to raise awareness or money around a good cause?

> *"The vision of a champion is bent over, drenched in sweat, at the point of exhaustion, when nobody else is looking."*
>
> —MIA HAMM

Handling Pressure to Achieve Results

There are situations where we see the "underdog" prevail in sporting competitions. Some of this success is attributed to the team having less pressure to perform (i.e., nobody expects them to win). With less pressure they are able to play aggressively while the favored team becomes conservative and tight, playing not to lose instead of playing to win. The 2011 NBA Championship, 2011 Stanley Cup Finals, and 2011 Super Bowl are all great examples. The Miami Heat, Vancouver Canucks, and Pittsburgh Steelers were heavy favorites (in Vegas) to win, yet the Dallas Mavericks, Boston Bruins, and Green Bay Packers prevailed respectfully.

We encounter similar pressures daily in our own lives. The greatest form of pressure is that which we place on ourselves to excel. Another huge form of pressure is that coming from your boss, rather than from within. (However, if you believe your boss or job is your greatest form of pressure then you need to reread Chapter Five as it is likely you aren't following your passion.)

Pressure directly flows from what we want to be and accomplish in life. On a daily basis, having the ability to complete our two goals for the day early in the morning helps relieve this pressure. Now, if you are a night owl, don't fret. It's difficult to fight our own individual biorhythms, so treat your two items as if they need to be done by noon tomorrow. Hence when you are toiling away at 11 p.m. on these goals, you are actually getting ahead by accomplishing tomorrow's tasks, today. This strategy will help avoid having these items loom over your head all day. Write your two items down at the appropriate time for you; this could be 9 p.m., yet you start working on these items at 9:15 p.m. and give yourself till 9 p.m. the next day to complete them. We all need to do what works best for us; Thomas Edison worked 24 hours a day, preferring to take 15-minute catnaps.[2]

As a business leader, keep in mind that employees may have different cycles and ways of working. Of course it is understandable that there are particular hours workers must be in the office, but in this technologically advanced world, there are plenty of ways to create flexibility, such as allowing some people to work from home. Other ways that leaders can alleviate pressure for employees is to foster an environment of sharing versus competition. We saw this earlier with Alan Mulally when he took over Ford and executives were more like rivals than teammates, so much so that nobody wanted to mark anything as red (problem).

> "The secret of getting ahead is getting started. The secret of getting started is breaking your complex overwhelming tasks into small manageable tasks, and then starting on the first one."
> —MARK TWAIN

The pressure on executives can be immense as well. For them, being fully transparent and using digital tools can be difficult if they try to handle it all on their own. They need to not only inform others about what they are thinking and doing but also request and process input from employees and customers. If you place the weight of the world on your shoulders it will be heavy. Make sure you offload this weight to your employees, customer, and board and use digital tools to accomplish these feedback loops.

When Inactivity Is Good

Action is great, but our body and mind occasionally need a break. To achieve everything we want in life many of us try to add more hours to the day. As a result most of us start to shortchange our bodies of sleep. "I'll sleep when I'm dead" is an often heard saying, though the irony is your death will come much quicker if this is your mantra. A study published in a 2009 issue of *Sleep* magazine followed 98,000 Japanese men and women ages 40 to 79 for just over 14 years. Those defined as short sleepers of both genders had a 1.3-fold increase in mortality rate compared with those achieving sufficient sleep. Another 2009 study followed 6,400 men and women for an average of eight years. The research concluded that those who suffered from sleep apnea (sleep disorder characterized by abnormal breathing) raised their risk of dying early by 46 percent. Most of our goals and visions will resemble more of a marathon than a sprint so we can't burn ourselves out before the finish line. You will achieve less in the short and long-term if you don't take care of your engine (body).

You Can't "Create More Time"

A striking fact about life is that no matter how much success or money we amass we still have the same amount of time during the day as every other human being on the planet, and this isn't going to change. Think about that, no matter what you or I do or how much money and influence we have, we can't get more actual time during a day than the next person. It's what we do with this time that matters. Many of us in life try to do the impossible and "create more time." In hopes of doing so, we may sleep less, but this is fruitless and ineffective.

Often we start this bad habit in college by pulling "all nighters" when studying for a test. One hundred twenty students were surveyed and it was found that those who had never pulled an all-nighter had an average grade point average (GPA) of 3.1 compared to 2.9 for those who had engaged in the practice.[3] A study from the *Archives of Internal Medicine* also supplies data supporting the inefficiencies of sleep deprivation. Sleep habits of 153 men and women were tracked by researchers for two weeks. Those in the study were then quarantined for five days and exposed to cold viruses (I hope they were paid a lot!). What was discovered is that the people who slept an average of less than seven hours per night were three times as likely to get sick as those who averaged at least eight hours. Other research showed dieters who logged 8.5 hours of sleep per night lost 56 percent more body fat than those with the *exact same diet*, but who were only able to get 5.5 hours of shuteye per night.[4]

One in five Americans sleeps less than six hours per night. *Harvard Women's Health Watch* suggests studies indicate insufficient sleep affects learning and memory. With the proper amount of sleep the brain is able to commit new information to memory via a process called memory consolidation. In studies, people who were allowed to sufficiently sleep after learning a task did better on subsequent tests than those not receiving the proper amount of sleep.[5]

> "It's not how much you get done that matters, it's what you've done."
> —@EQUALMAN

Aside from the learning and memory issues, the Harvard Medical School Special Health Report that reviewed all of these sleep studies concluded that insufficient sleep leads to problems with metabolism and weight, safety, mood, cardiovascular health, and disease.

Realistically, no matter what we do, we will all have occasional nights where we can't sleep. During these times it's better to get up and do something rather than lay awake in bed worrying about why we can't sleep. Go do something for an hour and then lay down on your back with your palms up and focus on your in-and-out breathing (preferrably do so while laying across the floor). For those that practice Yoga, this should seem familiar as it's a form of mediation typically performed at the end of a Yoga class. Even if you don't completely fall asleep in this position your body will feel more rested there than tossing and turning in bed all night. They key is that if we get the proper amount of rest during most days, an occasional bout with the pillow will be OK. When sleep issues become chronic, whether you are forcing it upon yourself or not, major problems can occur.[6]

Power Nap Your Way to Productivity

For years Japanese companies have been the gold standard in productivity. One of their secrets to success? They encourage employees to nap on the job. This raises the question: should we all take naps like kindergartners?

The University of California at Berkeley conducted a test that had one group nap in the afternoon while another group remained sleep free. They then had each group perform a memory test. The group given the nap outperformed the other group by 10 percent. "Sleep is not just for the body. It's very much for the brain," said study author Matthew Walker, an assistant professor at the University of California at Berkeley. Additionally, humans' memory generally decreases 10 percent in the afternoon, yet this group that napped was able to combat this 10 percent loss. Walker concluded, "This is further evidence that sleep plays a critical role in the processing of memories."[7]

In Japan, researchers suggest that the afternoon nap should last no more than 30 minutes to avoid being groggy. Nap salons are prevalent in Japan, where stressed out and tired workers can rent a daybed to relax for 30 minutes. Doctor Neil Stanley, a sleep expert at the Norfolk and Norwich University Hospital states, "a 20-minute nap gives you an amazing boost, it's much better than having a coffee. Even closing your eyes for 20 minutes is better than nothing."

American sleep expert Doctor Sara Mednick even describes taking a regular nap as a "lifesaving habit that can help improve your health and sex life, slim the waist, and boost work performance."[8]

There are no shortcuts in life; this includes sleep. Make the hours you are awake more effective by getting the proper rest. It will make your day-to-day hours quality over quantity and allow you to be on the planet longer to develop your legacy of leadership. If you were training for a marathon you wouldn't run a marathon every day; yet many of us attempt to do so with our digital tasks.

Weekly Unplug

Starting now, pick one day during the week when you will completely unplug from technology. That's right, no email, mobile phone, texting, tweets, etc. If this seems impossible, then you need this even more! If you can't go cold turkey, even for a day per week, start slow by selecting one day per month. I suggest a travel day or family gathering. Another gradual way to ease into the arrangement is you allow yourself three "passes" on your unplugged day where you can engage with technology for five minutes. You will find that you will be recharged (no pun intended) and your increased productivity on the other six days will make up for anything lost on the "unplug day."

Unplugging for a day *isn't easy* at first. University students that were placed into a "media blackout" started to feel withdrawal after only 24 hours. The study was completed by The University of Maryland Center for Media and the Public Agenda and included 1,000 students from 10 countries ranging from Argentina to Uganda. Quotes from study participants on how difficult it was do go without media for a day included:

> "Itching like a crackhead without multi-media."—U.S.
> "Feel Dead without it."—Argentina
> "Sickening."—Lebanon

Despite the difficulty, most students agreed that they envied people that weren't dependent on media. "I am always wondering why I become so dependent on these media now. When I was a child, I did not have these but I was also very happy every day. Why? Why is it like that today?" one Chinese student questioned aloud.[9] Monster.com founder Jeff Taylor offers this sage advice, "With emails available 24/7 through smartphones, it's incredibly difficult to turn work off; but it's important to turn it off. Most workers—even die-hard entrepreneurs—need to clear their minds and recharge their bodies."

Taylor turns off his BlackBerry at 8 p.m.—and doesn't hit the power-on button until 7 a.m. the next day. But he admits that schedule is not for everyone. Some people are incredibly productive from 9 to 11 p.m.—so they should work those hours, and then slice off some personal time during another part of the day.[10]

Get Active!

Often we trick ourselves into thinking we are active by telling ourselves "well I need to get into better shape before I go skiing" or "I need to wait and buy screenwriters' software before I begin writing my movie." When we find ourselves doing this, let's try and remember a story from Thomas Edison:

"The world is a dangerous place, not because of those who do evil, but because of those who look on and do nothing."

—ALBERT EINSTEIN

Once, when a new employee checked in at the lab in Menlo Park, New Jersey, he asked Edison for a copy of the lab rules. "There ain't no rules around here," said Edison. "We're trying to accomplish something." Accomplish he did. In a six-year span (1876-1882) Edison filed over 400 patents including ones for the phonograph, electric lighting, and power generation.[11]

We need to set long-term and short-term goals for ourselves in our personal and professional lives. Whether working toward two achievements from our index card, or smartphone list, or an annual revenue goal established at our company, we must take positive, consistent action today. We can create a digital log showing our successes over time while receiving input, feedback, and support from others. This digital log is part of our digital legacy and we want to make sure it speaks for itself. Don't waste time tweeting every little thing that happens to you in a day and remember that it is possible to alleviate some of the pressures of the modern world by occasionally unplugging from technology, grabbing a nap, or simply making sure you get enough sleep to stay on top of your game.

> *"The only thing constant in life is change."*
> —HERACLITUS

When we see items that need to be improved dramatically *we always wonder why somebody doesn't do something about it.* We are that somebody. Be that somebody that is part of the solution rather than simply part of the ongoing problem. Start taking action today!

SECTION THREE: ACT

Key Takeaways
- Be decisive
- Increase your rate of learning by increasing your rate of failure
- Leverage inertia: people in motion tend to stay in motion
- Accomplish two items toward your dream each day before engaging in the "day-to-day"
- Texts, email, and tweets can be a procrastinator's dream—don't fall into this trap
- If needed, use digital tools designed to keep you on the most important task
- Digitally unplug one day per week
- To perform your best you need proper rest
- Power nap your way to productivity
- Fail forward, fail fast, fail better
- Don't wait—take action toward your dream now!

MAP

1. Be firm in your destination, but flexible with your path

2. Your digital footprint reminds you, in real-time, how you are living your life

3. Set laughable goals

SIMPLE: success is the result of simplification & focus

TRUE: be true to your passion

ACT: nothing happens without action—take the first step

MAP: goals and visions are needed to get where you want to be

PEOPLE: success doesn't happen alone

CHAPTER TWELVE

Set Laughable Goals

"If you can dream it, you can do it."

—WALT DISNEY

There is a story of an individual (we'll call him Charlie) who was lifting weights near Tiger Woods in the fitness center of a golf club. As background, Charlie specialized in helping managers establish goals and the strategic plans necessary to achieve them. Charlie struck up a conversation with Tiger about goal setting, which went something like this:

Charlie to Tiger: "What is your ultimate goal?"

Tiger: "18"

Charlie: "That makes sense. Jack Nicklaus holds the record for winning the most major PGA Tour Events in history with 18. Obviously, you want to establish your legacy as the greatest golfer of all-time and surpass Jack's 18 major wins. At the age of 36 you (Tiger) have won 14 majors, so only 4 more and you are tied with Nicklaus."

Tiger: "That's not it."

Charlie (perplexed): "What does the 18 represent then?"

Tiger: "Each time I step onto the golf course my goal is 18. I want to shoot an 18."

Incredible, Tiger's goal is to shoot a hole-in-one for an entire round of golf! To give this context, the lowest round ever recorded for a PGA Tour Event is 59. Yet, Tiger wanted to shoot 18. Tiger considers this his "stretch" goal.

This is what great leaders do; they set an audacious road map for success, goals that others may even find laughable. A "laughable goal" is one that many people, especially your enemies or critics, will scoff at. Often their laughter may be the nervous kind, hoping you don't achieve your goal because they'd be jealous. Those that aren't laughing at your most audacious goals are the people you will want to surround yourself with. At some point their support may be necessary. The higher you set your goal the more you will need other people's help to achieve them. Are you setting your sights high enough? *Don't limit yourself when it comes to your dreams and goals.*

Determine What You Want and Go for It

Having a huge goal inspires us mentally and physically to overcome the hurdles and obstacles that we will encounter along our path. People *should* laugh at the audacity of our goals. If you weigh 300 pounds and say, "I want to drop 5 pounds by the end of the month," the statement doesn't inspire. If you say "I'm going to go from a size 50 pant waist to my high school size of 34 for my upcoming high school reunion," then that is ONE BIG HAIRY Goal. That is a map with a pot of gold at the end. If your goal is average and uninspiring, your effort will reflect this.

A good understanding of what you want in life will separate you from 99 percent of the crowd. Most of us don't define what we want. By going through the exercise of developing your map or vision for what you want today and tomorrow, you may not be 100 percent sure of what you want, but you will know what you don't want, and that is half the battle. Henry Ford believed people didn't know what they wanted until they saw it. With respect to the automobile, he said, "People don't know what they want. If I asked them they would say they wanted a faster horse."

If you are lucky, you know what you want in life and your object is to map out a path for this success. Although almost everyone desires to be happy, many of us don't know what we want out of life specifically. If you are struggling with this idea, try out this exercise. Use a spreadsheet (e.g., Google Docs, Microsoft Excel) and track by hour everything that you did that week. At the end of the week, take a day to decompress and then revisit this sheet. Mark in red anything you didn't enjoy doing, mark in yellow anything you found indifferent, mark in green anything you *really* enjoyed doing. Then start to plan or map out how to eliminate all the red and yellow items and focus on doing more of, and eventually almost exclusively all, the green items. Even once you get on a roll you should periodically perform this exercise to make sure you are still on the right track. This is a great way to digitally map your way to success.

Or try this one out. Pull up your most recent credit card and bank statements. There is an old saying that where you spend your money is where your heart resides. After reviewing your statements does this ring true for you? How and where we spend our money tells a lot about us to other people and ourselves.

It may be difficult to figure out what you want, but once you do, you must set a path and vision that inspires—then go for it. Recognize that there will be detours and new technology that spring up along the way, but this is just part of your journey.

What Do You Want to Be When You Grow Up?

What do you want to be when you grow up? This question is as applicable for those in your 50s and 60s as it was when you were twelve years old. Knowing what you want in life is the first half of enlightenment—knowing how to get it is the second.

Don't let anyone discourage you from your life's vision. Look to Barbara Walters, Bill Walton, and Lou Holtz for inspiration. All three suffer from various speech impediments. Yet, all excelled in the most unlikely field—broadcasting. Talk about fortitude and courage. They set a map for what they were passionate about and didn't stop until they reached their destination. All three of these individuals are some of the most highly sought after public speakers to deliver company keynotes. Why?

> "What you want said about you at your funeral is your own personal definition of success."
> —STEPHEN CONVEY

Because they know what it takes to overcome hurdles and become leaders and their motivational actions inspire others. If you keep striving toward the mapped out vision for you life, there will be no need to look behind you to see if there are followers, they will certainly be there.

DIGITAL DEEDS

Digital Video Stardom: 20 Tips

With the modern realm of digital media, new avenues such as YouTube are being utilized to help companies and individuals get on a path to success and reach their planned goals. Whether marketing a product or service, promoting a personal or professional endeavor, or simply sharing an event with friends,at some point you will be filmed and uploaded to YouTube, Vimeo, Facebook, or national television. It could be for a family reunion or for *The Ellen DeGeneres Show*. Whatever the situation, the below tips will help you be prepared to put your best face forward:

1. Relax your face, starting with the rest of your body. Make sure your hands aren't balled up and your shoulders aren't scrunched. Some people find it helpful to give a little self-massage to the temples and neck. Rubbing your palms together to generate warmth and placing them onto your closed eyes is another trick that works.
2. When you smile, specifically concentrate on raising your cheekbones. Raising your cheekbones will naturally give the illusion to the camera that your eyes are sparkling.

3. Focus on yoga-esque breaths that are deep and slow. This breathing technique will help relax your face and body and will also help prevent you from talking too fast.

4. When being interviewed, remember it is different than a normal conversation. Don't use non-verbal cues like nodding your head as it will appear like you are a "know it all" and are impatient for the question. It also conveys to the audience that you already know the answer. Nodding is a difficult habit to break so you may not get it right the first few times you are on camera, but with a little practice it will become second nature.

5. When possible, use a good microphone—they are worth the extra money.

6. Make sure the light is in your face and not behind you. Natural light is best at dawn and dusk. If you can shoot during these periods it will make you look your best.

7. Have good posture. Stand up against a wall and have your shoulders and the top of the back of your head pressed firmly against it. Then slowly walk away from the wall keeping this posture intact for the camera.

8. Overemphasize everything, including your words, excitement, volume, gestures, and eyes. Don't shout like you are scolding a misbehaving dog (see #2 about being relaxed), but you need to project like you are on stage performing a play. The first time I saw Magic Johnson being interviewed I thought, why is he shouting instead of talking in his normal voice? Then I found out the first few times I saw myself interviewed—if you are talking in your normal tone you come across as drab and unexcited. If the bubbly Magic Johnson has to take it up a notch to look excited on film, then we all need to!

9. Be concise. If you are filming your own video, make it less than two minutes. Better still, see if the video can be under a minute. If you are being interviewed, answer the question with your most powerful statement first and try to do so in one or two quick bullet points.

10. If you are wearing a suit jacket, tuck the tails of your coat under your behind and place your sitting bones firmly on them. This position will give a nice line on your shoulders and help avoid wrinkles. At the same time, if the fabric of your jacket becomes slack, it reminds you to sit up straight.

11. If offered hi-definition (HD) make-up, accept it. If you don't use it, you might look tired, shiny, and old on HD. If you are at home, apply base make-up with a brush to dramatically reduce shine and lines. If you don't have base make-up, use a cotton swap to quickly go over your face to at least remove the oil and dirt.
12. Make sure to stay hydrated and drink plenty of fluids beforehand. Have water nearby in case you need it. Avoid ice and sugary drinks. Sparkling water with lemon is the best.
13. The camera is your audience so spend the majority of the time looking into it. If you are on Skype/FaceTime don't watch your little image in the corner. If you are being interviewed ask the interviewer where you should place most of your eye contact. When you get on primetime television, make sure you know where the various cameras are and "work" each camera. If speaking on stage, ask the cameraman the best place to stand for optimal light on your face. Make sure you play to the camera for your major points of emphasis—you can use these for your highlight reel later.
14. Before you begin speaking, a good trick to set your natural voice is to hum happy birthday then immediately say, "The rain in Spain falls mainly on the plain."
15. Wear comfortable clothes and what you feel you look the best in. If you are comfortable then you will be confident. For Barack Obama, this might be a suit with a red tie, for Garth Brooks it might be jeans and an open collared black shirt. Try to be consistent in what you wear on video to make yourself more memorable. Think of Johnny Cash's "man in black" persona, Tiger Woods's red shirt on Sundays, Richard Simmons's exercise tank top, or Mark Zuckerberg's hooded sweatshirt. Don't wear clothing or items that distract the viewer or audience, such as a large broach, crazy tie, or a dress with a puffy or flowery design near the neck.
16. If you feel like you have a frog in your throat, eat some cantaloupe. This fruit acts as a natural lubricant and helps clear congestion.
17. Make sure you are yourself on camera. This can be difficult. Some speaking coaches say not to use your hands, but when I pay close attention to Jim Collins (Author of *From Good to*

Great and one of the best speakers in the world), he definitely does. The difference with him is that every movement he makes has a purpose, so the use of his hands assist his message rather than detract from it. So if you speak naturally with your hands, then do so, but make sure you raise them up so that they are in the frame of the camera. The worst thing is for a finger to be occasionally flying in and out of the frame. If the video is only showing your head then try and lower your hands so they have less of a chance to randomly fly into the frame. Lastly, never have your hands block your face, unless you are demonstrating being ashamed.

18. Use the tips mentioned here when filming others. Make them a star and they will shine brightly on you!

19. Have Fun!

20. Do post mortems. The beautiful thing about video is you can review. Act like you are the head coach of the New England Patriots and review video to get an advantage. How many "ums" do you say, are you slouching, do you look better with your glasses on or off, do you say "like" or other "pet" words too often? What little quirks do you have (dropping your head, slouching your shoulders, turning your back to the audience, shifty eyes)? Make note of these movements in your phone. Then, review the top three quirks you have the night before giving a presentation and the morning of the presentation. This will remind you to work on them.

Some of the best speakers you can learn from: Benjamin Zander, Dan Heath, Jim Collins, Seth Godin, Tim Sanders, Guy Kawasaki, Andy Stanley.

As improbable as it sounds, we can also take a lesson from the children's book *The Adventures of Peter Cottontail*:

The sun was shining, the Merry Little Breezes of Old Meadows, the birds were singing, and happiness, the glad, joyous happiness of springtime, was everywhere but in Peter Rabbit's heart. There seemed to be no room for anything but discontent. And such foolish discontent—discontent with his name! And yet, do you know there are lots of people just as foolish as Peter Rabbit.[1]

How many of us focus on little discontents rather than the big things we should be grateful for and the world of opportunity before us every day?

Harnessing Technology on the Road to Success

Opportunities are even more limitless and accessible now that we can leverage tools like YouTube, Twitter, iPad applications and more to make things happen, and happen quickly.

Let's say you are a small business owner. To help unwind at night you read and write while enjoying a glass of wine. You are excited as you just published your first novel, a science fiction piece. You go onto search.twitter.com and type in a search for "bookclub" and find out that many book clubs are using the hashtag #bookclub. You are fairly new to Twitter but you understand that #hashtags are used to help categorize conversations. Sure enough you discover that everyone using #bookclub is in a book club and they are discussing the current books they are reading.

You even find many using #scifibookclub in which users are reading science fiction books that you know and love. One group is discussing Isaac Asimov, your favorite author, so you chime in about how much you love Asimov's work. From there you start exchanging messages with a few of the members. They check your Twitter profile and find a link to your Website discussing your book. All of a sudden, three of these new contacts order your novel. You message them on Twitter that you hope they enjoy it, and suggest that if the book club wants to read it as next month's selection that you would be happy to video Skype in for a Q & A session. They select your novel and after the meeting concludes you ask everyone to go onto Amazon and rate your book. You see that your Twitter followers increased by 12 people; it's all the people from the book club. You find this so empowering and fun that you start to use the same method to reach out to the customers of your small business. This is just one simple example; but this is what I mean by digital opportunities being all around us if we are willing to simply listen and engage.

We should heed the sage advice that Jimmy Skunk gives Peter Rabbit:

> There's nothing in a name except
> Just what we choose to make it.
> It lies with us and no one else
> How other folks shall take it.
> It's what we do and what we say
> And how we live each passing day
> That makes it big or makes it small
> Or even worse than none at all.
> A name just stands for what we are;
> It's what we choose to make it.
> And that's the way and only way
> That other folks will take it.

In other words whether it's our name or other hurdle we've been burdened with, we shouldn't let anything stand in our path.

As is stated in the above passage, a name is just a name—it only takes on importance when we allow it to take on importance. Warren Moon graduated from the University of Washington as one of the country's top quarterbacks and winner of the 1978 Rose Bowl MVP award. He went undrafted, however, because he was an African American quarterback and refused to switch positions to Tight End. While African American quarterbacks are common in the league today, back when Moon graduated the thinking by NFL teams was that African Americans couldn't play this position. They were labeled as running quarterbacks, but not throwing quarterbacks. Moon was lumped into this group.

Moon, however, didn't let this moniker stick. Instead, he went to play football in the Canadian Football League as a quarterback. His team, the Edmonton Eskimos, went on to win an unprecedented 5 straight Grey Cups. Many NFL teams now came bidding for Moon's services and he went on to have a great career with the Houston Oilers, Minnesota Vikings, Seattle Seahawks, and Kansas City Chiefs. Moon was the first modern day African American quarterback inducted into the NFL Hall of Fame. All of this wouldn't have been possible if Moon had allowed others to label him. Some of us, like Moon, will have more hurdles to overcome than others do, but that will make the journey more interesting and rewarding.

> "If the majority was always right, then everybody would be rich."
>
> —BRIAN BILLICK

DIGITAL DEEDS

Don't Forget the Letter

When you forget to include the attachment to an email, text, or status update, it's the modern day equivalent of mailing a stamped and addressed envelope but forgetting to put your letter inside. If you turn on the proper settings on Gmail it will remind you if you said there was an attachment in the body of your text, but it wasn't included. You can also turn on features where it will offer suggestions on other people you might want to cc: based on the history of your emails. This helps to save time and embarrassment. The more time you save, the more time you have going after your goals in life.

Finding Our Path and Leading Others

As we previously discussed, Magic Johnson had a few failures when starting out as a businessman. Then, over time he started to map out his business vision. He wanted to focus on helping build up urban communities, places most businesses were afraid to venture. Once he had this vision it was easier for his company to identify opportunities.

"A lot of athletes go out and want to start sports bars or restaurants, and they do it without a vision of what they're going to add to their customers," Johnson says. "I can say that because I did it. But now I know what my vision is, and everything we consider has to fit that vision. Lots of opportunities come our way, and we ask ourselves as we look at every one whether it will bring something of value to the communities we serve.

"And as we make our way around those communities, my team now is always asking, 'What's missing?' We learned that African Americans are the No. 1 group of moviegoers in America, yet we didn't have theaters in our neighborhoods. That's when we started building Magic Johnson Theatres. If your vision is strong enough, focus isn't as much of a challenge. Things make sense or they don't."

Magic said he started out in business without a vision; but once he developed one everything became easier for him and his team. In life, the hardest person to lead is usually you. That is why much of this book focuses on taking ownership of your life in the digital age. You must first start with leading yourself. Once you are comfortable in your own skin, then others will began to follow in droves both offline and digitally (at a much larger scale). The hope is that this book will make becoming a digital leader a little easier, but it will be constant struggle. The beauty is that when we do find our path in life and can lead ourselves, it's amazing how quickly others will follow.

> *"If you think you can do a thing or think you can't do a thing, you're right."*[3]
> —HENRY FORD

DIGITAL DEEDS

Your Business's Mission

Does your business know its mission? Often, people at the same company are heading down different paths in regards to what they think is best for the business. Do this exercise with your company or organization. Randomly poll the majority of your employees by video recording them. Simply ask them three questions:

1. What's your business's reason for being?
2. What is your competitive advantage over the competition?
3. How is the business contributing to the greater good of society?

These are questions that you'd hope all of your employees have similar answers for. More times than not, though, the answers are not the same. It's then a good time to edit the video into a five minute compilation and have a meeting with all the employees to discuss their responses and get everyone on the same path.

Forrest Gump: Map

"You have to do the best with what God gave you," is advice to Forrest Gump from his mother. Gump's map in life is to make his Momma proud and to give his love in whatever capacity possible to Jenny (his boyhood crush and later his wife). It's a simple road map, but a hard one to follow without deviation.

By staying on his personal path, Gump positively influences others that have staggered off their own paths. This is particularly true of Lieutenant Dan. Gump saves the Lieutenant's life in Vietnam and then saves it again from a destructive spiral of alcohol and drugs by taking him on as a partner in his shrimp business. We also see it with Jenny. Without Forrest's example, she might have prematurely ended her life having been unable to endure several significant hardships.

Forrest ignored outside influencers that insisted he was a "fool" and "stupid" for taking his unconventional path, he stayed on his personal course. Gump simply wasn't distracted by the snide remarks of the naysayers.

To motivate their players, coaches in sports often prominently post disparaging remarks written about their team on their locker-room bulletin boards. We should either disregard the naysayers or, like sports underdogs, use their words to fuel our inner fire. Nothing propels us like the desire to prove others wrong; leverage this.

One of the action items in this book is to set huge visions. Some people will laugh about our ambitions, while others will quietly think we have no chance of making our dreams come true.

The fact that some people think our dreams are overreaching is a great thing. This may seem counterintuitive, but the fact is, if some people aren't a little skeptical, then our goals aren't grand enough! As I told the graduating business students at the University of Texas (McCombs) during my commencement address in Austin—*make it a habit to set laughable goals.*

If Forrest Gump said to people, "My vision is to practice ping-pong every day and become a better player." Most people would be disinterested and say "who cares?" or "that's nice." There aren't many naysayers when your visions aren't grand and specific. However, if Gump stated, "My vision is to become the *world champion* in ping-pong," this statement would certainly raise eyebrows and elicit skeptical responses of "impossible" or "are you mad, you've never even played before?"

Of the five STAMP concepts, Gump is strongest in the areas of **Simple** and **Action**. This is an important point. Each of us is going to be stronger in some STAMP areas than others. This is healthy. While it's not his strength, Gump still does a good job of staying true to his map, and in the end arrives at his desired destination in life.

While we want our goals to be big and hairy; don't misconstrue this with grandiose glory. "Big and hairy" are relative terms and different for each of us. This is made clear and poignant at the conclusion of the "Forrest Gump" film when Gump is shown contentedly mowing the local high school football field, and states, "And 'cause I was a gazillionaire, and I liked doing it so much, I cut that grass for free."

An Audacious Road Map to Success

Life is a journey, yet it is a short one. To get what we want out of life we need to set an audacious road map for success and set goals that some people will laugh at. When others say we can't reach our dreams or try to label us something that we aren't, we need to stay true to our map, visions, and goals. It's important to share our visions with friends, family, coworkers, employees, and others. The more they know, the more accountable they will hold us to them and help us along the way. Define what you want and strive toward your goals.

> *"Whatever course you decide upon, there is always someone to tell you that you are wrong. There are always difficulties arising which tempt you to believe that your critics are right. To map out a course of action and follow it to an end requires courage."*
>
> **—RALPH WALDO EMERSON**

CHAPTER THIRTEEN

Firm in Destination— Flexible in Path

"Leadership is a journey, not a destination.
It is a marathon, not a sprint.
It is a process, not an outcome."[1]
—JOHN DONAHOE, President of eBay

We develop our own road map for our journey through life. If this map were simply handed to us, the spontaneity and surprises that make life so vibrant would be eliminated. Yet, many of us abhor surprises when they present themselves.

Think about your family vacations. What stories are told and retold? The most memorable ones are usually about when things went wrong, or at least didn't go according to plan. There may be tales about a bear raiding your campsite, or when the thrill ride at Disney World unexpectedly stopped and left you hanging upside down, or the French waiter that kicked you out of his restaurant for speaking English. We talk about the challenges that we encounter and overcome. That is what travel is all about: getting out of our comfort zone and experiencing a sense of adventure. And, if we think about it, life is just one big adventure.

The same holds true when we are at work. If we are able to identify issues now that are similar to ones we've seen firsthand in the past, or draw on other leaders' experiences, that helps put us in a position of leadership. For example, when social media first came on the scene, many businesses, in particular those in the B2B space, pushed it aside as not being applicable. Yet, if they were able to draw on some of their past challenges they would have been able to see that they had faced a similar issue in a different form before. As funny as it seems today, many B2B companies thought that Google was only for B2C when it first came out. So just like social media, they pushed search aside. *History repeats itself because nobody listens the first time.* These leaders and companies wrongly believed that there would be a search engine similar to Google but tailored specifically for B2B, so they waited, and this engine never came to fruition. They failed to realize that, with digital advancements, whatever technology people use on a personal level, they will take into the business with them.

Other companies did the opposite when it came to social media. They went too far the other way. They tried to be a social media network by offering photo sharing, alerts, status updates, and more on their company website. Yet, if they would have thought about it, this same thing occurred at the turn of the century when portals (e.g., MyYahoo!) were the "Facebook" of that time. Some major telecoms started having users enable weather reports, sports scores, and financial news next to their phone bill. But, they found out that their customer would go to MyYahoo! for that other information (i.e., news, weather, stocks, games), they just wanted to receive and pay their bill on the telecom site and the more this process was complicated with other features the more frustrated they became; they just wanted to pay their bill!

As a digital leader you need to be able to identify potential issues. The best way to accomplish this when faced with a challenge is to ask the question to yourself and your cohorts: What are some of the bigger digital challenges we faced previously? What did we do well? What did we do poorly? Does the current challenge facing us share any similarities? With the ever-increasing pace of technology, instead of facing difficult technology questions a few times per year, we will deal with them a few times per week.

As of this writing, roughly over 50 percent of all companies block social media to their employees. Yet, if leaders in that company looked back a few years they'd realize that companies used to block Google, thinking employees just wasted time doing searches on Google. So whether it is in life or in business (I argue these are inseparable), we need to get out of our comfort zone and enjoy the adventure, as this will give us the experience we need moving forward to the bigger and better things that await us.

Now, you may be asking, don't we need to establish a map and goals before we start our adventure, whether as a business leader or in our life in general? Also, shouldn't this discussion about maps and paths have been covered off in Section One? Beyond the fact that the acronym MSTAP doesn't work as well at STAMP, there is an important reason why the subject of "Map" is not Section One. Proactive planning is important, but man plans and your God laughs, meaning that life is constantly changing, and we must be prepared to effectively respond and adapt.

Our needs and wants at the beginning of our lives are much different from the middle and the end—a beautiful balance. Many of us spend too much time dreaming and planning our path, rather than taking action and doing something concrete. That is why *simple*, *true*, and *action* were stressed in the first three sections of this book. I'm sure you know someone in your life that is an excellent planner, but never seems to start or accomplish anything. In life, you need to just go for it.

Why Plan at All?

If life is about being flexible, then why plan at all? Well, if we wake up in the morning and simply head to work hoping we look fine; things probably won't end well for us. Our hair will be disheveled, clothes rumpled, and our morning breath would not invite many conversations.

Instead, we do a little bit of mapping and planning in terms of having toothpaste, shampoo, and an ironed shirt, and we take time to shower. Conversely, what we don't want to do is primp until we look perfect, without a single hair out of place, as we would never leave the house and miss the entire day. So, what do we do? We adapt to change.

Some changes will be more gradual than others, for example, that which may occur in societal values or structures. Others, such as the rise of digital media, happen faster. Major events such as the 2008 financial crises seemed to happen in a flash, though the effects were long lasting. No matter what the situation is, however, change is inevitable and we must be willing to move with it, or be left behind. This concept has never been more true than in this era of digital media, social networking, and technological advancement. Think about the changes even happening within social networking—MySpace, the once predominant social networking website, is obsolete, while Facebook has become a global phenomenon within only a few years. However Facebook's end will come, the question is not if, but rather when. When Twitter first hit the mainstream media, many people were hesitant to adopt the new 140-character microblog, but as of 2011 there were around 200 million Twitter users worldwide.[2] If you do not harness these new resources, you will be missing out on a world of opportunity.

Having a plan is imperative, but to stick to it rigidly can create huge problems. Companies who are late adopters of digital technologies will fail compared to the ones that have been on the forefront of the digital revolution, evolving. As a leader, embrace these changing technologies throughout your company. Find ways to get employees and other executives involved and excited. If your map needs readjusting, then work on a plan that takes advantage of change, not on one that sticks the same course, especially if it will be detrimental to your image and revenue.

Mapping, planning, and having a vision are important, but it's being flexible when the unexpected occurs that is the key to digital success. Sometimes, however, external factors beyond our control will require us to take a different path toward our destination.

When I was doing work for one of the world's largest automotive companies, we ran several digital marketing initiatives comparing our wide car to other wide items found in life. For example, just as wider skis (parabolic shaped) give you better balance, the wide base of this car provided more steering control. We spent a day shooting photos of several interactions of this concept next to a giant golf driver from one of golf's best known brands. We were excited with what we'd done and sent word along to this golf manufacturer, letting them know when the campaign would run. What I, and others, had failed to do, however, was receive this company's prior approval. We'd assumed that they would be happy with the millions of dollars of media exposure they would be receiving for free with the inclusion. However, this was not the case and they indicated we could not run any of the images we had shot. Being flexible, we digitally altered the face and shape of the club so you couldn't see the brand name. Unfortunately this was still not good enough.

This was a big problem because I had cost the company several thousands of dollars—money that I most likely would have to pay back. More than that it made me look unprofessional in the eyes of my client. Trying to be flexible, I contacted another well-know golf manufacturer and explained what we were trying to do. Not only were they more than happy to participate, they were willing to give us 100 free golf clubs that we could use to raffle off at the dealerships and run online contests! Additionally, this gave us the idea to reach out to ski and snowboard manufacturers who were happy to contribute free items for our digital engagements with customers! By being flexible in our path we greatly benefitted from this particular challenge.

While we grasp the concept of flexibility in our personal lives sometimes we forget to apply this same adventurous attitude in our business lives. If you aren't flexible or adventurous in the digital decades ahead you will find a path that is difficult to follow to success.

Sour Apples to Success: Steve Jobs

Being flexible is highly encouraged throughout this chapter, yet you should be *inflexible* when it comes to anything that compromises being true to yourself (Chapter 6). How you arrive at your destination is often a winding road. The road is seldom paved with roses and you are likely to encounter some rotten apples along the way. These rotten apples will be part of the story, your story. This excerpt from Steve Jobs's commencement address at Stanford University in 2005 illustrates how circuitous our journey can be:

> Woz (Steve Wozniak) and I started Apple in my parents' garage when I was 20. We worked hard, and in 10 years Apple had grown, from just the two of us in a garage, into a $2 billion company with over 4,000 employees. We had just released our finest creation—the Macintosh—a year earlier, and I had just turned 30. And then I got fired.
>
> I didn't see it then, but it turned out that getting fired from Apple was the best thing that could have ever happened to me. The heaviness of being successful was replaced by the lightness of being a beginner again, less sure about everything.
>
> It freed me to enter one of the most creative periods of my life. During the next five years, I started a company named NeXT; another company named Pixar, and fell in love with an amazing woman who would become my wife.
>
> Your work is going to fill a large part of your life, and the only way to be truly satisfied is to do what you believe is great work. And the only way to do great work is to love what you do.
>
> If you haven't found it yet, keep looking. Don't settle. As with all matters of the heart, you'll know when you find it. And, like any great relationship, it just gets better and better as the years roll on. So keep looking until you find it. Don't settle.

Jobs's path was a different one than he envisioned but led to a positive result for all. Think about your own life. Looking back on a similar circumstance, what was the result? Did you use the experience and leverage it later to get you closer to your desired goals? Or did you allow these changes in path to negatively consume you? Maintain flexibility in your path but stay firm in your destination.

LIFE STAMPS

Oscar Morales

It sometimes takes courage to be a digital leader, and courage is something that 35-year-old Colombian software programmer Oscar Morales has in spades. He knew his mission in life would be to give back to society and to his home country of Colombia.

One day an opportunity to help his country presented itself to Morales and he took action. The news reported that FARC (Fuerzas Armadas Revolucionarias de Colombia), the ruthless guerilla, terrorist army in Colombia, would release a hostage boy. The boy had been born into captivity after his mother was captured and enslaved. It was found that FARC, however, didn't have this four-year-old boy— they had released him into the jungle two years prior. A search team then found the boy, but he was near death with a broken shoulder, malaria, and tuberculosis.

Morales was horrified by the story of the boy and tired of living in fear of the FARC. He believed others felt the same. He determined that part of his mission in life was to stand up against the FARC. Often, in previous protests against the FARC, people didn't reveal their identities for security purposes. Morales wanted to take a different route digitally. He started a Facebook page: One Million Voices against FARC. People's real identities would be used, harnessing the power of a collective voice. It was also dangerous, however, as several family members and Morales received death threats from the FARC. With the help of over 400,000 volunteers, in less than a month after starting the Facebook page, 12 million people flooded the streets in 200 cities and 40 countries across the globe in protest of the FARC.[3]

"We expected the idea to resound with a lot of people but not so much and not so quickly," said Morales.[4]

Morales said the campaign convinced people to say: "We don't tolerate the kidnappings and we want our freedom." Months later many freed hostages said they'd heard our protest in captivity on a radio and it gave them hope they'd survive. Also, a new law says former FARC members will only go to jail for eight years then they'll get education and housing; many FARC members left and rejoined society. They are quitting in large numbers."[5]

Morales points out that this movement couldn't have been made possible without Facebook, but it's also imperative to tie in offline activities to digital ones, "Online movements have greater possibilities of success when they are connected to present reality."[6] Morales identified an unexpected opportunity to contribute toward the betterment of society and he went for it.

Business Cycles

Flexibility is important in the new digital world. Many businesses historically set 10-year and 15-year plans. These planning periods were even longer in Japan and China. Business cycles, however, are becoming shorter and shorter. As a result, it is increasingly difficult for companies to stay on top of their industries. Since 1982, 21 of the 30 companies that make up the Dow Jones Industrial Average (DJIA) have been replaced by other companies. This statistic is incredible: in less than 20 years only 30 percent of the world's largest corporations were still considered significant enough to say in the DJIA.

AOL, Yahoo, MySpace, and eBay stayed on top of the mountain for years rather than decades. Facebook, Google, Apple, and others will face similar cycles. Or, to paraphrase Facebook founder Mark Zuckerberg, "Our competition hasn't been invented yet."

The CMO (chief marketing officer) of a Fortune 500 company asked me to help him build a five- to seven-year marketing plan. I explained that in 2007 Facebook wasn't a top 20 most visited site, but by 2011 it was the most visited site in the world. That was a span of less than five years. So I recommended that while a five- or 10-year planning horizon had value, his company would be better served by focusing on a six-month to two-year plan that was extremely flexible. Further, since the nature of their business environment was so uncertain, his firm should develop a range of alternate future (or "what if") scenarios with corresponding action plans. This setup would prepare the company to act immediately should any of these eventualities occur.

I was brought in to work with a small business that wanted to improve its mobile applications and mobile Website. The team started diving immediately into what it should look like, what products should be featured, the specific language, and other details. Some of the debate became a bit heated and then the question was asked, what is our goal? The room became quiet and nobody supplied an answer. Taking a step back we then mapped out four critical questions that must be asked at the start of any digital project:

1. **Goals**: What does success look like? What are we trying to accomplish, how are we going to measure it, and most importantly how is this helping our customer, client, or volunteers (non-profit)?

2. **Strategy**: What is our plan to get to our destination?

3. **Action**: What decisive actions are needed to execute the strategy?

4. **Rapid Contingency Plans**: The only thing we know for certain is that some items aren't going to go as planned. To the best of our knowledge what contingency plans can we put in place and be ready to execute?

> "There is no point getting caught up in the worst-case scenario because if it doesn't happen then you have wasted time. If it does happen then you have lived it twice."
> —MICHAEL J. FOX

Whether considering business, organizational, or personal development, clear goals, solid strategy, decisive action, and rapidly deployable contingency plans will serve you well.

DIGITAL DEEDS

Your Digital Compass

It's a good practice periodically to look back at a few days or weeks of your posts, emails, and texts. Is the content of your digital documentary in line with the visions you have for your life, or have you veered from your path? As I stressed in my book *Socialnomics*, we should no longer look back and say "what did I do with my life?" You can see changes in your life in real time in what you are posting.

Digital tools allow us to see what we are achieving (or not achieving) in real time. Take advantage of them by inspecting your digital footprints: are you walking toward your destination? If not, figure out how to take corrective action or work with the new challenges and changes you are facing. Remember, it's not the destination that's important, it's the journey—remember your past goals, but stay flexible in moving forward to achieve your new ones.

Shape Your Path

A marathon runner without a watch or distance markers, when asked how she is doing, doesn't have all the necessary information to answer that question. You need to shape your path, otherwise others could control your destiny. Although we may not always choose the right path in life, or the path may change, if we map our course, we at least have a sense of where we are and where we want to go.

And, it's easy to go the wrong way in the digital age. It used to be that we had the choice of if we wanted to sell our products online and how many banner ads we wanted to run pushing people to the site? Now the questions include: *Should we sell our products via mobile? What about Social Commerce? Should we block social media sites from our employees? Do our customers find it an invasion if we text them customer service responses? Is our presence on StumbleUpon great enough? Is my small business giving enough back to the local community—or are we negligent and subject to criticism on local blogs? Should our non-profit solicit digital volunteers or do we lose too much control? Does my small business have time to reach out to happy customers on Twitter or should I respond only to the negative ones? Should we allow our customers to rate our products online? As a B2B company should we be running community discussions on LinkedIn? Should my small business buy the international URL domains for my business name in case I want to expand in the future? Do we have all the international digital trademarks?*

Choice and change is good as long as it doesn't distract us from staying on our own personal yellow brick road to fulfillment. You will go down the wrong path when you set big goals and you will experience failure, but remember to fail fast, fail forward, and fail better as discussed earlier. Through all the challenges you face, remain flexible, without straying from your true mission in life.

> "People are like stained-glass windows. They sparkle and shine when the sun is out, but when the darkness sets in, their true beauty is revealed only if there is light from within."
> —ELISABETH KÜBLER-ROSS

CHAPTER FOURTEEN

Recreate Yourself

*"Life is what we make it,
always has been, always will be."*
—GRANDMA MOSES

An interesting exercise is to assume you were just fired from your current job. Or as Andy Grove, the CEO of Intel puts it: "If the board got rid of us and took over the company, what would they do differently than what we are currently doing? Why don't we do that right now, why don't we walk out that door and come back in and do what they (the board) would do?"

Taking Grove's thought process one-step further, ask yourself this question: If you, your company, or your product no longer existed what would be the loss to society? To your family? If your answer is it *wouldn't* create much of a void, you may reconsider your purpose. Don't forget to continuously pose the question asked earlier in the book, "What do I want to become when I grow up?" A digital leader is going to leave a permanent mark on this world. If you don't think a void will be created if you leave the position at your company, church, organization, or non-profit then you aren't creating a large enough footprint. Most likely you are being "nibbled to death" by ducks, meaning that you are focusing too much on trivial items, responding to the latest digital fire, and that you aren't progressing on your career or life map.

The good news is that it's never too late in life to go after your dreams or create a new map. As discussed earlier, one of the most successful entrepreneurs in history didn't get his start until the age of 52. Let's take a closer look at Ray Kroc's story.

Ray Kroc

"I was 52 years old. I had diabetes and incipient arthritis. I had lost my gall bladder and most of my thyroid gland in earlier campaigns, but I was convinced that the best was ahead."

—RAY KROC

"It's easy to have principles when you're rich. The important thing is to have principles when you're poor."

—RAY KROC

At the age of four, Ray Kroc's father took him to a phrenologist, a person who determines fate based on the shape of someone's skull. The phrenologist told young Ray Kroc that he would someday work in food service.[1]

It took five decades for this prediction to come to fruition, as Kroc tried his hand at driving an ambulance, selling paper cups, and even playing the piano. When the time came, it was well worth the wait for Kroc and for the world. As Ray Kroc said, "I was an overnight success all right, but 30 years is a long, long night."[2]

In 1954, as a 52-year-old multi-mixer salesman, Kroc visited the McDonald's brothers in San Bernadino, California, with the intent of selling them more multi-mixers for their malted milkshakes. The result is one of the greatest entrepreneurial stories in history.

"I went out to California because I'd never had someone order eight multi-mixers at once. So I went to the restaurant and I was amazed. I stood in line and talked with people and I said I've never stood in line for a hamburger in my life. They said, well, you would be glad you did here. They were serving hamburgers for 15¢, french fries for 10¢, and milkshakes for 20¢. And, basically, that was the menu. They had coke, orange, and root beer, but that was the menu. Very simple, very controlled, very clean, and very orderly and I said, that's for me."[3]

Ray didn't see his future in selling mulitmixers, instead his vision now was in burgers and fries. Despite the risks, Kroc's entrepreneurial spirit prevailed, and on April 15, 1955, he opened his first McDonald's in Des Plaines, Illinois. Three years later, in 1958, McDonald's sold its 100 millionth hamburger. By 1965 there would be over 700 McDonald's franchises. The success of the franchise grew based primarily on the mantra of ensuring all restaurants were consistent and clean throughout the world.[4]

> "If you work just for money, you'll never make it, but if you love what you're doing and you always put the customer first, success will be yours."
>
> —RAY KROC

Just as we will discuss in Section 5: People, Kroc understood that in order to achieve success he couldn't do it alone. Rather, he chose a different path: convincing both franchisees and suppliers to buy into the vision of not working *for* McDonald's, but *with* McDonald's. He promoted the slogan, "In business for yourself, but not by yourself." His philosophy was based on the simple principle of a three-legged stool: one leg was McDonald's, the second, the franchisees, and the third, McDonald's suppliers. The stool was only as strong as the three legs.

DIGITAL DEEDS

Selecting a Digital Mentor

Recreating yourself can be daunting. Selecting a digital mentor will help. Determine a leader you admire. Spend at least 20 minutes a day watching their his or her activity. Pay attention to:

- ► Who is he conversing with?
- ► What topics does she post and in what tone?
- ► Why does he post?
- ► When does she post?
- ► Where does he post and what tools or sites does he use?

The best digital mentor is generally someone that is in your industry or shares similar interests—someone that you find intriguing. Learn from these mentors and practice what they are doing.

> *"Luck is a dividend of sweat. The more you sweat, the luckier you get."*
> —RAY KROC

Kroc died on January 14, 1984 at the age of 82 and was estimated to be worth $500 million. His passion got him to this point. Even when confined to a wheelchair, Kroc still went to work in his San Diego office nearly every day. He kept a watchful eye over the McDonald's restaurant near this office, often phoning the manager to remind him to pick up the trash, clean his lot, and turn on the lights at night.

Taking a page from Ray Kroc, no matter how late in life, we can always find a passion that inspires us. Consider Dara Torres, who won an Olympic gold medal at the age of 41 when most swimmers she competed against where 17-21. Her key to success? "Treat people the way you want to be treated. And don't put an age limit on your dreams."

While neither Torres nor Kroc are digital savants, what they show is that it's never too late to recreate yourself. They did this the hard way, without benefit of the digital tools that we have at our disposal. If you are a grandmother that is in charge of fundraising for one of the world's largest non-profits, the concepts of digital leadership are just as applicable to you as they are to a teenager trying to become the next Lady Gaga. Having an attitude of "I'll never be able to learn all these new digital items or recreate myself as a digital leader" is a cop-out. First, nobody can stay abreast of all the digital challenges, secondly every advancement of technology is making the tools easier to use, not harder. A good example is Twitter. It take less than three minutes to sign up for an account and begin posting 140 characters or less.

> *"If you work just for money, you'll never make it, but if you love what you're doing and you always put the customer first, success will be yours."*
> —RAY KROC

Ric Elias Survivor of US Air Flight 1549

Ric Elias was one of the fortunate survivors of US Air flight 1549 that Captain "Sully" Sullenberger successfully landed in the Hudson River on January 15, 2009. He gave the following insight and advice at his talk at TED (Technology, Entertainment, Design) in March 2011 about three things he learned from the experience that brought him to make major changes in his life:

1. It all changes in an instant. We all have a bucket list and things we want to do in life. I thought of all the people I wanted to reach out to and couldn't. All the fences that I wanted to mend; all the experiences I wanted to have and never did.
2. I regretted the time I wasted with things that did not matter with people that do matter. I decided to eliminate negative energy from my life.
3. I had a sense of dying, it is not scary, it's almost as if we are preparing for it our entire lives. But, at the same time, it was very sad. I love my life. That sadness framed in one thought that I only wish for one thing. I only wish to see my kids grow up. . . Above all, the only goal in life I have is to be a good parent. I was given a miracle gift of not dying that day. I was given another gift, the ability to see into the future and come back and live differently.[5]

The Great Zamperini

We will all encounter hurdles and be wronged by people in our lives. Though we have no control over this fact, we do have control over our reaction to these negative experiences. Louis Zamperini's incredible story should cause us to pause whenever modern society or technology seems to overwhelm or derail us from our desired path and consider.

Louis Zamperini was born in 1917 and spent much of his youth as a mischievous child, often finding himself on the wrong side of the law. To corral this energy, his older brother

Pete encouraged him to join the high school track team. Soon, a star was born and Zamperini earned a scholarship to the University of Southern California (USC). At the age of 19, the handsome Zamperini was the youngest long distance runner to compete in the 1936 Olympics. While he was much overmatched in the race by the older competitors, Zamperini finished 8th and turned in one of the fastest last laps the world had ever seen. Hitler was impressed enough to invite Zamperini over to shake his hand. In 1938 Zamperini set a national collegiate mile record that would not be broken until 15 years later. Many speculated that Zamperini would be the first in history to run a mile under four minutes. Zamperini had his eyes set on gold for the 1940 Olympics, but alas this would never be.

The United States became engulfed in World War II and Zamperini was deployed to the South Pacific in 1942, assigned as a bombardier aboard a B-24 named the *Green Hornet*. After several successful combat missions, Zamperini and his crew crashed into the Ocean. Of the 11 crew members only three survived the crash, while eight perished. Zamperini and the two other survivors struggled to climb aboard a life raft. They were out of provisions after the first night. From there they had to survive by drinking rain water and eating any food they were able to catch. They would wait for an Albatross to land on the raft, kill it and eat the putrid meat. Occasionally they were fortunate enough to catch a pilot fish from the backs of the sharks that were constantly circling and bumping the bottom of the raft.

In an effort to avoid insanity, the three quizzed each other constantly and told stories about back home. On the fortieth day, one of the three crew members died and they had a burial at sea. On the forty-seventh day after drifting close to 2,000 miles they finally saw land. Their joy was short lived as they were captured by the Japanese and placed in a prison camp not registered with the Red Cross. The U.S. Government declared Zamperini dead and an entire country mourned.

The treatment of prisoners by the Japanese was so harsh that over 33 percent of all American prisoners captured in the

South Pacific died.[6] Till the end of the war, Zamperini was starved, tortured, and beaten daily, often to unconsciousness. Zamperini was one of the lucky ones to make it back home. However, his body had been so severely beaten that he'd never be able to run competitively again. He also suffered from severe post traumatic stress syndrome and turned to alcohol. Zamperini was on the brink of divorce when Billy Graham and his message helped turn Zamperini's life around. Zamperini was able to forgive his Japanese captors and returned several times to Japan in person. These guards that had treated him so harshly that they were incarcerated for war crimes were bewildered and confused when Zamperini offered them hugs and bibles instead of disdain.

Zamperini was able to turn his life around and in so doing he has touched the hearts and minds of thousands as he's traveled the world as a motivational speaker. He has become a living symbol of human determination. He returned to Japan in January 1998 to run a leg of the Olympic torch relay. Torrance High School, where he attended, has since named its home stadium Zamperini Stadium. The entrance plaza at USC's track & field stadium was named Louis Zamperini Plaza in 2004.

> *"We are stubborn on vision. We are flexible on details . . .We don't give up on things easily."*
> —**JEFF BEZOS**, Amazon

While Zamperini's path in life took a divergent course, he was able to overcome all of life's challenges and in doing so his destination ended right where he always wanted, in greatness. Zamperini was able to recreate himself under circumstances that I'd argue most of us will be fortunate to never have to face. So whenever we believe that it will be too difficult to change our path in order to achieve greatness, we should take inspiration from Zamperini. Or if we get in the mindset that there is only one way for us to achieve greatness, so that if we miss that window we will lose all hope. If Zamperini thought his only path to greatness was via track and field what a shame that would have been for all those lives he was able to touch. He was probably able to positively affect more people's lives than if he had won a gold medal. Digital leaders understand there are a multitude of paths and opportunities in order to effectively change our lives and in turn the lives of others.

Viral Videos: 5 Musts

If you find that you are unsatisfied with your personal or work life, look for a positive way to recreate yourself, or even your company. Changing who you are, or overhauling some aspect of your organization, may be the first step toward personal fulfillment. Video footage is a main component of your digital footprint, so use it to your personal or professional advantage in creating change.

Keep in mind that any video can potentially go viral, so you always want to act in a way that you can be proud of—once a video is online, it has a life of its own. If a video of yours goes viral, the size of your digital footprint is exponentially enlarged and, if it portrays you or your company in a positive light, you are fortunate to have achieved this notoriety. But "viral" isn't a video strategy: we cannot control what goes viral, the viewer does. We can, however, take five steps to give our video greater viral potential.

1. **Good Music:** Unless your video is of a cute baby or an extraordinary kitten, the music you select will be critical to its success. In various countries, YouTube's Content ID program allows you to use copyrighted music. As a quid pro quo, a pop-up window will display during your video listing the song title and artist and allowing users to click through to purchase the song. YouTube and the music label then share the revenue from the sale.

   My advice is to find successful viral videos that are similar to the one you want to produce, and determine what music they are using. You may seriously consider using the same music as it has proven to be successful, and the music owner isn't blocking it.

   Keep in mind that your idea will not be new—as of the writing of this book every minute there are 48 hours of video being uploaded to YouTube.[7] Review videos similar to what you want to do and take note of what is working and not working for these particular videos.

2. **Short and sweet:** Definitely keep your video under five minutes; preferably to a minute or less. In *Enchantment*, author Guy Kawasaki displayed data from research firm Visible Measures that showed 19.4 percent of viewers abandoned a video within the first 10 seconds, and by 60 seconds 44 percent had stopped watching.[8] Lead with your most eye-popping content to gain and hold viewer attention. Don't build to a crescendo that may never be viewed.

3. **Viewer is king:** Only *viewers* make videos go viral. Yet, often we produce videos from the vantage point of what we want to get out of them. This approach is wrong. We need to constantly ask, am I providing something of value for the viewers? What do they want to get out of it?

4. **Other purpose:** Don't produce a video simply hoping that it goes viral. Produce a video with a clear purpose in mind. If it goes viral because you adhered to the three suggestions above, it's a bonus!

5. **Share:** When people ask for your original file so they can use it in their presentations or for other purposes—share it. Sure, there will be a few that do so with malicious intent, but they will be in the minority. The majority will be adding distribution points and beacons for your great work. They may make the video into something cooler that you never dreamed of as well.

Guided by these five maxims I produced several videos explaining the power of social media. Viewers pushed these viral, and they became the world's most viewed social media videos.

Joe Pa

Joe Paterno, Penn State's famous football coach, says that his passion is teaching the youth of America. He does not do his teaching in the classroom, but rather on the football field. Aside from being a tremendous teacher, he has won more college football games than any coach in history. Joe Pa, as he is affectionately known, is still coaching in his 80s and has already been inducted into the Football Hall of Fame. He is truly a living legend.

Upon graduating from Brown in 1950, his father questioned his career choice of going into football. "For God's sake, what did you go to college for?" Rather than listen to his skeptical father, Joe went after his passion and never looked back, finding his dream come to life with Penn State. During his career, Paterno turned down lucrative offers to coach the University of Michigan Wolverines, Pittsburgh Steelers, and the New England Patriots.

When Penn State struggled to win football games between 2000 and 2004, many targeted Paterno and requested that he step down from the head coaching job. For Paterno this wasn't simply a job, this was his passion and he didn't want to abandon it. He was, however, self-aware enough to know that if he couldn't prepare the team to win, then he would be doing a disservice to those young men as well as the Penn State faithful.

In a speech to the Duquesne Club (Pittsburgh) in May of 2005, Paterno announced he would consider retirement if the 2005 football team had a disappointing season. "If we don't win some games, I've got to get my rear end out of here. Simple as that." [9] Penn State went on that year to become Champions of the Big Ten with an 11-1 mark, and defeated Florida State in the 2006 Orange Bowl. In 2010, the team finished in the Top 25. More importantly, they had the highest graduation rate of any Top 25 team and were in the 89 percentile of all the college football teams in the country.[10] At this writing (2011), Paterno is in his sixty-second year on the coaching staff at Penn State University. During his time on campus, "Joe Pa" can often be seen frequenting the campus creamery to enjoy his favorite ice cream, "Peachy Paterno."

Even if you are the most successful coach of all time, a Hall of Fame member, and have an ice cream named after you, you still will encounter hurdles going forward. You also will not be able to please everyone in life. The key is to keep trying. Don't ever assume you will reach the end of your path and put your feet up to relax.

"Joe Pa" continues to coach after 60 years because: a) he loves what he does, and b) he knows life is a journey, not a destination. If it were about the destination, he would have hung up his famous black sneakers and dark glasses after his first National Title. Yet, he kept at it and part of the fun of it was adapting to change. His core beliefs remained intact, but he changed with the times otherwise he wouldn't have been able to keep on winning. The same holds true for digital leaders, what works today most likely will not work tomorrow so we constantly need to evolve.

As this book went to press, news broke of a sexual scandal involving one of Paterno's top assistants who has been with Penn State for over 30 years. The major allegations are from 2002 and surround the sexual abuse of underage boys. While Paterno isn't criminally libel, it may turn out he is morally libel. This offline incident, not directly involving him, could tarnish his legacy forever. Will Paterno practice the items discussed throughout this book and maintain his legacy on Penn State's campus? Or will an ugly truth be revealed, tarnishing his reputation permanently? His legacy will be marred if it is found that he could have done more to stop these alleged crimes. If you surround yourself with the wrong people it will eventually bring you down. Consider how this case has unfolded, as it touches on everything discussed in this book on leadership and legacy. Paterno's ultimate legacy will be determined by what happens. More importantly, let us all pray for the victims involved.

Leaving a Void

We should make a habit of reviewing our digital footprint in real time. This action will help indicate if we are heading in the direction that we deserve. Also, we can determine if we are leaving a stamp that matters: Are we positively influencing others and the world? Are items we post being reposted? Are people responding or commenting on them? If we

> "I hoped for the best and planned for the worst."[11]
>
> —TIM FERRIS

do something offline are people posting positive items that contribute to our digital shadow?

Will there be a void left if we move from our current position and activities? When Bill Gates left Microsoft he left a void. When Steve Jobs passed he left a void. When Randy Pausch passed he left a void. When Joe Paterno retires he will leave a void. Are we just doing busy work or are we changing the world, either locally or globally? If the answer is that we aren't leaving a mark that matters then it is time for us to evolve or recreate ourselves. We can use digital tools to help us accomplish this goal moving forward.

SECTION FOUR: MAP

Key Takeaways
- ▶ Be firm in your destination, but flexible with your path
- ▶ Your digital footprint reminds you, in real time, how you are living your life
- ▶ Set laughable goals
- ▶ Success is a choice
- ▶ You only get when you give
- ▶ It's never too late to start
- ▶ Live as if you've been given a second chance at life

PEOPLE

1. Your friends and followers are digital currency: invest in them early and often

2. Nobody achieves greatness alone: learn to digitally and physically surround yourself with great people

3. Some items are still best handled offline

SIMPLE: success is the result of simplification & focus

TRUE: be true to your passion

ACT: nothing happens without action—take the first step

MAP: goals and visions are needed to get where you want to be

PEOPLE: success doesn't happen alone

CHAPTER FIFTEEN

Connections = Currency

"The problem with the world is we draw the circle of our family too small."

—MOTHER TERESA

How many friends do you have in your social networks? How many followers? How many are from foreign countries? What is your influence score? These questions are part of the younger generation's everyday dialogue. The ability to statistically measure our relationships is new, but the importance of our relationships is as old as time itself. Do you remember the old adage, "it's not what you know, it's who you know"? This statement is just as true today.

Dale Carnegie's *How to Win Friends and Influence People* was first published in 1936 and is still one of the bestselling books in the world. While we don't know what the digital landscape will look like tomorrow, we do know that relationships, both offline and digital, will be necessary for success. At some point in life we will all need to stand on others' shoulders to reach our goals.

A positive trend today is that individuals are being judged less on their personal accomplishments, and more on how they have helped improve society. This is often called "social good," and there are plenty of insightful books on the topic.

But I thought it was important to introduce the subject at the beginning of this chapter because it directly relates to how we can develop our best digital shadow.

Social Good

In 2010, I was fortunate to give a keynote speech in South Africa prior to the opening ceremonies of soccer's World Cup. While there, I heard an observation by Nelson Mandela (as paraphrased by Maya Angelou) that was fascinating. He said, "On a personal level people aren't likely to remember what you said or what you did, but the thing people will most likely remember about you is how you treated them." He also expounded that "It is better to lead from behind and to put others in front, especially when you celebrate victory when nice things occur. If you take the front line when there is danger, then people will appreciate your leadership."

The same idea holds true for companies as the public has become increasingly concerned with *how* organizations conduct their business. In the groundbreaking book *True North* by Bill George, former Novartis CEO Daniel Vasella said, "I can do what is right, based on my moral compass. At the end of the day, the only thing that matters is what we do for other people."[1]

At Levi Strauss, as much as 40 percent of management bonuses are based on measures of leadership in ethics, human relations, and effective communication.[2] Now that most communication is tracked in a digital format, companies are adopting similar policies out of necessity.

When I was interviewing author Malcolm Gladwell (*The Tipping Point* and *Outliers*) for this book, he indicated that a fundamental shift has occurred. He said that "consumers desire, and are demanding, partnerships with companies." Historically it would be tough as a customer to have an ongoing relationship with a company. With social and mobile technologies, however, staying connected and getting in touch with someone at a company or establishment is easier than ever before. This ability applies to large enterprises, small business, schools, universities, non-profits, and organizations. Now that customers know they have this option, they more readily demand it.

DIGITAL DEEDS

Giving 100 percent on LinkedIn

When a LinkedIn profile is deemed incomplete, it's most likely lacking recommendations from your peers, a profile photo or, perhaps, where you went to college. In the upper right of your LinkedIn profile is a bar that indicates what adjustments are required to get to 100%—it's that easy. Making sure your LinkedIn profile is 100% complete isn't just important for job seekers. Listed below are reasons why every person and company should have a complete LinkedIn profile to maintain connections:

1. LinkedIn profiles register high in Google and Bing search results, so it's important to have a good photo and well written text
2. Users with a 100 percent complete LinkedIn profile are 40 times more likely to receive an interview request than those that don't[3]
3. You need to network before you need your network: LinkedIn is a great tool for this process
4. Potential employees will review a company's LinkedIn page to determine if a company is worthy of their talents (yes, it cuts both ways)
5. Other parents will view your digital connections before considering you for car-pooling, book club, or bridge
6. Many will judge your stature based on the people you are digitally connected with. Professionally, the first place others will look is on LinkedIn
7. You can put hyperlinks in your profile that point to your websites or blogs providing a great source of traffic as well as "link-juice" (more people that link to your website). Google rewards this increased traffic by placing your websites/blogs higher in the search listings

Building Internal Connections and Community

A company is not only judged externally, but internally by employees as well. It's no fluke that the Starbucks brand was able to achieve success within the Facebook community. Employees that feel a strong connection to their company convey this affinity both in-person and digitally to the firm's consumers. The helpful Starbucks barista mentality that has been instilled in the company culture for decades has been appropriately and seamlessly incorporated into digital communities.

This connection was all based on Starbucks CEO Howard Schultz's vision. Schultz recalls how, at seven years old, he was forever changed by the news that his deliveryman father had slipped on a sheet of ice and broken his ankle. The accident cost Schultz's father his job and the family its health insurance and economic security. That experience eventually led Schultz to create a global business, one built not on lattes and Frappuccinos, but on the conviction that every worker deserves respect and healthcare. Even when Starbucks's stock was plummeting as a result of the recession that started in 2008, Schultz resisted suggestions to cut the costly health insurance for employees.

"Those early memories are with me all the time. I wanted to build the kind of company my father never had a chance to work for, where you would be valued and respected, no matter where you came from, the color of your skin, or your level of education," said Schultz.[4] Schultz never envisioned that this philosophy a few decades later would have a positive influence on Starbucks's social media endeavors. This should be a lesson to all of us that, in a fully transparent world, doing social good produces winners.

In his book *Onward* Schultz notes, "Customers are holding the companies they do business with—including Starbucks—to higher standards. No business can do well for its shareholders without first doing well by all the people the business touches. For us, that means doing our best to treat everyone with respect and dignity, from coffee farmers and baristas to customers and neighbors. I understand that striving to achieve profitability without sacrificing humanity sounds lofty. But I have always refused to abandon that purpose—even when Starbucks and I lost our way."[5]

At Starbucks, Schultz was willing to try new things. He wanted to give the customer more of a voice, so he launched a consumer friendly site called Greenstorm (later changed to My Starbucks Idea) to solicit ideas. Instead of having two to three folks from Starbucks marketing, he enlisted 50 Starbucks partners to help supply answers and responses to the customer. To date the site has received over 1,000 ideas and they've implemented 130 of them.

> *"The best and most beautiful things in the world cannot be seen or even touched—they must be felt with the heart."*
>
> **—HELEN KELLER**

The idea of the My Starbucks Idea site isn't what digital leadership is all about. Rather, it's about having the courage and confidence to trust 50 people to help grow and represent the brand. It's about fostering an online community, creating connections, and trusting your customers to behave appropriately within an online community. The community could have just as easily spiraled into a complaint board as a vehicle for positive change. Schultz readily admitted it wasn't possible to test every "what if" scenario. Schultz doesn't like to micromanage, especially when it comes to technology. Instead, Starbucks's digital success across a myriad of digital properties (Facebook, Twitter, Greenstorm) has grown because employees, customers, and partners equally share in its success. Schultz understood it wasn't his to control even if he wanted to and realized, despite the multitude of risks, that he had to trust in his partnership with customers and suppliers.

LIFE STAMPS
Homeless to Harvard

Whether you are climbing your way to the top or are trying to stay on top, you will need help from others. When help is offered, take it. Even if this help is from strangers; which in a digital world it often is.

While most of Liz Murray's success was the result of her hard work, she also understood she would need help along the way to get out of her predicament.

Liz Murray went from sleeping in the hallways of New York City to walking the halls of Harvard. Estranged from her father, Murray became homeless when her mother succumbed to AIDS. Murray completed her high school homework in train stations and hallways. The *New York Times* heard of a homeless high school student getting all A's and ran a story on Murray which helped change her life as it went viral.

"I began receiving handwritten letters of encouragement. Strangers showed up bearing brownies, clothes, books, and even hugs. I didn't realize how good people could be. But now I do, and I can say that the people who helped me have forever changed me. My willingness to be grateful for the things that I already have rather than dwelling on what I don't has helped. Let that be enough, and it will be all the freedom any of us need."[6]

How Many Friends Do You Have?

More and more people, especially potential employers, are checking individuals' digital influence—how many people one is connected to on various digital tools and how much influence they wield (www.klout.com) over these friends and followers. Employers understand that the more connections someone has, the more they serve as a miniature media outlet for the company and its brands. It also means that this person can help recruit others, whether it's for the company or to help coach a little league team.

New employees are the best tool for recruiting other rising stars to the company if the breadth of their network is extensive. As the CEO of Do Something, Nancy Lublin believes, "Millennials don't have traditional boundaries or an old-fashioned sense of privacy. They live out loud; sharing details of their lives with thousands of other people. . . I see their openness as a great opportunity. For instance, when our summer intern tweets and Facebooks about something he achieved at work that's free marketing for Do Something to the 1,500 people in his immediate network. I now ask job applicants how many Facebook friends and Twitter followers they have."[7] Many places are starting to employ similar tactics as Lublin. If you have two similar job candidates but one has 3,000 responsive and active people in her immediate network she is more likely to get hired for the position than someone with only 35 people in his network. The person with 3,000 will have more impact in terms of recruiting, getting the word out on new products, and having the ability to ask her larger network for input.

For their book *The Longevity Project*, psychologists Howard S. Friedman and Leslie R. Martin studied 1,500 boys and girls for up to eight decades (starting in 1921). Some key findings:

- ▶ Having good health, education, relationships, and a job you enjoy were major contributors to happiness
- ▶ People that were involved and focused on accomplishing things lived the longest
- ▶ People that took on challenges and were persistent lived longer than those who relaxed or retired too soon
- ▶ Involving yourself with activities and people that lead you to healthy habits and patterns is one of the best ways to turn your life around[8]

Occasionally we need to seclude ourselves and focus on the task at hand. However, this doesn't mean we need to do so *all the time*. In fact, based on the longevity project, constant seclusions will decrease our happiness, which in turn hurts our leadership capability. While it takes time to foster relationships both digitally and offline, they lead us to healthier habits and patterns. These people we have relationships with may ultimately be part of our group of followers.

Fostering relationships at your company or organization is also critical to accomplishing goals. Jim Keane, president of Steelcase, goes as far to say, despite all the complications with teams, that "teams are the only way to solve problems in a global, interconnected world."[9]

DIGITAL DEEDS

Creating Digital Legions

How do you develop relationships online? How do you create massive followings for your personal brand or product?

1. **Show that you care:** Social media users don't follow the most talented people or biggest brands. Instead they follow people and brands they believe care about them. People who have 10 million followers can't know every individual they are connected to online. However, these people still need to make their followers feel that they helped them achieve their fame or that the followers of a company are contributing to its continued success. When possible it needs to feel local. The more you can exhibit that you understand a person's local need the stronger the digital connection will become. There are simple ways to do this; for instance on LinkedIn you can see where someone went to college and include a reference to that campus (the more specific the better) in your digital conversations.

2. **Provide value:** Provide value to your audience. It's not what you are trying to accomplish, but rather what they are trying to accomplish that's important. Try and help them out. You only get when you give.

3. **Be honest and diligent:** Don't try to project a faultless persona, instead be yourself. The reasons that many celebrities have risen to popularity via digital beginnings is because they gave "behind the scenes" access into their lives, showing that they too have doubt, worry, and concern. Also, by not trying to portray an image of perfection, you are able to respond to many more fans and customers than if you are worried whether the proper wording is "effect" or "affect." Plus, have you ever noticed that "perfect people" lack in the likeability department?

The Magic Touch

Whether you are an individual or business, you need to associate with the right people. Don't be afraid to distance yourself from a friend or customer that isn't having a positive impact. This can be difficult to do, but necessary.

Now, I'm not suggesting that you abandon everyone. In some circumstances, if you can be a positive influence for another individual, please be one! It can be highly rewarding to positively influence someone else's life. Realistically, however, to have the greatest positive impact on your life and others, you need to select some relationships over others.

A good example is when a young man overcomes a difficult situation (e.g., economic, broken home, parent with substance abuse) and successfully lands in the National Basketball Association (NBA). It's imperative when this happens that the individual surround himself with the friends and family that have his best interests at heart. So often these young men fail to distance themselves from those that are purely using them to put money in their own pockets.

It's not uncommon to see an NBA rookie with a posse of "pilot fish" (fish that take free rides on whales, sharks) and more often than not the story ends in bankruptcy. When an NBA rookie's life changes dramatically for the better, he often doesn't make the appropriate changes for sustainable success. He fails to surround himself with the right people.

The majority of you reading this book are probably saying, "what does this have to do with me? I can't break a 100 in golf, let alone be a professional athlete." The example just happens to be an athletic one, but the concept of ensuring we surround ourselves with the right people, especially when we experience success, is applicable whether you drive an ice cream truck or own the dairy farm.

As discussed elsewhere in the book, one pro athlete that has experienced considerable success following his playing career is Magic Johnson. "When Kareem [Abdul-Jabbar] went broke and his agent took all his money, I think that changed my whole life," said Johnson.[10]

In order to achieve his goals, Johnson understood that he needed to disassociate from individuals that didn't have his best interests at heart. This task was hard for him, just as it will be hard for you or your company (firing bad customers). Firing bad customers may be a new concept to many companies, but some customers just aren't worth retaining—they actually cost the company money. Some bookstores and coffee shops that offer free WiFi and nice chairs often have to kick out patrons that aren't buying anything but are taking up space for potential customers. In your business, bad customers may be tying up your customer service or speaking ill of your product to others. A partnership is a two way street: good companies deserve good customers, just as good customers deserve good companies.

In the process, did Johnson turn his back on his true friends and his hometown of Lansing, Michigan? Hardly. Johnson is a fixture at Michigan State basketball games, his alma mater, and a place where a giant bronzed statue of him permanently resides on campus. He has given generously to the Lansing community both in time and money. However, on an individual basis, he realized that he needed to simply smile and wave to the old friend on the corner, and keep on driving.

Magic made his millions by investing in predominately black urban communities. Beyond a potential business opportunity, he felt this use of his money was the best way he could give back to the world. His efforts as a leader to create social good have resulted in financial success as well. Magic Johnson Enterprises' investment history includes partnerships with Starbucks, several inner city movie theaters, T.G.I. Friday's, 24 Hour Fitness, Sodexo, Aetna, and Best Buy. All told his business spreads across 89 cities in 21 states. In 2010 Magic sold 105 of his Starbucks franchises for an estimated $75-$100 million off an original investment of $405,000—quite a nice profit.[11] Forbes at one point calculated Johnson Enterprises' net worth at around $700 million.

Secret Agent L

A mysterious woman was going around Pittsburgh dropping off "random acts of kindness." These acts included little things like a $5 Starbucks gift card on a windshield, someone's parking meter being paid, or flowers on an office worker's desk. All of these gifts were accompanied by an inspirational note signed *Secret Agent L*.

The identity of *Secret Agent L* was revealed at a fundraiser for the National Alliance on Mental Illness. Pittsburgh blogger Laura Miller said she got the idea when one of her readers suggested, "Instead of giving me something for my birthday go do a random act of kindness for someone and you can call yourself *Secret Agent L*."

Millers's Twitter handle is @SecretAgentL and she says, "Social media has changed everything" by allowing her to count close to 2,000 volunteers doing random acts of kindness.[12]

Creating Connections as a Digital Leader

The old adage "it's not what you know, but who you know" has been taken to a whole new level in the digital age. Who we are connected to digitally can quickly open doors in all facets of our lives. It certainly doesn't replace face-to-face interaction at times, but it is a nice complement. It also allows us access to certain individuals (e.g., CEOs, celebrities, politicians) that were not accessible in the past.

To meet new people or foster existing relationships digitally we need to be less concerned with what's good for us and more concerned with what is good for society. What is the social good? We can do this by showcasing to our audience of potential followers that:

a. We care about them
b. We provide items and information of value to them
c. We are honest and diligent

"*Thousands of candle can be lit from a single candle, and the life of the candle will not be shortened. Happiness never decreases by being shared.*"

—**BUDDHA**

If we follow these rules, then we will never be short of connections—today's digital currency. These connections will also contribute to a favorable digital shadow. Because the world is fully transparent, good guys actually finish first. Most importantly, the more positive relationships we develop, the happier we will become.

CHAPTER SIXTEEN

Empower Others

"The older I get, the more I want to keep score.
Will people be better off when I quit
than when I started?"[1]
—BILL CLINTON

As discussed in the last chapter, connections are vital to anyone's success. As a digital leader, however, you can't act like Moses on the mountaintop delivering your commandments and expect everyone to follow. Great ideas can come from anywhere and anyone. As we've built up our connections, part of their value is the wisdom they will be able to supply. Every connection we have knows something that we do not. The key is making sure our connections feel empowered to not only share information, but to move forward and take initiative to help accomplish shared objectives. Timberland's CEO Jeff Swartz puts it this way, "You don't want to be led by someone that has a point of view and is clinging to it despite new data. My mind is open to insight whenever it comes and I'm flexible enough to respond to it."[2]

Bill George is the former CEO of Medtronic, Harvard professor, and author of *Authentic Leadership*. What he discovered during his research and career is even more applicable in a world where we are constantly connected. George concludes that empowerment is key:

To become authentic leaders, we must discard the myth that leadership means having legions of supporters following our direction as we ascend to the pinnacles of power. Only then can we realize that authentic leadership is about empowering others on their journeys . . . the transformation from "I" to "We" is the most important process leaders go through in becoming authentic.[3]

As a digital leader your main role is to create awareness and engagement. You need to provide enough information without causing confusion. You need to make people aware of the situation and help them understand it. The more they understand, the more engaged they become, and they will figure out each other's strengths and weaknesses to accomplish the task.

With the digital revolution, you actually gain more influence as a leader when you share information. Remember that influence has surpassed information in terms of importance because information is cheap and easily accessible. Sharing information, however, doesn't mean bombarding and overwhelming people with content. It's a difficult balance, but the key is to avoid providing too much information that results in confusion. One trick to help avoid giving out too much information is to try removing a sentence from a paragraph and seeing if the paragraph still makes sense; if so, the sentence probably isn't vital. Another trick is to simply keep all information to half a page or shorter.

If your non-profit is running a charitable 10K run and you send two volunteers a quick text telling them you are caught in traffic, then ask if they could please ensure vendor tents are OK and computer registration is up and running, you are instantly empowering your volunteers. The two volunteers quickly determine what needs to be done. Your one volunteer is great at vendor relations and he sets off to check on the tents, while the other volunteer heads over to make sure the computer registration program for runners check-in is ready to go. Along with empowerment and connections come partnerships and results.

Partnerships

Partnerships come in many different forms, but the key to successful ones are those in which two people, or groups, have different strengths. For example, talk shows that have two hosts that are too similar don't usually last long. The same is true in romance (opposites attract) and in business. The goal of the arrangement is to empower both partners, providing support with their unique capabilities.

Just like Magic Johnson understood he needed to surround himself with good basketball players on the court to win, in business he needed to surround himself with great business-people who possessed a different perspective. During an NBA game Magic famously turned to two successful businessmen sitting courtside and asked, "How do I get into business?"

That initial courtside question landed him a meeting with executive powerhouse Michael Ovitz (Creative Artists Agency). Despite being a living legend, Magic was humble, and knew he had to listen to people like Ovitz in order to learn and eventually succeed. Magic recalls (to Don Yeager of suc-cessmagazine.com) the first day that he met Ovitz:

> "I learned a couple of great lessons there with Michael Ovitz," says Johnson. "The first is that if you want to be successful, you have to be willing to use every connection you've got. The second thing I learned is that if you want someone to be your mentor, you better be ready to listen and be humbled," explains Johnson . . . "I had to prove to him I was serious and that I would listen . . . Michael Ovitz treated me like a man who had something to prove, and by that stage of my career, not many people treated me like that. I think I handled it right, and it made a great difference."[4]

Ovitz makes a good point in that we need to use every con-nection we have. Remember our connections only become currency when we actually reach out to others for assistance. If we have done things properly, our connections will be more than willing to help us as we've already helped them in the past! It's difficult to network when you are desperate for help; you must network before you need the network. We also all need to be humble; if we aren't humble then we may not be as open to partnering with others when it would behoove both parties. Magic explains that partnerships have helped him. "Don't be afraid to partner. I believe in partnerships—I have partnered my whole life. There is someone sitting there with expertise I can learn from, and they can learn from me. Then I can bring [that] back to those who live in urban America."[5] Companies need to do the same thing as Magic and treat customers like partners.

Partnerships today don't look like partnerships from the past which were often large and stagnant, with one partner having much more control over another. Instead, partnerships can often exist without contracts. In the case of Apple, a huge reason behind the success of the iPhone was the amount of applications that developers (not Apple) employees developed around the iPhone. In this fluid partnership, if Apple decides to take too favorable a path for itself (in terms of percentage of profits) then the developers may decide to build applications for another platform like Google's Android. Conversely, if the developers abuse the Apple platform by developing inappropriate content then Apple can ban the developers from the platform. In effect there is a tacit "working contract" between both parties. Both are dependent on shared success. In this same vein, if Google's social media network efforts fail, it will be due in large part to not appropriately fostering the necessary partnerships with developers and vendors to help build the platform.

Eliminating Draining Customers

It's also perfectly OK, and recommended, to eliminate customers that digitally drain the organization. To "digitally drain" means that your organization exhausts countless employee hours responding to negative comments on blogs or incendiary tweets from specific customers. These customers may inappropriately and negatively influence others digitally (one-to-one with potential customers) that are considering using your product or service and are wasting your time. Companies sometimes need to "fire" cantankerous customers in order to better serve their best customers. Such a decision can be difficult, but there are times when a customer or client may simply not be a good fit with your organization. With Facebook, Twitter, other online social networks, and mobile applications, you must perform this type of triage with customers that don't make good partners or be digitally drained by these underperformers.

We've already listed some digital listening tools to better determine star clients and customers from the malcontents. It has also become easier for companies to see if particular individuals or customers are a hassle for other companies. Companies can investigate others digital footprints and shadows to determine how much they are worth investing in, if at all.

> *"Children learn more from what you are than what you teach."*
>
> **—W.E.B. DUBOIS**

Oiling a squeaky wheel is much different than oiling a broken one. We need to discover these "broken" customers and move them to the junkyard while giving giant digital hugs to our deserving customers. Junkyard means that we no longer conduct business with this customer. Digital Hugs mean making sure we reply to customers positively posting, that we make it as personal as we can, that we solicit their opinions, and that we make them feel like part of the process. In the offline world, if we saw the customers this would mean the relationship was strong enough that we would emphatically hug them. Too often companies, non-profits, organizations, and small businesses digitally focus on the vocal negative minority and don't digitally hug their biggest supporters.

Brad Anderson, Best Buy's CEO, discovered that 100 million (about 20 percent) of Best Buy's customers were actually costing the company money. If they could focus their energy on the other 80 percent, he figured the stores would be more fun to shop in and they would actually increase their profitability.[6]

Zen of Digital Leadership

Many of the concepts, ideas, and digital tools discussed in this book shouldn't appear overly technical. In other words, realize that if you are a technical neophyte you can still excel in digital leadership. Conversely, if you are a digital savant, remember that offline behavior and leadership constructs of the past centuries are still important.

That being said, there is much that I have gone over in these pages. However when all else fails dealing digitally, you can never go wrong with simply following the golden rule:

> **Buddhism:** Hurt not others in ways that you yourself would find hurtful
>
> **Christianity:** Do unto others what you would have them do unto you: this sums up the Law and the Prophets
>
> **Hinduism:** This is the sum of duty: do naught unto others which would cause you pain if done to you
>
> **Islam:** No one of you is a believer until he desires for his brother that which he desires for himself
>
> **Judaism:** What is hateful to you, do not to your fellow man. That is the entire Law; all the rest is commentary

If you are truly overwhelmed with the digital revolution, the best approach digitally with your friends, family, coworkers, employees, and volunteers is to abide by the golden rule. This is the core to digitally empower others. Treat others how they would like to be treated. This should be easy for all of us. We all follow someone, so when it's our turn to digitally lead we need to remember what we like and don't like as followers.

Three days a week social gaming company Zynga brings in acupuncturists to work on employees. Cofounder Eric Schlermeyer believes it helps ward off illness and enables employees to be more emotionally balanced. "If you treat your employee like an Olympic athlete he/she will provide extraordinary value."[7] Simply put, support your employees and they will support you. Give them the extra attention and benefits they deserve and they will respond positively. By empowering your employees or customers, they will empower you.

Kevin Rose, the founder of digital application company Milk and former Digg CEO, has a $50 monthly expense allocation per employee for them to each buy flowers when needed, enabling employees to truly stop and smell the roses each day. "It's about realizing that beyond our world of writing code, there's a real world," explains Rose.[8]

Negative Posts

Shortly after you were born, a loving parent or relative probably put your feet into some form of malleable putty or plaster. This was designed to preserve your cute little feet for decades to come. This action is relevant for our discussion, because it is the purest your foot will ever be—smooth, no warts or blemishes. It is also the smallest your foot will ever be.

In relation to purity, we can't expect to go through life without getting our feet a little dirty; digital or otherwise. In time we will acquire blemishes on our feet. However, as our feet continue to grow, the percentage of impurities in relation to the size of the foot decrease. The same holds true when it comes to our goal for our digital footprints.

We can't expect to please everyone all the time; so we should expect a few negative digital posts associated with us. Many people and companies take the wrong reactive strategy of focusing all their attention on trying to remove these negative items. A better place to focus our efforts is to proactively post all the good things we are doing, or have someone else post them for us—our digital shadow. If you are following your passion and giving more than you are taking from people, positive digital posts are certain to follow.

If you proactively have hundreds of items out there, then the few negative items are just a small part of an overall story. Think about some of the good books you have read recently. If the book was only 5 pages and you didn't like 2 pages that is probably not a positive impression. However, if the book is 100 pages and you didn't like 2 of the pages, then these two pages are just a small part of a larger picture. We should take the same approach with our life story or company branding; the more pages we produce the less weight the negative items will merit.

Also keep in mind that not all negative comments are bad. If someone points out you have a poppy seed in your teeth prior to doing an interview via Skype or if a reader points out a factual error on your blog, that's helpful feedback. If you are a walking tour company in Amsterdam and you receive a negative review with a comment like "they never gave us a break; way too much walking," that review will be seen as a positive endorsement for those travelers that love walking.

Focus on Positive Feedback

As companies and individuals, we need to avoid the knee-jerk reaction of spending all our time dealing with, or worrying over, the vocal minority. Bazaarvoice, the world's leader in powering online reviews, has data indicating that 80 percent of people that review products with its U.S. clients give those products a four or five star rating (out of five stars). For its clients in the U.K., that figure jumps up to 88 percent. So we spend all our time concerned and working on negative comments when they only consist of 12-20 percent of our feedback. Let's make sure we focus on some of the positive feedback and ratings and continue to play to our strengths.

"The role of leaders is not to get other people to follow them but to empower others to lead,"

—BILL GEORGE, Medtronic CEO & Harvard Professor

Please understand I'm not saying ignore negative comments. I'm trying to get you to think differently than 99 percent of the world that puts negative comments first and foremost. Certainly we should address negative comments and concerns as they present a tremendous opportunity for improvement and to connect with, and empower, our customers.

FedEx has found that customers who had an issue the company was able to resolve are four times more likely to repeat business than those customers that never encountered a problem. Some of my biggest supporters today were my toughest book critiques a few years back when my first book *Socialnomics* was published. These people wanted to voice their concerns, and by reaching out to them and discussing their issues with the book, a relationship was built. The foundation of this relationship was our vested interest in the topic of the book. By engaging with the reader, I was able to empower them. By engaging with your customers, you will be doing the same.

If you reach out to customers digitally you will be amazed by the results. In the rare instance where this action doesn't work, remember to move on quickly—there are many other faithful followers to engage. Don't ignore positive posters.

DIGITAL DEEDS

"Huddle Up"

There is still no replacement for face-to-face communication in connecting with others and creating an empowered customer or employee base. Unproductive meetings, either corporate or personal, however, can be time wasters and morale deflators. The world has changed and we need to change with it. The next time a meeting is required try the following:

1. Send out a quick, well-defined agenda with goals
2. Remove the chairs and huddle like a sports team: people will get tired of standing inherently making the meeting shorter
3. The circular huddle also helps make everyone equal as there is no head of the table
4. Summarize verbally and electronically what was accomplished at the end of each meeting so that everyone knows what the action items are. This summary helps limit the number of future meetings.

Jim Donald, the former CEO of Starbucks, often had the positive habit of stopping one-hour meetings after 45 minutes and telling employees to use their extra 15 minutes to call someone they usually did not contact every day.[9]

Chris Brogan, former project manager and *New York Times* best-selling author, suggests doing all the running around and question-and-answer stuff before any status meeting. "Our meetings were never more than 10 minutes long, even when working on huge data center build-outs. Get decisions out of the way quickly. Never leave something up in the air, so we'd decide, and if the decision was a bad one, we'd fix it later."

Lessons Learned from Chilean Miners

In the fall of 2010, 33 Chilean miners were trapped 2,000 feet below the earth's surface for 69 days. Luis Urzua was the shift boss of the crew. Urzua didn't know it when his shift started, but his legacy would be secured as the main reason why all the miners were successfully rescued 69 days after their shift began. Urzua exhibited the five principles of STAMP discussed in this book to help triumph in the face of adversity. He wouldn't have been able to do so, however, if it wasn't for the relationship between the miners and their mutual support and empowerment of one another.

Simplify

From the beginning of the event, despite being trapped almost a half mile underground, Urzua stressed the importance of trying to make the days as normal as possible. He wanted the team to try and simulate a regular "shift" each and every day. Lights were turned on during the day and turned off at night. Urzua understood that in life it is much easier to get through one day, from sun up to sun down, than trying to combat the past and tomorrow: combating tomorrow or the past is an exercise in futility.

Yet, many of us who have *never* suffered such hardship as being trapped in a mine constantly worry about the past and future. We worry about unread emails, that a customer might post something negative about our company, that our children are going to grow up addicted to video games, or a thousand other things. Just as worrying about the past or tomorrow wouldn't help the miners it doesn't help any of us that want to become true digital leaders.

True

Urzua remained true to himself and the other miners. It would have been difficult for him to lead if the other 32 miners thought Urzua didn't have their best interests at heart. Much of this trust was built by Urzua's actions prior to the incident, not during the ordeal. A miner that had worked with Urzua prior to the incident described him as being "very protective of his people and obviously loves them, and would not have left until all his men were safely aboveground."[10]

This connection is important to note. We talked in this book about the importance of building your network before you need the network—a similar philosophy exists with trust. Build trust with customers, employees, and partners before you need it, rather than *when* you need it as this will prove to be much more effective. Fittingly, Urzua requested to be the last man lifted from the shaft after all the others were safe.

Action

Urzua made sure that in the early days while they were rationing the food supply (see below details under *Map*) that everyone ate at the same time and as a group. If everyone saw that they were each getting a meager teaspoon of tuna and a quarter cup of milk there would be less chance of bickering. Showing employees or customers that you care about them equally creates a better, lasting relationship.

Map

While Urzua simplified things to a day-to-day level, it was important as the leader to know a little about where they wanted to, or needed to, go. Most of the miners thought they would be rescued in a few days so it would have been easy to eat through all the rations of food quickly.

However, Urzua planned for the worst, but expected the best. It turns out this approach saved 33 lives. The miners weren't discovered in a few days, rather 17 full days. It was a full 69 days until their rescue. Urzua indicated they were lucky to ration the food supply, which was tuna, mackarel, peaches, and milk designed to last 48 hours. With Urzua's guidance they made the food last for all of those 17 days.

Luck is often made when preparation meets opportunity. Urzua said, "We saw the collapsed rock, many thought it would be two days before our discovery. But I knew otherwise." When the outside world first made contact by pounding a narrow hole into their location, the miners were so happy "everyone wanted to hug the hammer."[11]

Part of the miner's mapping was reminding the team of why they wanted to survive when it seemed hopeless. One miner's wife had a baby and he wanted to see his newborn. Another miner vowed to propose to his girlfriend. These visions helped them stay the course by making it mission focused. When we know our mission in life, everything else is simplified.

When we launch new ideas with our company or start using a new technology as a family it's best to prepare for the worst, but to expect the best. Run through and be prepared to tackle as many difficult scenarios as possible, but don't let fear limit your positive visions and expectations.

People

While trapped, if one or two miners were to abscond from the mission it could easily have snowballed into mutiny. Urzua lead by assigning each person a specific task—everyone had a role to play. With everyone seeing the plan Urzua laid out, teamwork was much easier to follow. By the end, the miners were so bonded that even after their removal they requested to stay on site (rather than go straight to the hospital) until every miner was safely lifted up from below.

"I can never be what I ought to be until you are what you ought to be."

—MARTIN LUTHER KING JR.

The cliché "what doesn't kill us, makes us stronger" can be at times seen as trite, but it is certainly true. Urzua was the last man rescued from the mine; a mine he entered as a shift boss and left as a national hero. Chilean President Sebastian Pinera greeted Urzua with, "You have been relieved, coming out last like a good captain. You have no idea how all Chileans shared with you your anguish, your hope, and your joy. You are not the same, and the country is not the same after this. You are an inspiration."[12]

Without Urzua's connection to his team, his ability to lead and empower the group, the ending of this story could have been much different. Thankfully, through mutual cooperation and careful planning, all 33 miners were saved.

DIGITAL DEEDS
Connecting with People

Here are three ways to connect with people online that will help lead to lasting relationships and empowerment for individuals, customers, employees, and other business partners.

Facebook Phonebook: Find mobile numbers using Facebook's Phonebook. If you ever need a phone number of one of your connections on Facebook they may have entered it on their profile. Go to Friends → Edit Friends → Phonebook. This will list all of your friends that have listed their phone numbers. Aren't friends with the person? Most likely someone in your social graph is connected to that person so start to network—hence why they are called social *networks*. You can do similar searches and networking on LinkedIn for phone numbers and emails.The key to remember is that *you need to network before you need the network*. In other words, the first time you reach out to people you shouldn't ask for a favor. In fact, you should do the opposite and do them a favor.

Facebook Groups: Easily share and communicate with smaller sets of friends. If you've accumulated hundreds of friends on Facebook and want an easier way to communicate with a few close ones, try setting up a group. From your home page, click "Create Group" in the left hand menu. Choose a group name and instantly add the friends you want involved. You can also choose what level of privacy you want for the group: open, closed, or secret. If you create a closed or secret group, only members will be able to see what is posted. Start one today for your family, book club, soccer team, or study group.

Status Tagging: Whenever you want to mention someone on Facebook, you can just type the @ symbol, start typing their name, and then choose them from the dropdown menu. They'll get an email notification that they've been tagged, similarly to how photo tags work. It's a quick and easy way to let your friends know to join the conversation.

The Power of Empowering Others

As a digital leader you need to empower your employees and family and make certain that everyone understands their role. Empowering others is one of the greatest gifts you can give the world today and leave behind for future generations. Living in a fully transparent world we can all see what others are doing and it's important for us to know how we fit in with others. When certain roles shift real time as a result of internal or external forces, it's important to communicate this change to everyone as it happens. We need to understand how we can help others on their journey and if we can help them digitally we need to do so in as many instances in which we are able. To this extent, if we ever become overwhelmed or confused by the technological advances that swirl around us, you can never go wrong if you follow the golden rule that has been passed down for generations: if you treat others how you'd like to be treated digitally you will never be short of support or fulfillment.

> *"I make a living from speaking, but it's from a lifetime spent listening."*
>
> —@EQUALMAN

CHAPTER SEVENTEEN

Digital Hugs

"People ask the difference between a leader and a boss . . . The leader works in the open, and the boss in covert. The leader leads, and the boss drives."

—THEODORE ROOSEVELT

Looking at the title of this chapter, you may ask, "What is a digital hug?" The basic idea is to ask yourself, "How do I help lift someone else up?" The process is one in which you help someone digitally with no concern for reciprocity or self-benefit. You have heard the term *pay-it-forward*, but now think in the digital mindset of *post-it-forward*.

If you were to take only one thing from this chapter it is simply this: you will attract more followers digitally in two days than you will in two months if you show interest in them versus trying to get them interested in you. A good example of this concept can be seen with any of our digital messages (e.g., texts, tweets, emails, etc.). Companies and individuals all too often push out messages that are of interest to them, rather than what is of interest to the recipient. A politician wouldn't preach about student loans to a group of senior citizens, just like she wouldn't preach about health care to students.

We sometimes forget these simple offline constructs when we attempt to amass digital legions. A good rule of thumb is if you have to think more than a few seconds whether or not a message will be relevant to the audience—it probably isn't. If you think you might be too old to be shopping at Abercrombie & Fitch, then, sorry, you are.

When Virtual Meets Reality

Many relationships today have digital origins. We are creating and cultivating relationships online. If, and when, we meet these people "in-person," we need to make a good first offline impression. Offline communication is much different than online communication, considering 93 percent of all communication is non-verbal.[1] Therefore, digitally we are only practicing 7 percent of all the communication possibilities afforded to us.

People are often surprised by how tall I am when they meet me in person. Even if we have been corresponding digitally for years, they have even seen me in numerous YouTube clips, and they already know I'm 6'6". Yet, there is something that simply can't replace that face-to-face encounter. Someone may project a lot of confidence digitally but in the real-word shrink like a wallflower. It's imperative in these offline meetings that you live up to expectations (feel free to insert your favorite online dating catastrophe here).

Maintaining Confidence

People want to be associated with confident individuals. Confident individuals are decisive, avoid self-promotion (others will promote them), view everything as an opportunity, and are generous in their compliments. These are traits we all desire to have and we hope that by associating with other confident individuals that we too will acquire these traits over time.

Physical posture and positioning play a major role in exuding confidence "offline." A good trick to maintain good physical posture—especially after pounding on a keyboard all day—is to periodically place your back and head against a wall. Pinch your shoulders together like you are squeezing a carrot between them while making sure you remain in contact with the wall. Put as much of the back of your head as you can against the wall (this forces your neck to be straight). Hold this position for a few breaths and then step away from the wall—you will notice a big difference in your posture the first time you do this. Make it a goal to keep practicing this movement until it is second nature. Sitting and typing, mobile phone use, and other modern contorted positions have adversely affected human posture. This simple "wall" trick is a great counterbalance to these negative positions.

To project confidence via Skype or other forms of videoconferencing, make sure the camera and viewing monitor are in line with your forehead or slightly above it. Most of us make the mistake of having the monitor or tablet below us so we end up constantly looking down. This position is habit forming and can affect our overall posture when we are away from our monitors. Looking down at the monitor also causes us to appear shriveled to the viewer, diminishing the desired projection of confidence.

As mentioned earlier, remember to look into the digital camera as much as possible instead of constantly looking at the person on screen. If you have trouble with this, tape a yellow sign near the camera exclaiming "look at me!" If you are constantly looking at the monitor as opposed to the camera it's analogous to looking at someone's belt-buckle during a conversation. The better you have the monitor and camera closely aligned the closer you are to stealing newscasters' tricks who read from a teleprompter.

A confident stance is just one part of your "offline" communication toolset. Other important aspects:

1. Make eye contact.
2. When shaking hands, be firm, but not bone crushing. If you struggle with this one, simply match the force of the other person's handshake.
3. If you have an outgoing personality and like to hug people, read the situation and if you aren't getting flashing red lights, then go for it. I realize this goes against every "behavior in the workplace" video that has ever been produced. However, go to Silicon Valley and walk around the hottest companies there. Do you think they are concerned that a hug might not

be politically correct? Do you think they are generating record profits because everyone has gone through sensitivity training? Times have changed. Work and life are blended together for those that have found their true calling. Not hugging your coworker would be akin to not hugging a close friend or a family member. Obviously if you determine that a coworker, friend, or family member doesn't like to be hugged then don't hug that person. Not sure? Ask them if they want to "hug it out." This may not sound professional or you're surprised to find this in a book, but people will line up to follow you if they know you genuinely care about their well-being.

4. When meeting face-to-face, shut your device lids and turn off monitors. If a call comes in don't even look at it. A Telstra survey showed over 51 percent of respondents admitted to secretly checking their smartphone during a *meeting*.[2] If you are expecting a call prior to the meeting, let the person know up front before the meeting starts that you may have to take a call. For example, "I apologize, but my wife is pregnant and she may call during this meeting and I'll have to take the call."

5. Remember the phone is there for your convenience, not the caller's convenience. If you are in a meeting and your desk phone rings, don't glance at the Caller ID—you'll be amazed at how great this makes the other person, or people, in the room feel.

6. Set distinct ringtones for important callers (e.g., mother, husband). Set all other ringtones to vibrate. This will help you give your full attention to the person you are currently having a conversation with.

7. Make mobile calls on long-open drives (use a hands-free device) on the highway or during a calm "outdoor" break—think of it as a smoking break, but replace the cigarette with your phone.

8. When leaving voicemail, be brief. Leave your name and phone number up front, even if the person knows you. Leave the most important info first (this mistake is a common one salespeople make). Also more and more people will have their voicemail translated to text so you want to lead with the headline. Remember that you don't like to receive long voicemails; your recipients don't either.

Having solid offline interpersonal communication skills will distinguish you as a leader. These skills are diminishing as we become more and more dependent on technology. A recent Nielsen study found that 4 out of 10 people surveyed have used their smartphone when trying to avoid a social encounter (11 percent admitted to accessing their smartphone while on the toilet).[3] Consider face-to-face meetings a gift and take advantage by giving them the full attention they deserve.

> "All of us have the spark of leadership in us . . .We're here for something. Life is about giving and living fully."[4]
>
> —YOUNG & RUBICAM
> CEO ANN FUDGE

DIGITAL DEEDS

Your Digital Voice and Tone

Since 93 percent of communication is non-verbal it's easy to convey the wrong tone or, worse, the wrong meaning in our digital messaging (e.g., texts, tweets, blogs, email). Here are a few tips to help you avoid such misunderstandings:

1. Greet the correspondent by name.
2. Use emoticons, for example, ☺ or ;), if appropriate.
3. Save the "Dear," "Mr.," and "Madam." Over 50 percent of the world's population is under 30 years old and aren't necessarily accustomed to, nor respond to, formal or business writing. (Note: In Asia and other parts of the world this formality, however, is still expected. Understand the different cultures you are dealing with and if unsure, err on the side of being more polite and formal.)
4. Use greetings like "Hi," "Hello," and "this is." Also use exclamation points where appropriate.
5. In most instances avoid complaints and sarcasm as these don't translate well digitally.
6. Sign-off with your name. This personalization can change the tone of your post and it only takes a second. Get in the habit of using friendly sign-offs like *Cheers, Best, Warm Regards*, or *Digital Hugs*. If near a holiday or weekend make sure to acknowledge it: *Have a great weekend* or *Happy Holidays!*

7. Proof before sending any digital communication or posting one online. One misplaced letter can throw off the meaning of the entire message (e.g., can't versus can) and will cause unnecessary confusion and clarification messages.

8. If you don't know an answer, send a quick response indicating you are checking into the question, but that it may take some time. This reply helps avoid the sender feeling ignored.

9. Some things are still best handled offline (e.g., if you are upset with your boss).

10. Praise publicly and criticize privately.

11. Try to avoid the use of "I" in your digital communication.

12. When you make a mistake offline or online, own up to it and get in front of it. Remember it's not usually *the crime* that is the issue it's *the cover-up.*

Concerned the written word is going down the drain with people injecting "LMAO" (Laugh My Ass Off) instead of using "that was funny"? Get over it. Language is constantly evolving. Think how different Shakespeare prose is to our 1990s textbooks. If you are too young to know what a textbook is, they were heavy and expensive. Make your language light and free.

Billy Jean People Queen

Billy Jean King is arguably one of the greatest tennis players of all time (39 Grand Slam Titles). Not only was King one of the world's greatest athletes, but similar to Muhammad Ali she has been influential in creating social change. She was the first prominent female athlete to publicly proclaim herself a lesbian. A strong advocate of women's rights, King defeated Bobby Riggs, a former Wimbledon men's singles champion, in the "Battle of the Sexes" (1973).

"The people of my hometown of Long Beach made a difference by helping me so that I in turn could help others. Just think of all the different people that came through for me in Long Beach; they believed in me. That is huge when people believe in you," said Billy Jean King on ESPN's Homecoming with Rick Reilly January 9, 2010.

Some of Billy Jean's success was based on the simple fact that people from her hometown believed in her. Are you letting people know you believe in them? If not, you should start today. It's easy to throw people digital bouquets of support and best of all it's free! Take inspiration from columnist Dan Savage who in September 2010 created www.itgetsbetter.org. This was in response to so many young lesbian, gay, bisexual, or transgender taking their own lives as a result of harassment or being bullied. The site's purpose was to inspire hope digitally.

It Gets Better Project (TM) turned into a worldwide movement, inspiring more than 25,000 user-created videos viewed more than 40 million times. To date, the project has received submissions from President Barack Obama, Secretary of State Hillary Clinton, Rep. Nancy Pelosi, Adam Lambert, Anne Hathaway, Colin Farrell, Matthew Morrison of *Glee*, Joe Jonas, Joel Madden, Ke$ha, Sarah Silverman, Tim Gunn, Ellen DeGeneres, Suze Orman, the staffs of The Gap, Google, Facebook, Pixar, the Broadway community, and many more. Notice how Google, Facebook, and Pixar didn't shy away from a controversial issue—that's digital leadership.

Forrest Gump | People

Many people enter and exit Forrest Gump's life, and most of them get more than they give from the generous Gump. Gump doesn't seem to mind, because he understands that true meaning in life isn't what you take, but rather what you leave behind. This comes across as he ruminates about the death of his wife, Jenny (at her gravestone):

> "You died on a Saturday morning. And I had you (Jenny) placed here under our tree. And I had that house of your father's bulldozed to the ground. Momma always said dyin' was a part of life. I sure wish it wasn't.
>
> Jenny, I don't know if Momma was right or if, if it's Lieutenant Dan. I don't know if we each have a destiny, or if

we're all just floating around accidental-like on a breeze, but I, I think maybe it's both. Maybe both is happening at the same time. I miss you, Jenny. If there's anything you need, I won't be far away."

Attract People to the Real You

Smile when you are talking or video conferencing and relax your face. These actions will change your voice so the person on the other end will hear your enthusiasm rather than indifference. When typing an important message, don't scrunch down until you are inches away from the screen. Instead, relax your shoulders and arms—this will help make the words you type relaxed, friendly, and welcoming.

"Pushing a company agenda on social media is like hurling water balloons at a porcupine."

—@EQUALMAN

Use your natural vernacular, don't try to be something you aren't. Your unique Digital DNA is what makes you interesting to others. Recall from earlier in the book how Gary Vaynerchuk started with episode one of *Wine Library TV* being subdued and serious. This strategy didn't work, as he was trying to be someone other than himself—he was trying to be a traditional wine connoisseur. *Traditional* doesn't stand out, so people didn't watch. They wanted the real Gary Vaynerchuk (brash, energetic, passionate) so Gary gave it to them and wine sales in excess of $50 million dollars resulted.

Digital Hugs: Criticism & Compliments

We need to push ourselves beyond our normal comfort levels. Without this necessary push, it is difficult to achieve progress. We are either going forward or we are going backward. You should not shy away from criticism; rather you should invite it as a healthy part of your life.

Often the best criticism can come from a close brother or sister. "Are you really wearing that shirt out?" "Your breath is terrible." The words hurt at the time, but you probably went and burned that shirt or popped a piece of spearmint gum into your mouth after the conversation. None of us is perfect. It is best to avoid destructive criticism, but welcome constructive criticism. People who avoid all criticism, however, will find success difficult to achieve.

When you receive constructive criticism digitally from a customer, this is a gift. They have taken the time to make you, your product, or your service better. Thank them for this gift and then do something with the advice. On your personal end, try and compliment three people per day digitally and, as a bonus, three people verbally. In person, make sure to look them in the eye. You will find looking people in the eye can be more challenging when you are speaking than when you are listening. To help overcome this difficulty, use the trick of focusing on one eye, then switching to the other eye during the conversation.

Attempt to eliminate the use of the word "I" in your offline and digital conversations for just one day. This may take a few attempts. Review your digital conversations to see when you are most apt to slip up. If your messages are riddled with Is, it can easily be misconstrued as self-promotion or that you are doing all the work. Whenever you can use the term "we" it helps to strengthen a digital relationship. This concept is important because we do not have the visual interpersonal communication signals online that we have in face-to-face conversations. To that extent if we are giving direction digitally it is often better to use "we" instead of "you."

Which of the following messages would you rather receive. "You need to get me the report by Thursday so that I have time to review for the executive meeting Friday" or "We should review the report Thursday so we are comfortable with the findings for the meeting Friday." The statements are saying the same thing: the report needs to be completed by Thursday. Yet, most would prefer receiving the second note because its digital tone is much more inclusive. The second note, unlike the first, sounds like the boss values the employees input ("we will review"), that there will be valuable discoveries made by the employee ("findings"), and that there is shared ownership and credit ("we are comfortable"). So even though the employee will not be in the room for the Friday meeting she knows her name will be tied to the findings. Make it a practice to periodically check your digital tone by acting like you were receiving the message you just typed from *your* boss.

Dream Dinner

Determine three people you admire, but have never met, that you'd love to have dinner with. Perhaps you've played this game with friends before. Well it's time to take it from a fun game to a reality. Write down your three people, don't be conservative here, go for broke: Carlos Slim, Richard Branson, Beyonce Knowles, Oprah, Tony Hsieh, Han Han, Nelson Mandella, Arnold Palmer, Bono, Mark Cuban, Barack Obama, Warren Buffet, Stephen King, or whomever else you might find inspiring. Ask yourself why you have selected these people. What do they bring to the table (no pun intended) or what do you want to learn or experience from them?

Now, use your network, creativity, and communication tools to set up a meeting with each one. Getting all three together at once will be a scheduling nightmare so I suggest meeting with them individually. Also, it doesn't have to be dinner—coffee or a 30-minute conversation is sometimes easier to achieve.

Think this plan is impossible to fulfill? Remember, in this day anything is possible—don't sell yourself short. It won't be easy, but you can do it. When trying to set up these meetings, always take the viewpoint of the person you are seeking out: what can *they* get from this meeting? It's not about what you can get. Look for connecting points and review their digital footprints and shadows to determine little known interests and hobbies of the person.

> *"I need you in order to be me. And you need me in order to be you."*
> —NELSON MANDELLA
> on the African concept of Ubuntu

Perhaps you share interest in the same charity? Maybe their son or daughter is in your industry and you can help them out. You write a blog that covers one of their hobbies and request a 10-minute interview. Often you might even share a common friend—if the world was small before, digital communication tools have made it pocket-sized by comparison.

The best part about this exercise is you have nothing to lose. You currently have never met these people and you don't have a meeting scheduled right now, so there is nowhere to go but up. It's a great feeling when someone asks what you are up to and your response is, "I'm trying to reach Kate Middleton so we can grab some tea together."

Turn Digital Hugs into Influence

No matter who we are or what we do, we have influence over others. It's our job to make sure it's a positive influence. We can influence others at any time, whether in person or digitally.

Nancy Gibbs, a well-known columnist for *Time Magazine*, pens:

> "I had many great teachers and professors and mentors over the years, but it was a young first-grade teacher who saw a crushed little girl, told by the grizzled senior teacher that I had used the word then too often in the first piece of writing I'd ever attempted, who swooped in with her gold star, stuck it atop the page and told me to keep writing . . . she sent me sailing off into the second grade, and a whole new world. She didn't invent me. But she invented a writer."[6]

"Friendship is the hardest thing in the world to explain. It's not something you learn in school. But if you haven't learned the meaning of friendship, you really haven't learned anything."
—MUHAMMAD ALI

Surround yourself with magnetic people—people that have a knack for attracting other people. Some of this magnetism via proximity will transfer to you. Digitally, we can now see who has friends and followers and the size of an individual's network. "A" magnets like Ashton Kutcher, Justin Bieber, Malcom Gladwell, or Seth Godin already have enough on their plates, they will be less able to help or develop a deep relationship with you. Rather focus your attention on connecting with those "B" magnets that are on the rise.

You can see who is gaining followers and growing their network in a particular field. Network with them and grow as they grow. Guy Kawasaki, who is an "A" magnet, was an Apple Evangelist before becoming a No. 1 selling author and founding several companies. He always stresses this idea by saying the "nobodies are the new somebody." Once again, remember to network before you need the network.

> *"Life's too short to worry about the color of the paper or the measurement of the drapes—what really matters are the people."[7]*
>
> —**BRAIN SCHWEITZER,** Governor of Montana

Go out of your way to thank someone in person and digitally every day. Look for reasons to praise people. View everyone that helps you as a volunteer. Even if these people work for you or are your son or daughter, everyone in life has the choice to help one another or not. Keep in mind that good people on your staff can always go work for someone else. If you feel your employees can't get up and leave, that they can't find work elsewhere, you may not have an exceptionally talented staff. You want to make sure you retain your best employees and, to do so, you need to show them how much you value them. Praise in public and if criticism is necessary do so in private.

Perform at least one random act of kindness per day: let a harried traveler ahead of you in a security line, tip a waitress 60 percent, shovel the snow off the sidewalk of a random house, pay the toll for the person behind you. Not only will you be making someone else's day, but you are likely to make yours as well.

DIGITAL DEEDS

A Family Tree of Thanks

Go to any free online family tree tool and either create your family tree or use one that another family member has already created. Annotate a note next to each person of significance that details:

1. a specific memory you shared together
2. what you respect about the person
3. what you have learned from that person

If the family tree itself is too complex, simply shoot them an email or post somewhere online about these three items. There's no time like the present to give out digital hugs like this one. As your fingers type, a smile will cross your face, and, soon, the person you are typing about will be smiling as well.

Listening to Others

The U.S. Constitution states it's the people, not the system, who create success. Creating a strong online and offline social network is the first step toward success. The second step is to make sure you *listen* to this network. Even if you don't take your network's advice, follow the old philosophy of knowing the rules before you break them. So many start-up companies are relocated to Silicon Vallley because their entrepreneur founders seek to surround themselves with experienced people. While many headstrong twenty-somethings may not always heed the advice of their mentors, they at least seek it. Mark Zuckerberg, for example, would admit that without the guidance of Sean Parker (Napster cofounder) he wouldn't have been so adamant about retaining so much control of the board and company. You become inherently more interesting to other people or groups not by speaking, but by listening to what is important to them. You need confidence to succeed, but you should go about it quietly, let others celebrate your successes louder than you do.

> "Leadership: The art of getting someone else to do something you want done because he wants to do it."
> —DWIGHT D. EISENHOWER

Treat digital posts like a first impression, what you say and do digitally is permanent. Make your exchanges as personal as possible. For example, on a tool like Twitter look to see what city the other person is from and take the extra time to spell their name correctly. "Thanks for the tip Tasha—I hope that Manchester United wins tonight!" Making digital communication or interaction personal digitally is analogous to remembering a friend's kids' names in the offline world. And don't forget: you will attract more followers digitally in two days than you will in two months if you show interest in them versus trying to get them interested in you.

SECTION 5: PEOPLE

Key Takeaways

▶ Your friends and followers are digital currency—invest in them early and often

▶ Nobody achieves greatness alone—learn to digitally and physically surround yourself with great people

▶ Go out of your way to thank and praise people digitally

▶ Make sure your LinkedIn profile is at 100 percent

▶ Consumers are demanding partnerships with companies

▶ The world demands succinct meetings and messages—adapt or die

▶ Learn the tricks of effective digital communication to avoid the wrong tone and misunderstandings (93 percent of communication is non-verbal)

▶ Praise publicly and criticize privately

▶ Some items are still best handled offline

▶ Give the person you are in conversation with your undivided attention

▶ Don't shy away from digital critics or criticism; it's a great method for improvement

▶ Exude confidence: confidence is a powerful magnet to attract friends and followers

▶ Make sure everyone surrounding you understands their role

▶ Face-to-face meetings help deepen relationships with digital origins

▶ Attract more followers by showing interest in them versus getting them interested in you

CONCLUSION

"The best of a book is not the thought which it contains, but the thought which it suggests . . ."
—JOHN GREENLEAF WHITTIER

Throughout this book, I stress that many of the leadership principles for the past centuries still apply today. In instances where technology has modified these principles I have attempted to show examples of how today's top leaders and aspiring leaders are making technology their friend rather than their foe. In today's digital world, opportunities are all around us.

In the past, these leadership habits may have simply been beneficial, rather than a necessity. Perhaps a leader cut a corner here or there and nobody noticed. Today, people will certainly discover leaders' shortcuts or subterfuge and hold them accountable in the court of digital public opinion. Whether you are a parent, politician, principal, or boss, the world is now fully transparent. As a result, those who aspire to carry the mantle of leadership must continually practice the five habits of the digital leader. If they do, they will discover that their influence on others is more vast than at any time in history. Remember, word-of-mouth has transformed into *world*-of-mouth.

Even if you don't consider yourself a leader, we are all creating a digital legacy that others can view not only today, but for centuries to come. Whether you are a hockey mom or run a small business, or both, you need to ask youself, is society benefiting from my actions today? Am I empowering others?

What will people find when they digitally search for me 100 years from now? Will my digital legacy provide value to future generations? If you are empowering others while benefitting future generations, then you are, indeed, a leader. We all have the potential to live our best life, inspire others, and leave a legacy that matters. Digital tools are keys that help us unlock our potential. Life, leadership, and legacy are an inseparable trinity. When you lead your best life, others will want to be led by you, and you will leave digital footprints and shadows that motivate other generations to achieve their best.

Success and happiness are truly a choice. By keeping life simple, acting on opportunities, staying true to your passions, and surrounding yourself with the right people, you'll take hold of your own life and be able to effectively lead others. Along the way, remember that failure can be your friend: you can be motivated by it and learn from it as long as you fail forward, fail fast, and fail better. Assume every day there are going to be challenges and embrace them without complaint— life would be boring without challenges.

Go for your dreams no matter how audacious they may seem. If nobody laughs at your goals, then set them higher. Those people who are supportive of your highest goals are the ones whose shoulders you will need to stand on. Remember that success is not a solitary pursuit; thank these people as you rise to the top.

My hope is that you learn from this book as much as I have during the process of writing it. I certainly will use it as a guide for the rest of my life and I hope you are able to do the same. Please don't hesitate to reach out to me if I can ever be of help.

Erik Qualman
equalman@gmail.com
twitter@equalman

ENDNOTES

Chapter 1

1. Howard Schultz & Joanne Gordon, *Onward*, Rodale 2011 New York, page 28, 31, 32.
2. http://www.avg.com/press-releases-news and http://www.businesswire.com/news/home/20101006006722/en/Digital-Birth-Online-World

Chapter 2

1. David Kirkpatrick, *Inside Facebook*, page 82.
2. Ibid, p. 54.
3. Josh Waitzkin, "The Multitasking Virus and the End of Learning? Part 1," *The Blog of Tim Ferris*, http://www.fourhourworkweek.com/blog/2008/05/25/the-multitasking-virus-and-the-end-of-learning-part-1/
4. "Is Multitasking Counterproductive?" American Management Association, June 19, 2007, http://www.amanet.org/training/articles/Is-Multitasking-Counterproductive.aspx
5. Ibid.
6. Ibid.
7. Ibid.
8. Brandon Keim, "Multitasking Muddles Brains, Even When the Computer is Off," *Wired Magazine*, August 24, 2009 http://www.wired.com/wiredscience/2009/08/multitasking/
9. Multitasking Is Counterproductive, CNN.com, December 6, 2001, http://www.umich.edu/~bcalab/articles/CNNArticle2001.pdf
10. Reader's Digest/Yahoo! Consumer Pulse Survey of attitudes and behavior toward digital technolgy was conducted in October 2010 by Ipsos OTX MediaCT. The survey included

2,003 U.S. residents between the ages of 18 and 64, split evenly between men and women. Of those, 40% have kids under 18.

11. Tanya Watkins, "The Myth About Multitasking," *Buzz About Science*, http://www.buzzaboutscience.com/myth-multitasking /cool-science/

12. Sandy Lindsey, "Stress S.O.S.," *Key Biscayne Magazine*, page 45, April 2011.

13. "More This, Less That," *Reader's Digest*, page 38, March 2011.

14. Richard Walsh, *Time Management: Proven Techniques for Making Every Minute Count*, Avon, MA: Adams Media, 2008.

15. Michael Austin, "Texting While Driving: How dangerous is it?" *Car & Driver*, June 2009, http://www.caranddriver.com /features/09q2/texting_while_driving_how_dangerous_is_it_ -feature/the_results_page_2

16. Tony Schwartz, "Alan Mulally Making Ford a Model of the Future," *HBR Blog Network*, http://blogs.hbr.org/schwartz /2010/04/alan-mulally-making-ford-a-mod.html

17. Guy Kawasaki, "The Stickiness Aptitude Test (SAT) and Ten Questions with Chip and Dan Heath," http://blog.guykawasaki .com/2007/01/the_stickiness_.html#axzz19JWbSkfc

18. Chip Heath and Dan Heath, *Made to Stick*, New York: Random House, 2007.

19. Jose Antonio Vargas, "Obama Raised Half a Billion Online," Washington Post http://voices.washingtonpost.com/44/2008 /11/20/obama_raised_half_a_billion_on.html

20. Rock The Vote Press Release, November 5, 2008, http://www. rockthevote.com/about/press-room/press-releases/youth-vote -rivals-largest-in.html

21. Projects for Students by Students, Oracle *ThinkQuest*, http:// library.thinkquest.org/20176/berlinwalltimeline.htm

22. Farewell Address to the Nation, http://www.ronaldreagan.com /sp_21.html

23. US News Staff, "Reagan Beats Lincoln and Kennedy as Most Popular President," *U.S. News*, February 12, 2009, http:// politics.usnews.com/opinion/articles/2009/02/12/reagan-beats -lincoln-and-kennedy-as-most-popular-president.html

24. The Internet Movie Database pulled on October 22, 2010, http://www.imdb.com/title/tt0109830/quotes

Chapter 3

1. A Complaint Free World, www.acomplaintfreeworld.org
2. Jeff Henderson, "Life Apps: The Encouragement App," Buckhead Church Podcast, www.gottman.com, April 16, 2011.
3. A Complaint Free World, www.acomplaintfreeworld.org
4. Jeff Henderson, "Life Apps: The Encouragement App," Buckhead Church Podcast, www.gottman.com, April 16, 2011.
5. Meryl David Landau, "Health Digest," *Reader's Digest*, December 2010, page 23.
6. Manju V, Breaking News: "Twitter joke trial sparks online outrage," *The Times of India*, http://timesofindia.indiatimes .com/city/mumbai/Twitter-joke-trial-sparks-online-outrage /articleshow/6921899.cms
7. Peter Shankman, "Be Careful What You Post," shankman.com, January 15, 2009, http://shankman.com/be-careful-what -you-post/
8. Jim Edwards, "Worst Twitter Post Ever: Ketchum Exec Insults Fedex Client on Mini-Blog" BNET, January 20, 2009, http:// www.bnet.com/blog/advertising-business/worst-twitter-post -ever-ketchum-exec-insults-fedex-client-on-mini-blog/256
9. Jeff Henderson, "Life Apps: The Encouragement App," Buckhead Church Podcast, www.gottman.com, April 16, 2011
10. Neil Pasricha, 1,000 Awesome Things: A time-ticking countdown of 1,000 aweesome things, 2011, http://1000awesomethings.com
11. Three As of Awesome paraphrased from Pasricha's talk at TED in September 2010.

Chapter 4

1. Tony Dungy & Nathan Whitaker, *Uncommon*, Tyndale House Publishers, Inc., February 21, 2011
2. David Kirkpatrick, *The Facebook Effect: The Inside Story of the Company That Is Connecting the World*. New York: Simon & Schuster, 2010
3. Jose Antonio Vargas, "The Face of Facebook: Mark Zuckerberg opens up," *The New Yorker*, September 20, 2010, http://www .newyorker.com/reporting/2010/09/20/100920fa_fact_vargas ?currentPage=all
4. Ibid.

5. David Kirkpatrick, *The Facebook Effect: The Inside Story of the Company That Is Connecting the World*, New York: Simon & Schuster, 2010.

6. Charlene Li, *Open Leadership: How Social Technology Can Transform the Way You Lead*, Hoboken, NJ: Jossey-Bass, 2010.

7. FoxNews, "Patriot's Cheerleader Fired After Swastika Photo," November 6, 2008, http://www.foxnews.com/story/0,2933 ,448044,00.html

8. "Social Media History Becomes a New Job Hurdle," via The New York Times | July 21, 2011 | 09:59 AM EDT on http://m.cnbc.com/us_news/43839704?refresh=true

9. Ibid.

10. Ibid.

Chapter 5

1. Margaret Rhodes, "Say No to PowerPoint Week," Fast Company, February 2011, page 20.

2. "Profile: Net-a-Porter's Natalie Massenet," *The Sunday Times*, April 4, 2010, http://women.timesonline.co.uk/tol/life_and _style/women/fashion/article7086909.ece?token=null&offset =12&page=2

3. Stephanie Thompson, "Extends $500 Million Business into Protein Bars and Waters," *AdAge*, November 7, 2006, http:// adage.com/article?article_id=112995ii

4. Emily Bryson York, "Kellogg: Digital ROI Surpasses That of TV," *AdAdge*, September 7, 2008, http://adage.com/article ?article_id=130747

5. Alex Salkever, "Behind the Breakaway Brands: Q&A with Hayes Roth," *Landor: Thinking in the News*, August, 2009, http://www.landor.com/index.cfm?do=thinking.inthenews _article&storyid=737&bhcp=1

6. Aaron Smith, "Americans and Text Messaging," Pew Internet Group, September 19, 2011, http://www.pewinternet.org/ Reports/2011/Cell-Phone-Texting-2011/Main-Report.aspx

7. The Radicati Group, September 26, 2011, http://www.radicati .com/?p=7674

8. Tom Watkins, "Researchers urge doctors to disclose sleep fatigue before surgery," cnn.com, December 29, 2010,

http://www.cnn.com/2010/HEALTH/12/29/sleepy.surgeons
/index.html

9. Mike Song, "America Wastes $540 Billion on Low Value
Email Each Year," Get Control, April 4, 2009, http://www
.getcontrol.net/ic540brelease.html

Chapter 6

1. Carl M. Cannon, "The New Bill Clinton," *Readers Digest*,
12/10-1/11, page 140.
2. "America's Beloved Friend," *Academy of Achievement*, http://
www.achievement.org/autodoc/page/win0int-2
3. Bill Keveney, "Dick Van Dyke Dances Through Life," *USA
Today*, April 27, 2011, http://www.usatoday.com/life/books
/news/2011-04-28-VanDyke28_CV_N.htm
4. "The Happiest Places in the World," *Delta Sky Magazine*,
January 2011, page 69.
5. Bill George, *True North: Discover Your Authentic Leadership*,
Hoboken, NJ: Jossey-Bass, 2007.
6. Ibid.
7. McDonald's All-Americans by College, accessed on March 24,
2011, http://statsheet.com/bhsb/mcplayers_by_college

Chapter 7

1. U.S. Census Bureua, World POPClock Projection, http://www
.census.gov/population/popclockworld.html
2. The Heard with Colin Cowheard, ESPN Radio Podcast,
March 1, 2011.
3. The Heard with Colin Cowheard, ESPN Radio Podcast, July
10, 2010.
4. Marcus Buckingham and Donald O. Clifton, *Now Discover
Your Strengths*. New York: Free Press, 2001.
5. Dale Carnegie Training, *Leadership Mastery: How to Challenge
Yourself and Others to Greatness* (Fireside, 2009).
6. Pablo S. Torre, "How (and Why) Athletes Go Broke," *Sports
Illustrated*, March 23, 2009, accessed on March 23, 2011,
http://sportsillustrated.cnn.com/vault/article/magazine
/MAG1153364/index.htm#ixzz1HQikJ0VT

7. David Kirkpatrick, *The Facebook Effect: The Inside Story of the Company That Is Connecting the World*. New York: Simon & Schuster, 2010.

8. Bill George, *Finding Your True North: A Personal Guide*, Hoboken, NJ: Jossey-Bass, 2008.

9. Josh B. Wardrop, "Something Wicked This Way Comes (Again)," *Playbill*, September, 2010, page 15.

10. "Ray Kroc: The Creator of McWorld," *BusinessWeek*, July 5, 2004, accessed March 23, 2011, http://www.businessweek.com /magazine/content/04_27/b3890021_mz072.htm

11. "American Cultural History 1900-1909," *Lone Star College— Kingwood*, accessed March 23, 2011, http://kclibrary.lonestar .edu/decade00.html

12. Advertisement for book *Brandwashed*, September 2011.

13. Dr. Luis Dilner, "Dr. Luisa Dillner's guide to . . . life expectancy," *The Guardian*, March 22, 2011, accessed March 23, 2011, http://www.guardian.co.uk/lifeandstyle/2011/mar/22 /luisa-dillners-guide-life-expectancy

14. Bill George, *Finding Your True North: A Personal Guide*, Hoboken, NJ: Jossey-Bass, 2008.

15. Howard Schultz & Joanne Gordon, *Onward*, Rodale 2011 New York, page xii.

Chapter 8

1. Howard Schultz & Joanne Gordon, *Onward*, Rodale 2011 New York, page 56.

2. *Fortune*, November 9, 1998.

3. Leaner Kahney, "The 10 Commandments of Steve," *Newsweek*, page 35, September 2011.

4. Biography for Thomas A. Edison http://www.imdb.com/name /nm0249379/bio

5. "Professor Stephen Hawking's Disability Advice," accessed on March 25, 2011, http://www.hawking.org.uk/index.php/ disability/disabilityadvice

6. Sally Schultheiss, "Make it Matter: A Playground for Kids With Special Needs," *Reader's Digest*, September 2009, http:// www.rd.com/make-it-matter-make-a-difference/make-it

-matter-a-playground-for-kids-with-special-neeeds
/article156346.html

7. "Our World Now," *Delta Sky Magazine*, January 2011, page 63.

8. Timothy Ferris, *The 4-Hour Workweek: Escape 9-5, Live Anywhere, and Join the New Rich, Expanded and Updated*, New York: Crown Archetype, 2007.

Chapter 9

1. Melissa Krisch, "Stop Procrastinating—Right Now!" goodhousekeeping.com, June 10, 2011, www.goodhousekeeping.com/health/emotional/procrastination-get-done

2. John Tierney, "The Price of Dithering," *The New York Times*, March 24, 2008, accessed March 26, 2011, http://tierneylab.blogs.nytimes.com/2008/03/24/the-price-of-dithering/

3. Read More: "What Are You Waiting For?" *Reader's Digest*, March 2011 and *Good Housekeeping* "Stop Procrastinating—Right Now!" http://www.goodhousekeeping.com/health/emotional/procrastination-get-done, June 2011

4. Jerry B. Harvey, *The Abilene Paradox and Other Meditations on Management*. Hoboken, NJ: Jossey-Bass, 1988.

Chapter 10

1. John Greathouse, "Ten Tips from Amazon Founder Jeff Bezos,' September 8, 2011, http://technorati.com/business/article/ten-startup-tips-from-amazon-founder/page-2/

2. http://www.strategicbusinessteam.com/famous-small-business-quotes/famous-jeff-bezos-quotes-on-business-leadership-and-strategy/

3. Jared Spool, "The Question That Makes Amazon $2.7 Billion Of Revenue," March 28, 2009, http://articles.businessinsider.com/2009-03-28/tech/30041571_1_new-review-negative-reviews-review-system

4. Don Yeager, "Magic Johnson's Fastbreak Into Business," successsmagazine.com, http://www.successmagazine.com/magic-touch/PARAMS/article/1127/channel/22#]

5. Charles Hallman, "The Magic Business Potion: Invest in Urban American," *Minnesota Spokesman-Recorder*, October 19,

2010, http://www.tcdailyplanet.net/news/2010/10/13 /magic-business-potion-invest-urban-america

6. http://www.30secondmba.com/user/mark-zuckerberg; video
7. http://www.30secondmba.com/user/vivian-schiller; video
8. Sridhar Pappu, "mike on a mission," *Fast Company*, page 100, September 2011.
9. http://inoveryourhead.net/you-need-tension/
10. "America's Beloved Friend," *Academy of Achievement*, http:// www.achievement.org/autodoc/page/win0int-2
11. Bill George, *Finding Your True North: A Personal Guide*, Hoboken, NJ: Jossey-Bass, 2008.
12. John Akers, "Remembering Coach John Wooden," *Basketball Times*, June 7, 2010, http://www.basketballtimesonline .com/2010/06/remembering-coach-john-wooden.html
13. Larry Birds Competitive Fire Thing of the Past in the NBA by Mike Cole July 15, 2010, nba.com http://www.nba.com/pacers /news/web_100715.html
14. Larry Getlen, "The Miracle that is Kobayashi," *The Black Table*, May 19, 2005, http://www.blacktable.com/getlen050519 .htm
15. Aaron Strout, "Less than 5 Percent of Fortune 500 CEOs on Twitter," *Common Sense*, June 10, 2011, http://blog.wcgworld .com/2011/06/less-than-5-percent-of-fortune-500-ceos -on-twitter

Chapter 11

1. Just Disney, http://www.justdisney.com/disneyland/history .html
2. Thomas Alva Edison http://fecha.org/edison.htm
3. "Students Who Pull All-Nighters Have Lower GPAs," *AP*, www.foxnes/com/story/0,2933,316796,00.html, study conducted by Pamela Thacher of St. Lawrence University.
4. Meryl David Landau, "Health Digest," *Reader's Digest*, December 2010, page 30.
5. Harvard Health Publications, "Importance of Sleep: Six reasons not to scrimp on sleep," January, 2006 http://www .health.harvard.edu/press_releases/importance_of_sleep _and_health

6. A majority of sleep study data was pulled from the excerpt from a 2010 Harvard Medical School Special Health Report "Improving Sleep" http://www.health.harvard.edu/special _health_reports/improving-sleep-a-guide-to-a-good -nights-rest

7. Charina Flores, "Afternoon Nap Is the New Trend in Productivity?" *biznik*, March 8, 2010, http://biznik.com/ articles/afternoon-nap-is-the-new-trend-in-productivity

8. Denise Winterman, "Are You Getting Enough," *BBC News*, November 28, 2007, http://news.bbc.co.uk/2/hi/7114661.stm

9. Jacqui Cheng, "Students Face Withdrawal, Distress When Cut Off From Internet, *US Airways Magazine*, June 11, 2011, pages 28-30.

10. Rod Millington, "Life partners avoid talking shop outside the office," *USA Today*, May 12, page 3B.

11. The Thomas Edison Center at Menlo Park website http:// www.menloparkmuseum.org/

Chapter 12

1. Thomas W. Burgess 1877 Dover Publications

2. Don Yeager, "Magic Johnson's Fastbreak Into Business," *successmagazine.com*, http://www.successmagazine.com/magic -touch/PARAMS/article/1127/channel/22#

3. Henry Ford Quotes: http://www.smallbusinessnotes.com /history/quotations/author/ford.html

Chapter 13

1. Bill George, *True North: Discover Your Authentic Leadership*, Hoboken, NJ: Jossey-Bass, 2007.

2. Erick Schonfeld, "Costolo: Twitter Now Has 190 Million Users Tweeting 65 Million Times a Day," *TechCrunch*, June 8, 2010, http://techcrunch.com/2010/06/08/twitter-190-million-users/

3. One Young World, "Oscar Morales," http://www. oneyoungworld.com/counsellors/detail.asp?cns_ID=21

4. Ibid.

5. Oscar Morales, "How I used to protest Farc," metro.co.uk http://www.metro.co.uk/news/812277-oscar-morales-how-i -used-facebook-to-protest-against-farc#ixzz1b3SAb500

6. Oscar Morales, "Ten Questions with Oscar Morales," movement.org http://www.movements.org/blog/entry/10-questions-with-oscar-morales-oscarmoralesg

Chapter 14

1. Woopidoo! Biographies, accessed on 11/01/2010 from http://www.woopidoo.com/biography/ray-kroc/index.htm
2. The Ray Kroc Story http://www.mcdonalds.com/us/en/our_story/our_history/the_ray_kroc_story.html
3. CNBC Video Founder of McDonald's Ray Krock http://www.cnbc.com/id/15840232?video=477180493&play=1
4. McDonald's History, http://www.aboutmcdonalds.com/mcd/our_company/mcd_history.html
5. Ric Elias, "3 things I learned while my plane crashed," (TED Talks March 2011 Long Beach, CA)
6. Niall Ferguson (2004), "Prisoner Taking and Prisoner Killing in the Age of Total War: Towards a Political Economy of Military Defeat," War in History 11 (2), p. 186 via Wikipedia http://en.wikipedia.org/wiki/Prisoner_of_war#cite_note-30
7. "New YouTube Statistics: 48 Hours of Video Uploaded Per Minute, 3 Billion Views Per Day," May 25, 2011, http://searchenginewatch.com/article/2073962/New-YouTube-Statistics-48-Hours-of-Video-Uploaded-Per-Minute-3-Billion-Views-Per-Day
8. Guy Kawasaki, *Enchantment*, page 146, Portfolio Penguin 2011.
9. Chico Harlan, "Paterno puts career on line," *Pittsburgh Post-Gazette*, May 13, 2005. http://www.post-gazette.com/pg/05133/504023.stm
10. Jennifer Gish, "Joe Paterno a Man to Admire," *Centre Daily Times* http://www.centredaily.com/2010/09/04/2188489/joe-paterno-a-man-to-admire.html
11. The 4-Hour Workweek, Expanded and Updated: Expanded and Updated, With Over 100 New Pages of Cutting-Edge Content.

Chapter 15

1. Bill George, *True North: Discover Your Authentic Leadership*, Hoboken, NJ: Jossey-Bass, 2007.
2. Leadership Mastery: How to Challenge Yourself and Others to Greatness by Dale Carnegie Training location 159
3. LinkedIn, http://learn.linkedin.com/job-seekers/
4. Bill George, *True North: Discover Your Authentic Leadership*, Hoboken, NJ: Jossey-Bass, 2007.
5. Howard Schultz & Joanne Gordon, *Onward*, Rodale 2011 New York, page xiv & xiii.
6. Liz Murray, "Freedom from Want," *Reader's Digest*, page 106-109, March 2011.
7. Nancy Lublin, "In Defense of Millennials," *Fast Company*, October 2010 page 72.
8. Beth Dreher, "For a Long Life Watch Your Attitude," *Reader's Digest*, page 29-31, March 2011 and Howard S. Friedman, PhD, Leslie R. Martin, PhD, The Longevity Project: Surprising Discoveries for Health and Long Life from the Landmark Eight-Decade Study, Hudson Street Press, March 2011.
9. www.30secondmba.com
10. Charles Hallman, "Magic urges athletes to become businessmen," *Minnesota Spokesman Recorder*, October 13, 2010 http://www.spokesman-recorder.com/news/article/article.asp?NewsID=105595&sID=42&ItemSource=L
11. Broderick Turner, "Magic Johnson liquidates another asset: his interest in Starbucks," *Los Angeles Times*, October 19, 2010, http://dailyme.com/story/2010101900005291/magic-johnson-liquidates-asset-interest-starbucks.html
12. CNN HLN August 5, 2010

Chapter 16

1. Carl M. Cannon, "The New Bill Clinton," *Reader's Digest*, 12/10-1/11, page 140.
2. CEO in Transition, *30 Second MBA*, Interview with Jeff Swartz. http://www.30secondmba.com/question/ceo-transition?video_id=7bc4619cb083

3. Bill George is the former CEO of Medtronic, Harvard Professor and author of *Authentic Leadership*

4. Don Yeager, "Magic Johnson's Fastbreak Into Business," successmagazine.com, http://www.successmagazine.com /magic-touch/PARAMS/article/1127/channel/22#

5. Charles Hallman, "The Magic Business Potion: Invest in Urban American," *Minnesota Spokesman-Recorder,* October 19, 2010, http://www.tcdailyplanet.net/news/2010/10/13/magic -business-potion-invest-urban-america

6. Seth Godin, *All Marketers Are Liars*, Portfolio Hardcover, November 12, 2009.

7. Hans Villarcia, "Buddhist Geeks: The Conference," *Fast Company*, page 20, July/August 2011.

8. Hans Villarcia, "Buddhist Geeks: The Conference," *Fast Company*, page 20, July/August 2011.

9. Howard Schultz & Joanne Gordon, *Onward*, Rodale 2011 New York, page 21.

10. *San Francisco Examiner,* October 13, 2010, by Eva Vergara http://www.sfexaminer.com/nation/shift-leader-luis-urzua -imposed-order-control-helped-miners-stay-calm-104908894 .html#ixzz12UKrx38E

11. Ibid.

12. Ibid.

Chapter 17

1. Susan Heathfield, "Listen with your Eyes," about.com, accessed 6/24/2012, http://humanresources.about.com/od /interpersonalcommunicatio1/a/nonverbal_com.htm

2. Louisa Hearn, "Mobile distractions make a mockery of meetings," thecourier.com.au, June 24, 2011, http://www .thecourier.com.au/news/national/national/general/mobile -distractions-make-mockery-of-meetings/2206072.aspx

3. "Smartphones Popular While on the Toilet," July 11, 2011, http://www.goldcoast.com.au/article/2011/07/11/331631_gold -coast-news.html

4. Bill George, *True North: Discover Your Authentic Leadership*, Hoboken, NJ: Jossey-Bass, 2007.

5. David Kirkpatrick, *The Facebook Effect: The Inside Story of the Company That Is Connecting the World*. New York: Simon & Schuster, 2010.
6. Nancy Gibss, "Essay," *Time Magazine*, November 22, 2010 page 108.
7. Myatt Murphy, "Peak Performance," *Delta Sky Magazine*, January 2011, page 110.

INDEX

ABOUT ERIK QUALMAN

Erik Qualman has been called a Digital Dale Carnegie and *Fast Company* listed him as a Top 100 Digital Influencer. His last book *Socialnomics* made Amazon's #1 Best Selling List in the US, Japan, UK, Canada, Portugal, Italy, China, Korea, and Germany.

Socialnomics was a finalist for the "2010 Book of the Year" awarded by the American Marketing Association. Qualman produced "Social Media Revolution," the most watched social media video series in the world which has been used for training everywhere from NASA to the National Guard.

Qualman has advised and given keynotes with the following: Coach, IBM, Facebook, UGG Australia, GM, Starbucks, M&M/Mars, Cartier, Montblanc, TEDx, Polo, UGG Australia, Nokia, Google, and more. Qualman gave the commencement address to the 2011 graduating class of McCombs Business School (University of Texas).

Qualman is a frequently requested International speaker and has been highlighted in numerous media outlets including: *BusinessWeek*, The *New York Times*, *WSJ*, *Mashable*, *USA Today*, *Financial Times*, *Forbes*, *Fortune*, *CBS Nightly News*, and *The Huffington Post*. He has been fortunate to share the stage with Julie Andrews, Al Gore, Tony Hawk, Sarah Palin, Jose Socrates (Prime Minister of Portugal), Alan Mulally (Ford CEO), Lee Scott (CEO/Chairman Walmart), Sergio Marchionne (Chrysler/Fiat CEO) and many others.

Qualman is an MBA Professor at the Hult International Business School. For the past 18 years he has helped grow the digital capabilities of many companies including Cadillac, EarthLink, EF Education, Yahoo, Travelzoo and AT&T. He is the founder and owner of socialnomics.com which PC Magazine ranked as a Top 10 Social Media Blog.

Qualman sits on the Advisory Boards of Manumatix, ShopVisible and Bazaarvoice Inc. He holds a BA from Michigan State University and an MBA from The University of Texas. He was Academic All-Big Ten in basketball at Michigan State University and still finds time to follow his beloved Spartans and Longhorns while living in Boston with his wife and daughter.

CPSIA information can be obtained
at www.ICGtesting.com
Printed in the USA
LVOW13*2241270117

522457LV00005BA/8/P